Critical Social Psychology

Critical Social Psychology
An Introduction

Brendan Gough

and

Majella McFadden

palgrave

First published 2001 by
PALGRAVE
Houndmills, Basingstoke, Hampshire RG21 6XS and
175 Fifth Avenue, New York, N.Y. 10010
Companies and representatives throughout the world

PALGRAVE is the new global academic imprint of
St. Martin's Press LLC Scholarly and Reference Division and
Palgrave Publishers Ltd (formerly Macmillan Press Ltd).

ISBN 0–333–77646–1

This book is printed on paper suitable for recycling and made from fully managed and sustained forest sources.

A catalogue record for this book is available from the British Library.

10   9   8   7   6   5   4   3   2
10   09   08   07   06   05   04   03

Typeset in Great Britain by
Aarontype Limited, Easton, Bristol

Printed in Great Britain by
Creative Print and Design (Wales), Ebbw Vale

For our families

Contents

List of Boxes

Preface

This textbook is designed for students taking introductory courses in (critical) social psychology, although it could also feature as a preliminary text for more advanced (critical) social psychology modules. As the title suggests, a key aim is to make students aware of contemporary developments and debates in critical social psychology, with an emphasis on rendering often complex concepts and issues as accessible as possible. Our attempt at summarizing and illustrating this challenging material is a response to the relative lack of available introductory texts on critical social psychology and related areas. With a few notable exceptions, existing books dealing with critical social psychology themes tend to target academic audiences and largely comprise theoretical discussions (e.g. Parker, 1992; Fox and Prilleltensky, 1997). Consequently, we have found it somewhat difficult to identify many 'student-friendly' references in the course of teaching critical social psychology to Level 2 students and have had to rely on a diverse range of book chapters and journal articles. Student feedback, however, has consistently lamented the absence of a dedicated critical social psychology text.

In an effort to maximize student understanding we have deployed various devices throughout the text. Each chapter contains:

- 'critical thinking' boxes, which aim to stimulate reflection on the relevant topic with various questions and exercises;
- illustrative material in boxes, which present details of contemporary 'critical' research studies and quotations from theorists on important themes;
- a glossary, where key terms are defined (students often find the vocabulary of critical social psychology difficult);
- reference to two key readings, carefully selected to provide further insights into pertinent areas.

In summarizing and simplifying the terrain of critical social psychology in this way we are conscious of presenting an account which does not do justice to its breadth and diversity. We do hope, however, that students will use this text as an opening into the world of critical social psychology and we do encourage further reading to garner greater sensitivity to the various strands and debates which exist.

It is still true that the majority of social psychology courses are dominated by cognitive-experimental traditions, as evidenced by the preponderance of 'mainstream' (largely North American) mass market texts (e.g. Baron and Byrne, 1999). And courses dealing with critical social psychology themes often feature in other 'non-psychological' places, such as cultural studies, gender modules or specialist third level units. In other words, it is rare that 'mainstream' and 'critical' approaches are discussed in the one course/text. Our book represents an effort to consider both perspectives in relation to a range of relevant social psychological topics. It mimics the structure of established mainstream social psychology texts, thereby enabling comparison, but also highlights 'critical' work in each area. In this way students can immediately discern key differences between the traditions and are in a position to assess their relative worth in the context of existing research and 'knowledge'. So, this book can operate as a complementary text for courses informed by cognitive-experimental social psychology and as a core text for courses dedicated to introducing critical social psychology. Although this topic-based structure helps create an accessible text for students, it must be borne in mind that common themes and debates affect each area and these central issues are stressed throughout. For example, the idea of 'knowledge' as social production is constantly underlined.

However, we must stress that what follows is not an 'objective' or 'neutral' presentation of contemporary social psychology. Rather, our agenda is mainly to promote critical social psychology perspectives as we feel these offer more sophisticated and convincing accounts of social psychological phenomena compared with cognitive-experimental approaches. This agenda is elaborated within the first three chapters especially, which deal directly with questions of social psychological theory and method and their interconnectedness. Students are advised to read these first (at least Chapter 1) to become familiar with the terminology and general orientation of critical social psychology before exploring subsequent chapters. Chapters 4 to 9 may be read in any order, since they all contrast 'mainstream' and 'critical' approaches to 'classic' topics in social psychology, such as social influence and prejudice, and present arguments for adopting critical positions in these areas. The final chapter reviews key features of critical social psychology and highlights important debates and differences within critical social psychology mentioned in the first three chapters. In the light of ongoing discussions, it is stressed that critical social psychology cannot be considered a unified or unproblematic school of thought, but that concepts used and issues raised within critical social psychology offer valuable insights into contemporary social life.

We hope you find this book useful.

BRENDAN GOUGH
MAJELLA MCFADDEN

Acknowledgements

Thanks to Frances Arnold for helpful editorial input, colleagues who provided invaluable reviews of drafts, and Katy Day for advice on Chapter 8.

BRENDAN GOUGH
MAJELLA MCFADDEN

Critical Social Psychology: An Introduction

1

This introductory chapter will highlight:

- Diversity within (social) psychology
- Key influences on the development of critical social psychology
- Important themes within critical social psychology
- Methods favoured by critical social psychologists

Introduction

Just as the discipline of psychology can be broken down into many different sub-disciplines (developmental, clinical, educational, etc.) and perspectives (cognitive, psychodynamic, humanistic, etc.), so too can social psychology be separated into different fragments. A convenient, though simplistic, way of classifying distinct strands is in terms of approaches which place the individual at the centre of analysis, i.e. psychological social psychology (PSP), and those which emphasize the social dimension to experience, i.e. sociological social psychology (SSP). For example, in studying conformity a PSP approach might focus on 'personality', perhaps devising a scale to distinguish between acquiescent and resistant 'types' of people. On the other hand, an SSP explanation of conformity might focus on aspects of the social situation such as 'peer pressure' as well as wider institutional and cultural expectations such as 'respect for authority'. It is important, however, not to see these two 'camps' as diametrically opposed, since psychological perspectives usually reserve a role for social factors and sociological theories often allow for some form of individual or local autonomy. The aim of this text is to contrast these two versions of social psychology, highlighting differences in the explanations offered for various phenomena such as gender and aggression, both between and within the two camps.

But in contrast to other textbooks which claim to offer a neutral or 'objective' presentation of the many theories and studies which make up contemporary social psychology, we explicitly argue in favour of a social psychology which stresses the social embeddedness of experience. However, as well as following an SSP model, we also advocate a social psychology which is 'critical': in other words, a social psychology which challenges social institutions and practices – including the discipline of psychology – that contribute to forms of inequality and oppression. There is already a history of such critical work in social psychology, as Griffin (1995) notes, including research which has engaged with the impact of unemployment on a community during the 1930s (cited in Jahoda et al., 1972) and research on fascist ideology (e.g. Billig, 1978), but the present day has seen a renewed interest in critical psychology. In studying racism, for example, a critical social psychologist might well highlight and interrogate prevailing ideals and claims which locate the 'causes' of racism within the individual (thereby neglecting institutional cultures) or within the minority group in question (blaming the victims for their predicament) (see Wetherell and Potter, 1992). So, we are advertising a social psychology which gets involved in 'society', which adopts particular positions in important debates on many different issues such as prejudice, violence, 'mental illness', unemployment, crime, etc. – a strange, perhaps alien, departure for students more familiar with the detached 'scientific' stance assumed by many – mainly cognitive-experimental and biological – social psychologists.

The purpose of this chapter is to introduce you to key concepts and debates within what is now known widely as 'critical social psychology' (e.g. Ibañez and Iñiguez, 1997), sometimes condensed to 'critical psychology' (e.g. Fox and Prilleltensky, 1997). This branch of social psychology has flourished in the last fifteen years and has resulted in many new courses, conferences and assorted publications, not only in the UK: there are 'critical' fragments developing in Australia, the USA and parts of Europe. However, given the relative youth of this burgeoning movement and an unfortunate tendency towards complex vocabulary, there is a need for introductory texts such as this to clearly present to a student audience terms and issues which are central to critical social psychologists. The immediate objective of this chapter is to consider significant influences on the development of critical social psychology, notably Marxism, feminism and social constructionism, before summarizing key themes within critical social psychology. Also, some discussion of methods used within critical social psychology will be presented, with relevant examples provided to give a flavour of what critical social psychologists do in practice, although Chapter 3 is devoted to this area.

CRITICAL THINKING ON PSYCHOLOGY

We are suggesting that psychologists should situate themselves and their work within society and develop a critical attitude towards psychological 'knowledge' and its applications. For example, research on sexuality might highlight accounts by marginalized groups (e.g. lesbian women and gay men) in order to challenge psychological theories which present such groups as 'deviant' or 'abnormal' (see Kitzinger, 1997). Can you think of any other areas where critical social psychologists might wish to intervene in this way?

Critical social psychology: key influences

Critical social psychology emerges from and is informed by a range of other theoretical traditions usually absent from or on the margins of 'scientific' psychology. Marxist and feminist approaches clearly offer critical analyses of social class and gender relations and tend to stress power, conflict and ideology. Also, 'postmodern' and social constructionist ideas have proved very influential, with concepts such as the social constitution of reality, discourse and subjectivity central. Below, then, each framework is considered in terms of its contribution to critical social psychology.

Marxism

There are many forms of Marxism and differences of interpretation between the various camps but it would not be too controversial to assert that Marxism is about the theory and practice of class struggle. Instead of the psychological focus on the individual, we have the sociological spotlight on relations between groups or social classes within a broader system of economic structures and institutions, i.e. capitalism. As any introductory sociological text will document, this relationship between classes is considered conflictual, where economic conditions are said to sustain competitive and destructive forms of social relations. In the world of work, it is asserted that the worker is dehumanized and commodified by virtue of the drive for efficiency and profit – the benefits of which are returned mainly to owners and managers rather than to 'ordinary' workers. Within the capitalist system, there is little interest or scope for facilitating human needs for social support, creativity, stimulation and identification with work processes and products (see Parker and Spears, 1996). Consequently, there is a tension between the goals of the business, such as profit, and those of the workers, such as fulfilment; in other words, a class struggle which manifests itself outside work in society in terms of largely distinct consumption patterns (e.g. a preference for sherry or beer) and leisure pursuits (e.g. a taste for classical or dance music).

This account is greatly simplified, of course, and in contemporary society it could be argued that the boundaries between classes are more difficult to detect, or have even disappeared in the midst of a modern 'classless' society. Nonetheless, the emphasis on power differentials and conflict around class is an important one for critical social psychologists who are interested in highlighting and challenging inequalities in any form (see Brown, 1974). As well as documenting class relations ('reproduction') Marxist approaches also assert a commitment to social change ('transformation'), that is, an effort to resist and overthrow prevailing systems of discrimination and alienation. This concern and vision about an alternative, oppression-free society is shared by many critical social psychologists. Forms of Marxist theory have also concentrated on 'ideology', loosely defined as 'knowledge' which works to obscure exploitation and oppression, including psychological theories (see Ingleby, 1972). The notion of competition as natural and healthy would be one example of an ideological norm which could well be used to justify the subordination of particular individuals and groups ('survival of the fittest', etc.). A Marxist or critical social psychologist might prefer to emphasize competing ideals, for example around collaboration and equality. Finally, both Marxism and critical social psychology have in common a project of critical empirical research aimed at exploring local instances of class inequalities and struggles. For further discussion of the relationship between Marxism and psychology, see Parker and Spears (1996) – a flavour of this text is given in Box 1.1. Notwithstanding the importance of Marxist analyses, critical social psychology is also interested in difference and relations which arise from other social categories and identities, notably gender, as the next section on feminism suggests.

CRITICAL THINKING ON SOCIAL CLASS

A Marxist analysis highlights differences and inequalities between members of distinct social class groups. Can you think of any such differences between 'working-class' and 'middle-class' groups? To which social class group do you 'belong', if any? Or is social class less important than other social categories (e.g. gender, race) in terms of influencing social status and experience? Discuss!

Box 1.1 Marxism and Psychology (Parker and Spears, 1996: 2)

The authors see Marxism as a theoretical research programme and political movement devoted simultaneously to comprehending the historical development and dynamics of society through attention to underlying structures of economic exploitation, and to revolutioniz-ing social relations through the praxis of the oppressed and their allies. While the central category is that of class, the architecture of capitalist society in the over-industrialized world, of the bureaucratic remnants of the Stalinist states in some countries, and of the colon-ized third world, are also locked into place by structures of patriarchal and racist domination. The theoretical framework of Marxism for radical psychologists includes, as interconnected sets of analysis, an account of commodification, alienation and individualization.

Feminism

Some scholars, notably socialist feminists, have sought to integrate Feminist and Marxist ideas to produce a critique of 'patriarchal capitalism', where the family is highlighted as the nucleus of female subordination and control. Nonetheless, in most classic forms of Marxism, gender is neglected or relegated to secondary status in the analysis of class relations. The importance of feminism lies in its clear and critical focus on gender as a means of organizing social relations and inequalities. Feminists have consistently underlined the oppression of all women within male-centred heterosexual social institutions and practices (e.g. Millett, 1970; Rich, 1980). For example, sexual violence has been analysed in terms of sustaining male power and control over women generally through producing a climate of fear keeping women 'in their place' (Kelly, 1988). Women as a group have been presented as second-class citizens across various social spheres, including education, employment and family life, a position justified by ideologies of femininity in which women were defined as mothers, carers and housekeepers.

Through engagement with recent social theory (e.g. post-structuralism), however, feminism has recognized the often different experiences of women from various backgrounds, thereby calling into question the notion of women as a coherent, self-contained group with common issues and goals (see Wilkinson, 1986; 1996). Indeed, early forms of feminism have been criticized for reflecting the concerns of mostly white, middle-class women, and as a result contemporary feminism (or feminisms) embodies a much more diverse – and sometimes conflicting – range of positions (see Wilkinson, 1996, and Box 6.1 in Chapter 6). One key ongoing debate for example revolves around the extent to which women can be considered a unified group – are there some problems shared by all women or do considerations of class, race, ethnicity, sexuality, etc. disrupt any claims of universal experiences? For example, one current discussion concerns the perspective on heterosexuality, with many lesbian feminists arguing for a rejection of this institution whilst other voices suggest potential ways for women to progress within heterosexual frameworks (see Wilkinson and Kitzinger, 1993). Feminism is a term which is very much contested in contemporary literature, a category which is subject to continuous debate (see Griffin, 1995).

From a critical social psychology perspective, situating the individual within the gendered social relations is an attractive and important move, as is the critical focus on power and gendered inequalities. Also, feminist researchers have been at the forefront of critiquing 'scientific' methods in psychology and have advocated more democratic, inclusive and reflexive forms of research which seek to give voice to participants and break down barriers between researcher and researched (Stanley, 1990; Wilkinson, 1988). In general, feminists and gay and lesbian scholars have been among the most cogent and vociferous critics of mainstream psychological theories and methods which have furnished 'norms' around gender and sexuality with scientific authority and contributed to the marginalization of women and homosexuality (e.g. Burman, 1990; Kitzinger, 1987). In fact, the journal *Feminism & Psychology* has provided a key forum for research challenging forms of sexism, heterosexism, racism and class oppression both within and beyond the discipline of (social) psychology (e.g. Bhavnani and Phoenix, 1994; Kitzinger *et al.*, 1992; Walkerdine, 1996).

Box 1.2   (a) Feminist psychology (Wilkinson, 1997)

Wilkinson describes feminist psychology as psychological theory and practice which is explicitly informed by the political goals of the feminist movement. Although feminism embraces a plurality of definitions and viewpoints, these different versions of feminism are said to share two common themes (Unger and Crawford, 1992). First, that feminism places a high value on women, considering them as worthy of study in their own right, not just in comparison with men. Second, that feminism recognizes the need for social change on behalf of women: i.e. feminist psychology is explicitly political.

(b) Lesbian and gay psychology (Kitzinger, 1997)

Kitzinger notes an important shift since the 1970s towards the creation of a lesbian and gay psychology that challenges the whole notion of homosexuality as pathology, investigates the reasons for prejudice and discrimination against lesbians and gay men, develops theoretical and practical responses to lesbian and gay concerns, and attempts to create effective changes in the world such that lesbians and gay men might be spared some of the injustices to which they are currently subjected.

CRITICAL THINKING ON GENDER

Feminist social psychologists provide a critical focus on gender, with some arguing that sex differences are innate, whilst others point to societal factors. In what ways, if any, do you think men and women are different – and how would you explain such differences?

The emergence of social constructionism

This critique of psychology has also been facilitated by the emergence of a new movement or 'paradigm' called social constructionism. Recent versions of feminism (and Marxism) within social psychology and beyond have been informed by concepts presented by social constructionism. Now, there are various terms currently in circulation which overlap with or which are even used interchangeably with social constructionism, including 'post-modernism', 'post-structuralism', 'deconstructionism', etc. We will not concern ourselves here with the often subtle and much debated differences in and disputes over meanings which characterize the theoretical literature (but see Burr, 1995 for a clear overview). Rather, we will attempt to convey some key assumptions which frame most contemporary thinking within a broadly defined social constructionist movement.

The first and crucial point to make is that social constructionism represents a 'turn to language' in social theory. In other words, there is an emphasis on representation, meaning and interpretation. This particular focus is hardly new in the social sciences. Indeed, there are many precursors to this linguistic turn, including 'symbolic inter-actionism' (Mead, 1934), which portrays identity as (re-)constructed during social interactions, and 'ethnomethodology' (Garfinkel, 1967), which focuses on everyday language use as social practice. It is interesting that these theories have historically been presented in other disciplines such as sociology and anthropology and have only recently been taken up within social psychology. In fact, a key moment in the modern development of social constructionism is the publication of Berger and Luckman's seminal (1967) text *The Social Construction of Reality*, in which these sociologists examine the joint creation and negotiation of shared realities between people.

Box 1.3   Language and social construction (Burr, 1995)

'Our ways of understanding the world come not from objective reality but from other people, past and present. We are born into a world where the conceptual frameworks and categories used by people in our culture already exist. These categories are acquired by all people as they develop the use of language and are thus reproduced every day by everyone who shares a culture and a language. This means that the way people think, the very categories and concepts that provide a framework of meaning for them, are provided by the language that they use.

By placing centre-stage the everyday interactions between people and seeing these as actively producing the forms of knowledge we take for granted and their associated phenomena, it follows that language too has to be more than a way of simply express-ing ourselves. When people talk to each other, the world gets constructed. Our use of language can therefore be thought of as a form of action, and some social constructionists take this "perfor-mative" role of language as their focus of interest.' (Burr, 1995: 6–7).

Within social psychology itself, certain landmarks are also identifiable. For example, Gergen's (1973) paper, 'Social Psychology as History', located the discipline within particular cultural and historical settings, thereby undermining claims about scientific objectivity; if the knowledge produced by social psychology only makes sense within specific (Western, individualist) contexts then aspirations of 'truth' and generality can be seen as misguided. Whilst Gergen was writing from the USA, some colleagues in the UK such as Harré (Harré, 1979; Harré and Secord, 1972) were also turning to language and its operation in everyday activity. The 1980s and 1990s saw a development of this work with a more 'poststructuralist' flavour, an emphasis on meaning as fluid and unstable. A germinal text here is *Changing the Subject* by Henriques *et al.* (1984), a book which emerged from critical engagements with post-structuralism, psychoanalysis and ideology featured in the since-expired journal *Ideology & Consciousness* (Adlam *et al.*, 1977). This edited volume has proved very influential in the subsequent development of critical social psychology and offers a profound critique of psychology as an individualistic, affirmative enterprise. Drawing principally on the theoretical work of French psychoanalyst Jacques Lacan and philosopher Michel Foucault, two of the most important figures invoked by critical social psychology, there is a call to re-view 'the subject' (i.e. the individual) as produced or constructed by social and ideological forces.

Other more recent 'critical' key texts include Potter and Wetherell's (1987) *Discourse and Social Psychology*, the authors being active members of the University of Loughborough Discourse and Rhetoric Group, and Burman and Parker's (1993) *Discourse Analytic Research*, a product of the Manchester Metropolitan University Discourse Unit. Feminist, gay and lesbian and black social psychologists have produced influential works on discourse, subjectivity and power (e.g. Burman, 1990; Bhavnani and Phoenix, 1994; Wilkinson and Kitzinger, 1995). Other dedicated critical social psychology sites are emerging all the time, such as the Centre for Critical Psychology at Nepean University, Sydney, and new journals have recently been introduced, such as the *Annual Review of Critical Psychology*. The fledgling discipline of critical social psychology has blossomed of late, with whole conferences, seminars and websites now devoted to debating and applying critical ideas. Returning to key themes within social constructionism which have been taken up by critical social psychology, the following section presents a brief summary of these, using relevant examples.

CRITICAL THINKING ON LANGUAGE

Social constructionism highlights the role of language in defining ('constructing') reality. This creative use of language is evident when there is more than one version of the same event. Think of three 'objects' (e.g. 'housework'; 'whale hunting'; 'children') and list the different ways in which each is explained or constructed. For example, 'housework' might be defined as 'not proper work' or as 'a valuable contribution to society'. Discuss the reasons for such diverse meanings. Who uses particular constructions, and for what ends?

Critical social psychology: key themes

It is important to stress at this point that, as with any other (sub-) discipline, there are some disagreements and debates within critical social psychology itself. Indeed, it has been disputed that social constructionism necessarily offers a coherent base for critical social psychology since social constructionist arguments can be used to present a case for relativism, a stance which undermines the authority of 'taken for granted' knowledge, treats all accounts or discourses as equal and renders problematic the connections between language and 'reality' (see Edwards and Potter, 1993; Parker, 1998). This perspective allows us to critically interrogate claims about 'truth' and 'reality' (e.g. in 'scientific' psychology) but can make it difficult to argue *for* a particular or critical version of reality, as some feminist writers point out in their efforts to hold on to a view of social relations centred on the patriarchal oppression of women (e.g. Gavey, 1997; Gill, 1995; but see Hepburn, 2000 for a defence of relativism within feminism). Indeed, feminism has a stake in privileging and promoting women-centred experiences and voices, and this debate between recognizing differences between women according to constructions of race, class, sexual orientation, etc. and highlighting common experiences by virtue of gender, continues to figure in the literature (e.g. Burman, 1998). These issues are addressed elsewhere in the book (see Chapter 3), but for the moment we shall limit ourselves to four statements commonly associated with social constructionism which would unite most critical social psychologists:

- the individual is (always, already) located in society;
- the individual is (at least partially) positioned within systems of difference/inequality;

- power is linked to language and representation ('discourse/s');
- research should aim to challenge oppression and promote social change.

The individual and the social

The point here is that it is difficult and perhaps artificial to separate the individual from society. It is contended that the individual is constantly connected to the social world in many ways and at various different levels. We can think of 'the social' on at least two levels – the interpersonal and the societal. The former obviously pertains to social interactions and relationships in which the individual is involved, whilst the latter relates to broader social norms and practices. Both levels of the social will surround and penetrate the individual, impacting on personal identity and public practice.

Consider the example of alcohol consumption. Your experience and presentation of drinking might well be different when with your partner/spouse from when in the company of mates, or with your parents, for example. The place or situation in which drinking takes place could have an impact – the local pub, a cafe-bar, a club, a restaurant, at home, etc. all present different opportunities and constraints on drinking behaviour (depending on the company too, of course). And then prevailing cultural ideals around gender and class, for example, could frame the drinking event: there is a well-established association between (working-class) masculinity and drinking and fighting in UK culture (but not in Southern European culture), whilst women who drink pints of beer may be seen to contravene traditional definitions of femininity (and subject to unfavourable judgements, even harassment) (see Canaan, 1996; Kaminer and Dixon, 1997). Even when drinking alone the social is ever-present; in fact, lone drinking is very much constructed as a more 'masculine' pursuit and may be connected to an inability to face one's emotions (again, a traditionally 'masculine' deficiency) or to problems in a relationship or stress at work or college.

Everyday talk and interaction, then, can be seen to rehearse and re-work prevailing cultural ideals. In discussing football, for example, shared norms around gender, sport, competition, etc. are accessed and replayed. When male players are described as 'girls' or 'poofs' this draws on commonly held understandings of masculinity as physical, strong, fearless, and so forth (and femininity/male homosexuality as weak, passive and ineffective). The pursuit and celebration of victory can even be seen as reproducing capitalist notions of competition and profit at the expense of 'weaker' others.

These examples highlight the social embeddedness of individual activities; indeed, it challenges this notion of the individual itself, standing apart from the social and enjoying control over her/his actions. This argument is supported further if we examine the historical and cultural variation in individual and social practices. For example, self-expression is encouraged in Western societies whereas self-discipline is promoted in Oriental societies, thereby amounting to different customs and forms of interaction in different countries (see Chapter 4). Similarly, social norms and rituals vary across time. Excessive alcohol consumption was previously explained in terms of individual weakness or lack of discipline, whereas the dominant contemporary account points to the notion of illness, with 'alcoholism' deemed beyond the control of individuals. Such variation in ideals and practices across time and place draws attention to the local and transitory nature of what we regard as 'knowledge'.

This is not to suggest, however, that the individual is at the mercy of cultural and historical forces; that would be a deterministic stance which allows for no human agency or autonomy. Most critical social psychologists would suggest that the individual has room to manoeuvre within given social constraints; some women can and do defy conventional expectations by consuming lots of beer and behaving 'laddishly' whilst many working-class men are not interested in fighting when on a night out. The debate about how much autonomy a person has – and how to conceptualize this – is one which is complex and ongoing within critical social psychology.

CRITICAL THINKING ON DRINKING

In researching how alcohol use is defined, critical social psychology points to the impact of social and cultural expectations. Considering your own drinking habits, to what extent do you think that 'social' factors such as gender, class and culture influence these?

The individual and social inequalities

With the critical social psychology focus on social norms comes an interest in power and ideology. It is fairly clear that certain groups in a given society are disproportionately subjected to discrimination or abuse and given little access to power. Many examples pertaining to race, gender, class, sexuality, dis/ability, occupational status, etc. can be cited here. As the above alcohol example suggests, cultural expectations serve to enable or limit drinking behaviour according to gender, generally tolerating male drunkenness ('boys will be boys') and discouraging female pub/lic pleasure ('a woman's place is in the home'). Following a feminist or critical analysis, such gendered notions concerning alcohol consumption can in turn be related to patriarchal social structures and institutions (see Day, 2000; Gough and Edwards, 1998; Kaminer and Dixon, 1997).

If we consider the arena of sexuality, for example, what is 'normal' in most cultures is defined largely in terms of married heterosexuality: that is, a man and a woman engaged in a committed and intimate relationship overseen by the state and usually culminating in children. This 'norm' is supported by institutions such as the family, the law, education and most religions and is promoted in advertisements, soap operas and films. By contrast, gay and lesbian sexualities are marginalized, receiving little or no public acknowledgement, tolerance or rights and are often defined as pathological (deviant, abnormal, etc. – see Coyle and Kitzinger, 2001). Consequently, the experiences of gay men and women will be coloured by the way in which they are negatively positioned within society, excluded from mainstream roles and lifestyle and subjected to much prejudice and discrimination. That is not to say that lesbian women and gay men are automatically or completely oppressed by virtue of their sexuality – many may not choose to participate fully in mainstream heterosexist society anyway. The point is that representations of homosexuality as sick and dangerous will inevitably curtail aspects of gay men's and lesbian women's lives.

Any individual will, at times, face forms of prejudice and discrimination based on the social construction of race, class, sexuality, disability, etc. Even white, middle-class men, traditionally granted power and status, can be thought of as vulnerable in some areas – for example, immersed in stressful work situations or out of touch with their emotions – although the extent of this 'suffering' is open for debate (see Gough and Peace, 2000; Griffin, 1991). The point is that no individual is separate from social relations and systems of difference which serve to position people in various, often inequitable, ways. And social psychology is often implicated in the oppression of particular groups and individuals, as Box 1.4 on the practices of 'abnormal' psychology illustrates.

Box 1.4   A critique of the *Diagnostic and Statistical Manual (DSM)* used to identify mental disorders (Hare-Mustin and Marecek, 1997)

The authors contend that the *DSM*'s shift to a medicalized frame of reference coincided with the shift to conservatism in national politics in the United States and elsewhere that began in the 1980s and continues to the present. By framing psychological disorders as counterparts of physical illness, it is suggested that *DSM* focuses clinicians' attention on the individual separated from the social context. Further, it is argued that *DSM* downplays the potential negative effects of discriminatory treatment, urban disarray, widening social and economic inequalities, and the growing impoverishment of the poor and the working classes. In this way, the mental health professions help conceal the costs incurred to society when wealth is concentrated among a privileged few and when the state relinquishes its commitment to the welfare of the least fortunate members of society.

CRITICAL THINKING ON SELF IN SOCIETY

Critical social psychology draws attention to the various social positions which people inhabit. One individual will therefore be positioned in many different ways, with some positions more powerful or positive than others. Think about the social identity categories which you 'fit' into (male/female, gay/straight, working/middle-class, etc.). Which identities do you think are currently more privileged and which are more oppressed? Why?

Discourse/power

For critical social psychology, power is intimately bound up with language and representation. In this view, language is active, that is, used to create or 'construct' meanings rather than some neutral reflection of 'reality' – the idea that 'knowledge' produces rather than describes a reality. To proclaim heterosexuality as normal and homosexuality as alien, for example, is not to state the nature of things – male homosexuality was the norm in Ancient Greece – but to produce one powerful version of reality within contemporary society. Moreover, such language can be used towards certain political and social ends, in this case to criminalize and pathologize gay and lesbian identities and practices. For example, constructions of the military around ideals of heterosexual masculinity can work to exclude women and gay men, etc. from access, full participation or promotion. So, any given social construction/ interpretation/ perspective can be deployed towards certain actions or consequences.

The term 'discourse' is widely used here following the work of Foucault, and is a term which has been usefully defined as a 'set of statements which construct an object' (Parker, 1992: 5). Foucault used the term in his famous historical (or 'genealogical') studies of surveillance and regulation around sexuality, madness and criminality to suggest that language is intimately connected to the operation of power and social control of 'problematic' subjects – perverse, mad and dangerous individuals. With its power to classify or diagnose and prescribe management techniques and treatments for difficult individuals, psychology was implicated in the disciplinary architecture of modern society (more on Foucault throughout the text).

To illustrate the concept of discourse, think about what it means to be unemployed. A popular discourse around this 'object' relates to notions of individual responsibility, infamously highlighted by 1980s Conservative un/employment policy which urged people to 'get on your bike' in order to find work. So, ideas and practices which centre around this 'individualistic' view suggest that the unemployed are to blame for their situation and place the onus on unemployed men and women to find work, or show that they are actively seeking employment. Within this discourse it becomes easy to position the unemployed as lazy or parasitic and for the unemployed themselves to feel ashamed, guilty or desperate. Again, this discourse which defines unemployment as a problem for individuals is but one possible way of presenting this 'object', although again a rather dominant perception in contemporary society. Nonetheless, there is potential to envisage alternative discourses, such as framing unemployment in terms of economic or global forces or as a positive life choice, discourses which imply radically different images of the unemployed (see Henriques *et al.*, 1984).

CRITICAL THINKING ON UN/EMPLOYMENT

As suggested above, prevailing social norms or 'discourses' can largely shape experiences of un/employment. Think about someone you know who is unemployed or think back to a time when you were unemployed. How do they or how did you explain the situation, and how are they or how were you viewed by others? What other 'discourses' are/were available?

Power/resistance

In light of the above, critical social psychology encourages researchers to examine how discourses are used to subordinate and silence particular individuals and groups in society. Consequently, there is a commitment to social change whereby alternative meanings are marshalled which could be of use to those who are marginalized. The work of feminist and gay scholars can be mentioned here in relation to struggles to challenge conventional notions around femininity/masculinity and heterosexuality/homosexuality and to present competing discourses, images and practices (e.g. Kitzinger, 1987; Wilkinson, 1986). More recently, for example, a visible lobby in support of disabled groups has emerged to critique prevailing images of disabled people as passive victims and have advocated more positive representations depicting activity, creativity and independence. And the recent controversy in the UK concerning the murder of Stephen Lawrence, a black teenager, has highlighted the prevalence of 'institutional racism' and has prompted a critical examination of race relations within dominant institutions such as the police.

So, ideas and practices once accepted uncritically as natural or true or proper – the man is the breadwinner, black people are less intelligent, motherhood is the pinnacle of femininity, and so on – are now subjected to critique. Critical social psychologists therefore seek to perform research which undermines claims to reality or truth, to interrogate 'taken-for-granted' knowledge and to liase with relevant action groups in the community to promote change. In its 'truest' form, such work is known as 'action research', where participants and researchers engage in dialogue and set the research agenda and practice together (e.g. Rheinharz, 1992).

CRITICAL THINKING ON SOCIAL CHANGE

Critical social psychology aims to change as well as understand society. Concentrating on a specific area such as work or the family, try to identify current ideals and practices – and their effects. If you

feel that any commonly used meanings/practices operate oppres-
sively, what arguments could you use to undermine these and what
alternative representations can you imagine?

Critical social psychology:
research methods

In general, critical psychologists tend to favour the use of qualitative
methods in research. Following the social constructionist argument
that all knowledge is constructed, links between theoretical stance
and choice of research method/s become clear. If a 'natural science'
approach is adopted (as it has been by cognitive psychologists, for
example) then quantitative methods such as experiments and questionnaires tend to be favoured because they supposedly produce
'objective' or factual knowledge about the phenomenon in question.
Critical social psychology, on the other hand, usually adopts a
constructionist 'epistemology' (theory of knowledge) and highlights
the diversity of perspectives and positions presented in talk – and the
interpersonal and social functions that particular accounts serve. For
example, a study of national identity could question people from
different racial and ethnic backgrounds to identify the range of definitions of nationhood on offer and then link these to distinctive political
goals and issues. You could imagine that definitions of 'Irishness' would
differ between the North and South of Ireland and between religious and
political groups within the island. A preference for 'British' or 'Scots
Irish' might be attributed to Northern Protestants and Loyalists in the
light of their identification with the UK and historical links with
Scottish religion, whilst many Catholics and Republicans might well
favour 'Irish' or even 'Celtic' given their aspirations towards Irish
unification and the celebration of Gaelic culture.

With the emphasis on language, critical social psychology research
often amounts to an examination of 'texts', whether these already exist
(e.g. newspaper articles, advertisements, etc.) or are produced by the
research process (e.g. interview transcripts, diary sheets, etc.). Data
collection then can proceed by a variety of methods, including archival
searches, interviews, focus groups, diaries, participant observations,
and so on. The role of the researcher here tends to be much more
involved than the 'detached scientists mode' favoured by cognitive-
experimental social psychology. Thus, observation methods tend to

emphasize researcher participation rather than distance – the difference between joining in a group's activities and watching from the sidelines. Also, critical social psychology data collection tends towards less rather than more structured formats, thereby enabling participants to (partially) determine the course of the conversation or activity. In general, then, critical social psychology research aims for an inclusive and engaged approach in order to facilitate the gathering of rich data in which participants have had a voice.

In terms of data analysis, the popular preference for critical social psychology is discourse analysis (see Burman and Parker, 1993; Potter and Wetherell, 1987). Although there are different forms of debates around this approach, the main aim is to carefully examine a text, highlight recurrent patterns of talk and to locate such talk within social and political ideals and practices. A study of motherhood, for example, in which new mothers talk about feeling depressed and unable to cope with parenting, might be used to critique the discourse of motherhood that implies that women are naturally equipped to nurture and train children, with fathers notably absent, presumed working. Comments such as 'I don't feel I can live up to the expectations' and 'It looks easy for most other women' would reinforce this analysis (see Phoenix *et al.*, 1991, for critical discussion of motherhood).

This is not to suggest that qualitative, critical research is straightforward or problem-free. On the contrary, there are numerous practical and theoretical issues to be negotiated when undertaking research of this nature. Because the researcher is involved in data collection and is responsible for interpreting data, accusations of bias and subjectitity would be easy to make. There is difficulty in attempting to generalize findings also, since most qualitative studies involve small numbers because data collection, transcription and analysis is so time-consuming. However, such problems only arise if one subscribes to the natural scientific model which emphasizes neutrality and objectivity. It has been argued that qualitative research represents a distinct form of enquiry and as such requires different criteria to assess quality and validity (see Banister *et al.*, 1994).

Box 1.5   The theory–method connection

Within mainstream psychology, choice of research method/s is framed as a technical matter – the research question simply dictates the most appropriate method/s to be used. If the relationship between extroversion and psychological health is to be investigated, a questionnaire study might well be selected whereby relevant questionnaires are presented to subjects and correlations subsequently computed. If the aim is to predict the effect of one variable X on another variable Y, an experiment might be devised where the two variables are isolated, X systematically altered and the impact on Y observed. But social constructionism suggests that the way the research question is framed in the first place presumes a prior theoretical, and methodological, stance. Questions about relationships between variables suggest a natural scientific 'epistemology' (theory of knowledge), whilst those concerning 'the experience of ...' (e.g. being hospitalized) presume a humanistic or phenomenological orientation. In other words, the terminology within the research question follows from a particular worldview and tends to imply specific research methods. A study of the experience of hospitalization will inevitably use methods which allow participants to describe their experience, such as interviews and diary methods. The majority of social psychology textbooks, however, devote a discrete chapter to 'methods', a strategy which gives the impression that theory is separate from choice of method. And although we do provide a 'methods' chapter in this textbook (Chapter 3), we certainly do not wish to reinforce the traditional separation of theory and method. Our rationale is simply presentational – as students you may well be familiar with this format and we wish therefore to encourage critical comparisons with other texts – and we try to emphasize how theory and methods are related throughout the book.

In this vein it has been suggested that 'the personal' inevitably affects the research process (qualitative *and* quantitative research) in terms of choice of topic, methods adopted, forms of analysis and conclusions reached. Consequently, it is recommended that the researcher makes available his/her position/s so that the analysis can be judged from an informed perspective – a practice known as 'reflexivity'. Similarly, as much detail as possible about the study is presented so that an assessment of procedures and format can be made – a strategy known as 'transparency'. With this in mind, notions of bias and generalization become meaningless. Such issues are developed and discussed further in Chapter 3. On a final note, it must be stressed that critical work does not necessarily stop at research: there is often a concern with social change, with practical interventions aimed at assisting the oppressed (see Nightingale and Neilands, 1997; Parker, 1999).

Summary

To sum up, critical social psychology can be viewed as a school of thought operating within and against (social) psychology which prioritizes the study of discourse, power and subjectivity. With some precedents in social psychology but more recently influenced by perspectives such as Marxism, feminism and social constructionism, there is an emphasis on locating the individual within society in relation to systems of difference and inequality. Also, power tends to be linked to language and representation ('discourse/s'); and there is typically a commitment to research which strives to challenge oppression and promote progressive social change.

It is hoped that you have acquired a flavour of critical social psychology from this introductory chapter. Don't worry if you have not understood every point here – it is inevitable that a new and unfamiliar terminology will provoke some confusion and anxiety. In the chapters which follow, the above concepts and issues will be explored in much more detail using relevant and up-to-date examples gleaned from contemporary critical social psychology research, and important issues and debates will also be covered.

Key references

Burr, V. (1995) 'What is Social Constructionism?', Introduction to *An Introduction to Social Constructionism* (London: Routledge). An accessible introduction to key themes within and influences on social constructionism, emphasizing the contrast with 'traditional' psychology.

Parker, I. (1999) 'Critical Psychology: Critical Links', *Annual Review of Critical Psychology*, 1: 3–18 (concurrently published in *Radical Psychology*). A useful historical overview documenting the origins and development of critical social psychology within the UK over the past few decades.

A Critical Look at Cognitive-Experimental Social Psychology

2

This chapter will highlight the:
• Historical emergence of social psychology
• Humanistic 'crisis' within the discipline
• Rise of cognitive social psychology
• Attempt to produce a distinctive European social psychology
• Analysis of social psychology as social control
• Virtues of a critical social psychology.

Introduction

Having been introduced to critical social psychology, it is important now to place it the context of social psychology as a whole. As stated in the first chapter, critical social psychology represents a relatively recent school of thought whilst social psychology as a discrete discipline has been in existence for over a hundred years! Of course, over the years the form/s of social psychology have fluctuated as new perspectives and topics have been taken up and later overtaken by different concerns. Yet, throughout, much social psychological theory and research has been underpinned by common assumptions. For example, a prevailing view in the mainstream is that social psychology is a science which studies the effects of social factors on the individual. According to Baron and Byrne's (1999: 6) definition, for example, social psychology is 'the scientific field that seeks to understand the nature and causes of individual behaviour and thought in social situations'. This dominant orientation has informed the largely quantitative research conducted and the emphasis on the individual as the key unit of analysis. For example, experimental studies of 'social facilitation' have sought to measure the effects of the presence of other people on an individual's performance (e.g. Zajonc, 1965).

During the late 1960s and early 1970s many social psychologists became dissatisfied with the discipline's near obsession with quantification and its perceived irrelevance to ordinary people's lives, a period widely depicted as a 'crisis' for social psychology (see Armistead, 1974). There was a subsequent humanistic call for research which would explore meanings used by people in daily interaction. Apart from a certain degree of methodological change, however, no great or lasting impact was made on mainstream social psychology, which by this time had embraced the cognitive revolution. Indeed, a European focus on inter-group phenomena which began by addressing the social dimensions to identity and relationships proceeded to reduce the level of analysis to cognitive processes. Hence the contemporary focus on 'social cognition', on how the human mind processes 'social' information in predictable (but flawed) ways. This recent history of social psychology is recounted below and the contemporary preoccupation with matters inside people's heads criticized. A critical social psychology analysis is then developed which situates the disciplinary focus on cognition in relation to wider cultural discourses and institutions implicated in social control. The chapter ends by reaffirming the case for a social psychology which is genuinely social and which engages critically with society.

The historical emergence of social psychology

The roots of (social) psychology have been traced back to Greek and Roman civilization, but most writers focus on the modern age, dated roughly from the mid-1600s to the twentieth century (see Sahakian, 1982; Still, 1996). The philosophy of Descartes (1596–1650) in particular is pinpointed as an important foundation. Briefly, Descartes argued for a separation between mind and body – the 'Cartesian' split – and that human reason and experience can be used to gain knowledge about the world. This call to 'empiricism' (or 'scientific' data collection) has been enthusiastically embraced by modern social psychologists.

A scientific enterprise

(Social) psychology as a separate discipline is typically traced back to the mid nineteenth century, during a period characterized as a time of great social and scientific change. The modern or 'enlightenment' philosophy underlying this upheaval centres on scientific reason, progress and liberal humanism (Parker, 1989). In other words, there was a march towards building 'civilization', advancing society beyond the superstition, stagnation and irrationality which was said to characterize earlier 'darker' periods. The discoveries and successes of the physical sciences at this time made a great impression on philosophers who were moved to abandon speculation in favour of a more applied analysis of the human condition. Although 'introspection' – the disciplined examination of one's consciousness – was emerging as a tool for investigating the human mind, the rigour and precision offered by the methods of the natural sciences proved irresistible in the quest for knowledge about human behaviour. Indeed, the utilitarian philosopher J.S. Mill positively urged human science to embrace scientific principles and methods (see Hammersley, 1989).

The nascent discipline of (social) psychology was concerned to distinguish itself from 'unscientific' philosophical or everyday thinking, deemed partial, contradictory and inadequate. For example, note the conflict between the following two proverbs: 'absence makes the heart grow fonder' and 'familiarity breeds contempt'. A primary function advertised by (social) psychology was the capability of 'testing' opposing ideas under scientific conditions in order to establish the circumstances under which specific principles applied. Perhaps it would find 'absence makes the heart grow fonder' more relevant for romantic relationships, and 'familiarity breeds contempt' more appropriate for relationships with work colleagues or family members. At any rate, the rise of 'behaviourism' was set in motion, with a focus on visible, concrete behaviours amenable to measurement and analysis rather than the intangible activities of the mind. Stainton-Rogers et al. (1995) speak about a shift from nineteenth-century engineering to twentieth-century 'humaneering'. A study by Norman Triplett in 1898 on the influence of other people on sporting performance is widely cited as the first social psychology experiment (Box 2.1).

So, mainstream social psychology adopted a scientific model and indeed continues to employ quantitative experimental methods to investigate the behaviour of individuals in social situations. Quite often, social psychologists attempt to reproduce specific social scenarios in the laboratory, so that particular variables are more easily isolated and controlled for study. For example, to study conformity, Asch (1952) exposed subjects to a condition in which they experienced social pressure to go against the evidence of their senses concerning

Box 2.1   The first social psychology experiment? (Triplett,1898)

Norman Triplett's (1898) paper on 'The Dynamogenic Factors in Pacemaking and Competition' is widely cited as the earliest publication in social psychology. Whilst studying the official bicycle records from the Racing Board of the League of American Wheelmen for the 1897 season, he realized that those cyclists who competed against others performed better than those who cycled alone against the clock. Triplett attributed this phenomenon to the energizing force of competition, a hypothesis which he tested by observing children winding up a fishing reel, both alone and in conjunction with others. He found that, on average, winding time was faster when the children worked side by side rather than alone. This study has proved influential on subsequent 'social facilitation' research, although the effects of other people on performance have been found to be variable (see Zajonc, 1965).

various comparisons of line length (many 'subjects' were confederates of the experimenter and were instructed to give incorrect answers – see Chapter 5).

Sometimes social psychologists venture into the 'field' and attempt to manipulate elements of naturally occurring situations. For example, to study altruistic behaviour, a confederate would assume various guises on a train (tramp, businessperson, etc.) and feign some seizure or collapse whilst psychologists recorded the responses of bystanders (Latane and Darley, 1970). In both research situations, the experimenter controls aspects of the situation and measures or observes the resulting responses of the often unwitting subjects. Experiments remain very popular as a tool for social psychological investigation, although other quantitative (e.g. questionnaires) and qualitative (e.g. interviews) methods are also used, occasionally together.

CRITICAL THINKING ON SCIENTIFIC PSYCHOLOGY

Since its inception, (social) psychology has attempted to emulate the philosophy and methods of natural science. But can human activities be captured sufficiently by scientific methods (e.g. experiments, questionnaires)? Give examples of human behaviours which can and cannot be measured, predicted and controlled.

The above account clearly emphasizes the dominance of quantitative or experimental traditions within social psychology. Whilst such practices have largely shaped the character of modern social psychology, it is also important to highlight other, more 'social' approaches. The early work of Wundt in the late 1800s, for example, pioneered a form of 'volkerpsychologie', a study of the cultural understandings and practices which informed human consciousness. Dilthey founded the hermeneutic (or interpretative) school, proposing a psychology which examined 'the systems of culture, commerce, law, religion, art and scholarship and the outer organisation of society in family, community, church and state' (1976: 90, cited in Still, 1996). This emphasis on societal relations and systems of meaning was taken up by other prominent figures such as George Herbert Mead and John Dewey during the early decades of the twentieth century. Sigmund Freud, of course, was also interested in psychosexual socialization and his work was adopted to further understand the origins and persistence of fascist ideology (e.g. Adorno *et al.*, 1950). But such contributions have been marginalized by mainstream social psychology in favour of a scientific approach to the study of self-contained individuals. Nonetheless, social psychology has also been interested in exploring, understanding and 'solving' social problems, as the next section suggests.

Addressing social problems

The social psychological pursuit of knowledge could not be accurately described as an impartial, scientific endeavour, for there was – and is – a great concern with tackling social issues and improving the individual's quality of life. This orientation can be found in Comte during the mid nineteenth century, who proclaimed that the then emerging science of 'la morale' would combine biological with sociological knowledge to help explain and provide solutions to moral problems in society. The view that there is nothing as practical as a good theory has often been cited and there have been repeated calls to 'give psychology away' to the people (Miller, 1969). In this sense, there is a departure from a purely scientific or objective approach as particular values (human betterment, equality, etc.) are adopted. This focus is emphasized in textbooks, where a major aim of social psychology is to 'seek out sound knowledge of human nature' in order to 'make social institutions and practices better suited to human needs' (Tiffin *et al.*, 1940: 23), or to consider 'how such (social psychological) knowledge might be used to alleviate some of problems plaguing us in the world today' (Aronson, 1988: preface) (both cited in Stainton-Rogers *et al.*, 1995).

For example, there is a body of social psychological work dedicated to understanding and controlling human aggression (e.g. Berkowitz, 1962). Social agendas are tackled as if they were easy to isolate, measure and resolve by means of scientific methods. Stainton-Rogers *et al.* (1995) liken this 'liberal humanistic' endeavour to missionary evangelizing, in which the social psychologist is depicted as holding or discovering the 'truth' and redeeming society with it.

Box 2.2   Social psychology as moral crusade

Throughout the century, social psychology has painted itself as socially responsive and responsible. According to Gergen (1973), the subject-matter of social psychology has often been dictated by prevailing social issues. For example, the horrors of the Second World War prompted much research on social influence (obedience, conformity, compliance), a key question being how people could be persuaded or coerced to co-operate in the extermination of specific social groups (e.g. Milgram, 1974). Similarly, a research programme on altruism was engendered by the lack of public intervention in the course of the murder of a young woman ('Kitty Genovese') – 'bystander apathy' (Latane and Darley, 1970). Social issues have figured prominently in the social psychological literature, covering a range of topics, including prejudice and discrimination (racism, sexism, homophobia, etc.), marital breakdown, eyewitness testimony and interpersonal violence. Implicit in such work is the image of the social psychologist as concerned expert, eager and qualified to 'make a difference' to the world through the application of 'scientific' knowledge.

But in studying and accounting for social problems, *individual* factors tend to be emphasized. For example, research on occupational discrimination against woman (lower salaries, less status, etc., compared to men) has focused on women themselves rather than prevailing sexist norms and practices. Thus, women have been found to hold lower career expectations than men, a finding related to numerous other factors, such as:

- women anticipate taking more time off work than men;
- they recognize the 'reality' of unequal pay and conditions more than do men;
- they perceive relatively low levels of pay as more fair than do men, and
- they compare themselves more with other women rather than men (Jackson *et al.*, 1992).

Somewhat ironically for research on sexism, it is women who are virtually held responsible for inequitable and seemingly unchangeable working practices! The preoccupation with individual factors (expectations, cognitions, etc.) rather than social factors (institutions, norms, etc.) is developed and criticized in the next section.

CRITICAL THINKING ON SOCIAL PROBLEMS

Looking at the various topics studied by social psychologists suggests a desire to address social issues such as racism and stress. Yet research and theories tend to focus on individual characteristics and cognitions rather than social or cultural factors. Consider one social problem such as aggression or sexism and discuss the various individual and social factors that might be involved. Which explanation/s seem more plausible?

A study of individuals

In the ways social psychology defines and studies 'social' phenomena, society often becomes invisible or constant in favour of a focus on and vocabulary of individual behaviour. The 'social' is reduced to that which can be easily observed or measured, including:

- the presence of others (in altruism research, a key variable is the number of people present which deters the subject from responding altruistically to a person in need);
- the small group (the identification of 'task-centred' and 'people-centred' leaders has proved a popular research project);
- social/cultural categories (many 'traits' and behaviours have been examined in terms of differences between men and women, distinct age groups, nationalities, subcultures, etc.).

Those aspects of society considered too complex or ambiguous to quantify – 'sociological' concepts such as ideology, social relations and institutional practices – are overlooked and projected on to other social science disciplines. In striving to isolate and measure particular concrete aspects of the social situation and individual responses to these, 'social' psychological research manufactures and promotes a de-socialized conception of the individual. As Kvale (1992) notes, culture is taken as accidental and local, while psychological processes are depicted as fixed and universal. The individual is prioritized, but the image of the individual is of a rather passive and simplistic stimulus-response machine.

The study below (Box 2.3) is an example of social psychological research which uses social categories but which fails to analyse the social meanings which impinge on, in this case, gender. Although the testosterone–aggression relationship was found to apply to both sexes, the fact that testosterone is a 'male' sex hormone means that men are more likely to aggress.

Box 2.3 Sex differences in aggression: individual biology over society

Although social psychologists acknowledge the role of social situational factors in explanations of aggression, research continues which also stresses biological influences. In particular, the notion that there are (natural) sex differences between men and women in levels of violence persists. For example, research by Harris *et al*. (1996) investigated the role of 'sex hormones' in aggression. Participants were firstly required to complete questionnaires designed to measure tendencies to behave aggressively and tendencies to be helpful and nurturing in a range of situations. Items used to indicate aggression included: 'I have trouble controlling my temper' and 'If somebody hits me, I hit back', whilst items used to record prosocial behaviour included: 'I often take people under my wing' and 'I like helping other people'. The researchers also obtained two measures of testosterone, a 'male' sex hormone. The results depicted a correlation between testosterone and aggression, with higher levels associated with aggressive tendencies and lower levels with more prosocial behaviours – for both sexes. It was also found that increases in testosterone accompanied instances of aggression, suggesting a causal rather than merely correlational relationship.

But cultural practices and norms around masculinity and femininity are not taken into account, such as the greater power and privilege afforded many men and the reinforcement they receive for being 'tough' and unemotional. Instead, mainstream social psychologists often treat social categories and the alleged differences between them as neutral and constant when, in fact, groups who differ according to gender, race, sexuality, social class, etc. are represented and treated in different and complex ways in society in the first place. Critical social psychology argues that the discourses and practices around social identities need to be acknowledged – and challenged – by social psychologists.

To reiterate, mainstream social psychology has so far been characterized and criticized as a scientific endeavour interested in addressing social issues but doing so from a stance of individualism. The tension between the 'scientific' (technical, value-free) and 'applied' (practical, humanistic) concerns of the discipline have also been highlighted. A debate between these two strands has continued throughout recent times, although the mid-century brought with it some disappointment that theoretical developments were being neglected in favour of pragmatic questions. Brewster-Smith (1983) argues that the subsequent post-war lapse in applied social psychology in favour of technical and theoretical questions facilitated the image of social psychology as a pure science, a more powerful and privileged position where issues around theory, measurement and methodology were prioritized. But this orientation within the discipline soon generated an amount of dissatisfaction, as the next section discusses.

Humanistic 'crisis'

Although alternative approaches within and outside mainstream social psychology did exist, it was during the late 1960s and early 1970s when criticism became more vociferous and organized, with objections raised in particular about the perceived irrelevance of social psychology to people's lives (see Armistead, 1974). There were concerns about the artificial and highly technical nature of social psychological investigation, the outcome of which was described variously as 'elegantly polished triviality' (Allport, 1968: 29) and, in the words of Toffler (1981: 141–2), 'obsessive emphasis on quantified detail without context, on progressively finer and finer measurement of smaller and smaller problems, leaves us knowing more and more about less and less'. Indeed, Kline (1988) remarks that the nature of experimental (social) psychology tends to attract neurotic introverts who happily detach themselves from emotional and social contexts! As a result of such observations there was something of a clamour for different approaches which could enable the exploration and further understanding of individuals and groups in more naturalistic ways (e.g. Gross, 1974). The focus of this critique then largely centred on method, with orthodox quantitative methods regarded as constraining participants in the push for numerical data. Methods such as experiments and questionnaires were considered to limit individual choice, as subjects were required to select responses from a preordained list or task.

Pausing to reflect on the social psychology experiment, it becomes clear that the typical subject is placed in a strange environment with limited knowledge about the purpose of the study and is instructed to perform often bizarre tasks, the outcomes of which are rarely made known to them. In contrast, the experimenter is aware, active and dynamic in the research process and is in a more powerful position (Jourard, 1972). The subject's own understanding of the situation is neglected and marshalled into the experimenter's cul-de-sac of meanings and measurements (Brown, 1980). This selective focus on particular variables and their effects led to the charge of 'determinism', i.e. the containment of individual freedom in the experimental situation. The related charge of 'reductionism' referred to the subsequent explanations of behaviour, usually linking complex human phenomena to a few quantifiable factors.

Consequently, a new improved social psychology was sought. In particular, qualitative methods were advocated as more worthwhile, interesting and relevant. Methods such as participant observation, role-playing, repertory grids, etc. were favoured as they allowed for a focus on meaning and experience. An interest in studying the rules and roles which people negotiated in real life settings developed under the umbrella of 'ethogenics' (Harré and Secord, 1972). Central to this framework is the notion that behaviour, or action, can be explained in terms of the actor's 'social competence', i.e. the knowledge an individual possesses about what is appropriate to do or say in distinct social situations. This approach draws heavily from (micro)sociology (e.g. Garfinkel, 1967; Goffman, 1959) and is concerned to study the conventions adhered to by social actors in their everyday settings. It is the task of the ethogenicist to elicit the nature of the (often implicit) norms which prompt action, typically by examining the actors' accounts. Such accounts are located in various 'texts', including interview transcripts, newspaper clippings, diaries and observational notes.

**Box 2.4   An ethogenic approach to football violence
(Marsh et al., 1978)**

The hypothesis here was that even such apparently disordered behaviour as that perceived on football terraces was structured by underlying rules. A body of accounts was analysed, comprising interviews and conversations with fans as well as video recordings of behaviour on the terraces. Following analysis, two types of account were identified, one stressing disorder and violence, the other order and safety. It was concluded that both types of accounting were necessary for the fans' behaviour: on the one hand an image of excitement and risk could be sustained by stories of aggression, whilst on the other hand talk of safety reinforced the perception that injury was unlikely. With the benefit of the observational data, which depicted few scenes of violence, it was argued that the safety account was 'correct', whereas the violence account was merely a constructed version of reality which functioned to promote certain positive images of the fans (as tough, adventurous, etc.).

CRITICAL THINKING ON THE SUBJECT-MATTER OF SOCIAL PSYCHOLOGY

The ethogenics approach suggests that social psychologists should direct their attention towards the meanings and practices which people negotiate in everyday life. What are the advantages and disadvantages of this form of research compared to the examination of behavioural responses in a laboratory setting?

However, such work remained at the margins of the discipline, as concepts such as meaning and perception were assimilated by the burgeoning (social) cognitive approach and reconfigured as internal phenomena ('scripts', 'schemas', etc.) governed by a central processing mechanism. This fact was lamented in the late 1970s when it was recognized that social psychology had largely failed to become more relevant: 'psychology failed for being ahistorical, for not applying to itself the standards it applied to others, for fancying itself value-free, and for continuing indulgence in the Newtonian fantasy' (Leahey, 1992: 481).

The rise of cognitive social psychology

With the advent of computers, (social) psychological attention shifted from behaviour back to mind again and the investigation of mental or cognitive processes. But this was no return to introspective approaches; rather, cognitive processes were defined in ways which enabled scientific study so that various questionnaires, tests and experimental tasks could be designed and used. This 'social cognition' approach remains fairly dominant in contemporary social psychology as all manner of topics from the self to prejudice and aggression are interpreted in terms of cognitive concepts such as 'schema', 'retrieval', 'scripts' and 'prototypes'. In order to test hypotheses about cognitive processes, subjects are typically presented with information from which they have to make judgements about people and situations. They might be asked to attribute the 'cause' of a particular action (internal or external?), remember as much as they can about a story read some time before (which details are omitted, distorted, etc.?), decide which candidate to employ from a selection of curricula vitae (does gender/race/sexuality, etc. of 'candidate' influence choice?), and so on.

Often this work 'demonstrates' various 'errors' or 'biases' in human thinking which social psychologists attribute to 'cognitive heuristics' or information-processing 'rules of thumb' which we access to make decisions. Brehm and Kassin (1993) provide a table of the main types with accompanying descriptions and examples (see Box 2.5).

Box 2.5 Evidence of faulty human thinking (Brehm and Kassin, 1993: 112)

In their textbook on social psychology, Brehm and Kassin (1993) outline a number of heuristics or cognitive shortcuts which people are said to use to simplify social perception. Three such heuristics are detailed below.

Representativeness refers to the tendency to assume, despite compelling odds to the contrary, that someone belongs to a particular group because s/he resembles or 'represents' a typical member of that group. For example, a study by Kahneman and Tversky (1973) found that people who read about a conservative man who enjoys maths puzzles and has no interest in social or political issues, they guess that s/he is an engineer rather than a lawyer – even though s/he was said to be randomly selected from a group containing 70 lawyers and 30 engineers.

Framing refers to the tendency to be influenced by the way something is presented or 'framed'. For example, Levin *et al*. (1988) found that people are more likely to recommend a new medical treatment if described as having a 50 per cent success rate rather than a 50 per cent failure rate.

Simulation refers to the tendency to predict and explain the outcome of an event on the basis of how easy it is to imagine an alternative script or 'simulations' of that event. For example, Miller *et al*. (1990) found that when people hear that a passenger was killed in an airline crash, they find the death more tragic if the person had just switched from another flight ('if only ...') than if they think that the person scheduled for weeks to take the trip.

Interesting and creative though many of these experiments are, the cognitive model can be subjected to the humanistic criticisms levelled at previous behaviourist-dominated versions of social psychology. The 'scientific' orientation within social cognition again means a preoccupation with measurable responses from subjects who have little awareness of the research aims. This emphasis on method therefore treats individuals and their minds as objects which can be isolated and their activities recorded under various predetermined conditions. In this way cognitive social psychologists subscribe to methodological behaviourism, with the processes of perception often reduced to biological or computational models (see Gergen, 1989).

CRITICAL THINKING ON COGNITION

Social cognition research highlights various shortcuts and 'errors' deployed by individuals under specific experimental conditions. But is it important that the human mind is not completely 'scientific' or logical? Discuss!

Also, the overwhelming focus on cognitive biases, shortcuts and errors establishes a contrast between faulty, irrational human thinking and correct, logical scientific thinking. Given that cognitive social psychologists adopt a scientific posture we can presume that they exempt themselves from the mundane mistakes committed by the lay person's mind. Again there is this distinction in operation between 'ordinary' and 'scientific/psychological' reasoning which privileges the latter and therefore helps reinforce the expert status of the discipline (see Stainton-Rogers *et al.*, 1995).

Critical writers have in fact pointed to the 'language games' deployed by psychologists in the promotion of their work as scientific; many scientists have been found guilty of persisting with beliefs/ hypotheses even when the evidence does not support these (see Kuhn, 1970). Finally, the focus on individuals – or individuals' thought processes – makes for a de-socialized discipline where social relationships and practices surrounding the individual are obscured.

A European social psychology

In the UK and Europe, however, there have been attempts since the 1960s to forge a uniquely Euro-centric social psychology interested in the individual-in-society. Spearheaded by figures such as Marie Jahoda and Henri Tajfel, the ethos of this movement is summed up by Jaspers (1986: 3, 10, 14):

> Social psychology needed another forum, intellectually independent from the one provided by our colleagues in the U.S. ...

> which must include a direct concern between individual psychological functioning and large-scale social processes which shape this functioning and are shaped by it ...

> should not ideas, problems, issues come first? Perhaps this is in part where the difference in focus between European and North American social psychology is to be found. The most noticeable contributions to European social psychology...took on problems of a much wider scope.

Two influential contributions to this distinctive Anglo-European are Social Identity Theory (e.g. Tajfel, 1978) and the Theory of Social Representations (e.g. Moscovici, 1981). Both perspectives will be summarized to provide a flavour of apparently more social forms of social psychology, although it will be argued that particular assumptions and methods adopted undermine claims for alternative, social analysis.

Social identity theory (SIT)

The theory (e.g. Tajfel, 1978) distinguishes social from personal identity, defining the former as those aspects of self based upon their social group/category membership with the latter referring to individual traits. It is also assumed that personal and social identities are context-dependent such that they generate diverse forms of action, that is, interpersonal and inter-group activities respectively. Further, it is asserted that everyone has an interest in preserving and enhancing self-esteem and the theory concentrates on how group members work to promote a positive image of their group – and by implication, themselves. Acknowledging that societies contain many groups perceived to occupy different social positions, the theory suggests that membership of 'subordinate' groups will impact negatively on self-esteem, and vice versa. As a result, group members will act to either maintain or improve the status quo, and several strategies are reported.

For example, if social mobility is thought feasible, the individual may attempt to pass into a higher status group. Such an individualistic measure will be encouraged by the dominant group since it leaves the inter-group status quo unchanged – and therefore the superior position of the dominant group. Alternatively, if inter-group boundaries are perceived to be tight, minority group measures such as social creativity may be adopted, whereby inter-group comparison dimensions might be changed (e.g. using sporting prowess instead of economic success) or other social groups chosen for comparison ('at least we're not as poor as them' etc.). Social competition might also be taken on as a strategy and can range from political protest and passive resistance to physical damage and terrorism. In contrast, the dominant group will counter any threats to its position by re-emphasising traditional justifications of the status quo and deploying fresh defences (see Hogg and Abrams, 1988).

With this inter-group focus, SIT has sought to locate the individual within social processes. However, in many respects the theory can be criticized for perpetuating some of the problems it sought to overcome. For example, an image of the individual as mechanically responding to social conditions and cognitive structures is presented, thereby echoing the determinism inherent in US cognitive-experimental research. And despite a professed interest in the social dimension of identity and experience, much SIT research has been conducted in the laboratory using the 'minimal group paradigm', whereby subjects are arranged into artificial groups and their biased in-group behaviours recorded (e.g. Tajfel and Billig, 1973). When relevant work has been conducted in the field, some of the theory's assumptions have been found wanting in the light of social complexity and flexibility. For example, evidence of communal and co-operative behaviour in women's groups casts SIT as a male-centred and simplistic framework (Williams, 1984), whilst research on the Northern Irish conflict points to diverse and inconsistent use of meanings and practices around key 'identities', such as 'British' and 'Irish' (e.g. Gallagher, 1988). In sum, the theory neglects to account for variability and conflict in the words and actions produced by group members in social interaction (see Billig, 1985).

The theory of social representations

In Moscovici's (1984: 948) words, this theory is an attempt to realize the goal of transforming social psychology into an 'anthropological and historical science' by fostering a properly social account of human action and meaning. The term 'social representation' is said to contain two dimensions – abstract concepts and concrete images – which together help define or explain an object. For example, the word 'psychology' can be referenced by concepts such as 'mind', 'psyche', 'personality', etc. and exemplified by a portrait of Freud or the brain or an attitude scale, etc. Social representations are said to circulate in the social world and are drawn upon by individuals to make sense of or make familiar a social phenomenon and to communicate with others. New or difficult concepts are first 'anchored' to existing representations (e.g. 'road rage' is linked to stress) and then 'objectified' or transformed into more concrete images (e.g. a 'crazed' driver, a crash victim). As such, social representations refer to commonsense understandings of academic or abstract ideas. It is assumed that different social groups will apply distinct social representations of an object.

An influential study on the social representations of health and illness in France was conducted by Herzlich (1973). In-depth, semi-structured interviews were carried out with 80 participants, most from the city (Paris) and a few from the countryside. In general, it was found that health and illness were understood as opposites, with health represented as something internal to individuals whilst illness was construed as an external force which can strike at any time. Moreover, illness was commonly associated with city life whereas life in the country was regarded as healthy. However, although much research in this tradition has employed qualitative methods to examine multiple accounts, it has been argued that the theory resorts to cognitive and individualist assumptions. In fact, the individual is presented as possessing the power to select and use those social representations deemed appropriate at a given time, and social representations themselves are situated within individual minds rather than social relations (see Parker, 1989).

In sum, it has been argued that the work of Tajfel, Moscovici and colleagues have managed to usher in only superficial changes which are easily contained within the existing USA-centred experimental-cognitive perspective (Ibanez, 1990). Within such work, the social functions and institutional power of the discipline are not addressed. Critical social psychologists, however, have analysed the social position and principal practices of experimental-cognitive social psychology, emphasizing its participation in regimes of social control.

CRITICAL THINKING ON EURO v. US SOCIAL PSYCHOLOGY

As mentioned, there has been a concerted effort to distinguish a European from a US social psychology. Why do you think social psychology has developed (to some extent) differently in Europe (an interest in groups) compared to the USA (a focus on individuals)?

Social psychology as social control

Since the late 1960s critics outside the discipline – and more recently within – have challenged the form and functions of mainstream social psychology, as evidenced by texts such as *Deconstructing Social Psychology* (Parker and Shotter, 1990). Within this literature social psychology is situated in the wider context of Western capitalism (Laing, 1967), imperialism (Rose, 1985) and patriarchy (Wilkinson, 1986). This critique is allied with and draws upon various traditions, such as Marxism (e.g. Parker and Spears, 1996), feminism (e.g. Wilkinson, 1986) and social constructionism (e.g. Burr, 1995), which in various ways produce troubling accounts of the modern period and its prevailing values of science, progress and individualism. The critical spotlight is cast on the institutional and disciplinary role of social psychology as bolstering existing inequalities of power by leaving them unexamined. According to this view the social psychologist performs the role of social engineer, helping to maintain the status quo by concentrating the gaze on individuals and not society (see Stainton-Rogers *et al.*, 1995).

A specific and influential critique of (social) psychology was generated in the 1960s by the 'anti-psychiatry' movement (e.g. Laing, 1967). At that time – and indeed currently – psychiatry and clinical psychology were informed by a medical–scientific framework in which patients/clients were viewed as sick or abnormal and subjected to a variety of techniques to cure or control 'problematic' symptoms ('anti-psychotic' drugs, behaviour modification, etc.). Diagnoses and treatments were directed at the level of individuals and components of individuals (brains, behaviours, etc.), with little or no attempt to understand the individual in social and cultural contexts. In countering the prevailing philosophy, critical theorists and practitioners suggested replacing the notion of 'mental illness' with interpretations of strange or disturbing behaviour in terms of relationship, communication and cultural factors. Szasz (1961) argued that 'mental illness' was a myth, a self-serving creation by dominant academic and professional bodies which fed into establishment concerns about the control of 'deviance'. Within the anti-psychiatry movement, there was a preference for situating problems within families and wider culture rather than locating these inside individuals. For example, Laing (1960) studied communication difficulties within families and linked these to broader material and ideological forces based around capitalism and patriarchy.

CRITICAL THINKING ON MENTAL ILLNESS

Clearly there are biological dimensions to 'mental illness'. But do you think medical explanations and treatments have been overused? Discuss other factors that might contribute to 'madness'.

Later feminist critiques connected women's 'madness' with the construction of femininity in the nuclear family and in patriarchal society in general where the female is depicted in a range of conflicting and demeaning ways. For example, Wilkinson (1991: 8) highlights the role of psychology in obscuring the socio-political context of women's lives – and the feminist critique of this practice:

Feminist [social] psychologists have also been critical of the harm that psychology (and the popularisation of psychological ideas) has wrought in women's lives: primarily (but not exclusively) through the location of responsibility – and also pathology – within the individual, to the total neglect of social and political oppression.

More generally, feminist social psychologists have challenged the tendency of (social) psychology to cast women as inferior to men, as:

inconsistent, emotionally stable, lacking in a strong conscience or superego, weaker, 'nurturing' rather than productive, 'intuitive' rather than intelligent, and, if they are 'normal', suited to the home and family. (Weisstein, 1993: 207).

The force and momentum of anti-psychiatry, feminist and other (black, gay and lesbian, etc.) scholarship and political activity has produced a broader, critical, anti-psychological orientation within and beyond mainstream (social) psychology (e.g. Burman, 1990; Ussher, 1991; Wilkinson and Kitzinger, 1995). The focus of much contemporary critique tends to be on the use of technical jargon by (social) psychology and the ideological and practical functions this serves.

Discourse/ideology

The 'knowledge' produced by mainstream (social) psychology has been construed as a form of 'mystification', as summed up by Laing (1967: 52): 'a positive (i.e. scientific) description can only perpetuate the alienation which it cannot itself describe ... which it consequently disguises and masks more'. Similarly, Argyris (1975) argues that the model of the person conveyed by psychology presents a de-natured, competitive, rational and gain-oriented individual. The 'knowledge' produced by social psychologists then can be thought of as ideological in its promotion of particular ('objective', 'individualistic') analyses of social phenomena and its suppression of 'other' potential forms of explanation (emphasizing the social embeddedness of self and experience). Another way of regarding social psychological knowledge is as a form of 'fiction', i.e. a particular and partial construction of reality rather than an accurate reflection of reality (see Kvale, 1992; Parker and Shotter, 1990). This point has led some 'post-modern' commentators to argue for the incorporation of fictional accounts into social psychological analyses, a move which repositions social psychology as art rather than science (see Sass, 1992). Indeed, in some of the chapters which follow, we deliberately draw upon accounts from novels as well as social psychological studies in order to illuminate specific points.

Ideological practices present as natural or correct ways of thinking and social structures which actually favour the interests of a particular class or group. It could be argued that social psychology has offered social theories and technical solutions to social problems which promote white, male middle-class interests. This view led some people towards a Marxist analysis of the individual-in-society:

> Psychology, like the ruling-class forms of production/distribution it supports, believes in a pessimistic humanity for which 'original sin', 'instinct', or 'inappropriate response' dictate the need for social control. Marxism counters such an attitude with its own view of humanity ... transcending the past in the creation of newness ... Instead of passive pawns, we become active creators. (Brown, 1974: 165–6, cited in Sapsford and Dallos, 1996)

Foucault (1977) in particular emphasizes the 'governmental' role of human sciences such as social psychology within the institutions and practices of modern life. In light of its individualistic orientation, social psychology is implicated in producing a 'regime of truth' which bolsters dominant Western culture. Of course, defining subjects as measurable variables provides grounds for a range of institutional activities such as personnel selection, patient diagnosis, performance appraisal, etc. Foucauldian critics construe such classificatory practices as a form of policing a range of 'problematic' subjects: 'masturbating children and hysterical women, feebleminded children and recruits to the armed forces, workers suffering fatigue or industrial accidents, unstable shell-shocked soldiers, lying, bedwetting or naughty children' (Rose, 1989: 122). So, the production, nature and application of social psychological knowledge reflects the powerful position of the discipline in the containment of subversive identities, thereby ensuring social control.

For example, social psychology played a key role in taming the massive influx of immigrants to North America at the turn of the century. Although useful as workers for the massive industrialization and urbanization projects, the issue of controlling immigrant labour became important. Hence the emergence of Taylorism, or 'scientific management', a regime which advocated the subdivision of work tasks so that performance could be readily monitored and measured (see Parker, 1990). Similarly, Cartwright (1979: 84) has pointed to the USA government funding of research in the wake of the Second World War on numerous research topics, including: 'building civilian morale and combating demoralisation; domestic attitudes, needs, and information; enemy morale and psychological warfare; military administration; international relations; and psychological problems of a wartime economy'.

But the discipline of social psychology does not simply impose its knowledge on a docile public. Rather, as Foucault has pointed out, power is not possessed by privileged groups – it is dispersed among the population in often complex and subtle ways. Over the past twenty years or so, power has been analysed in terms of ideology or discourse (e.g. Billig *et al.*, 1988). Instead of conceiving ideology as a system of beliefs external to individuals designed to obscure the 'truth' of class inequalities (thus inflicting people with 'false consciousness'), Althusser (1984) presents ideology as a set of relationships between individuals and social worlds within which we negotiate meanings and identities about ourselves and others. For example, individuals discover themselves as students, husbands, fathers, etc. by being recognized as such by other people and society in general, as all these roles are already established and familiar. Ideology therefore helps to (dis)locate people in the world through providing identity slots which individuals fill with little or no choice in the matter. This reading of ideology obviously introduces more complexity to identity by linking it with social structures in a dynamic, multifaceted way (see Chapter 4). With Foucault, the power/discourse dimension is complemented by an equal emphasis on resistance, that subjects are produced by ideology but can also position themselves outside particular representations.

CRITICAL THINKING ON IDEOLOGY AND SOCIAL CONTROL

Do you agree that social psychology has played a role in the oppression of particular groups and the maintenance of the social order? What can social psychologists do to resist the discipline of social psychology?

Revisiting critical social psychology

To reiterate, critical social psychology is concerned to contest the knowledge and practices which characterize mainstream experimental-cognitive social psychology. As Chapter 1 suggests, critical social psychology emphasizes the 'social construction of reality' and is sceptical of scientific social psychological claims of neutrality and fact-finding. Instead, the aims, methods and outcomes of social psychology are highlighted as ideological, as producing forms of knowledge which obscure and therefore reinforce power differentials in society. This point is emphasized by Wilkinson (1991: 7–8) in relation to the (social) psychological formulation of women, but can also be applied to other groups subordinated in terms of race, ethnicity, social class, sexual orientation, etc.:

> psychology's theories often exclude women, or distort our experiences – by assimilating it to male norms or man-made stereotypes, or by regarding 'women' as a unitary category, to be understood only in comparison with the unitary category 'men' . . . Similarly, psychology [screens out] . . . the existence and operation of social and structural inequalities between and within social groups (power differentials are written out).

Whether the focus is on individuals or groups, social relations, differences and conflicts are not recognized or held constant, so that the ensuing 'knowledge' is stripped of relevance and insight. When devising and measuring 'internal' entities such as 'personality', 'attitude', 'motivation', 'intelligence', 'need for achievement', etc., and comparing different social groups on these dimensions, social psychology paints a rather simplistic, static and de-socialized picture of the phenomenon in question. In contrast, critical social psychology points to social complexity, contradiction and construction, thereby disrupting social psychological narratives of 'objectivity' and 'progress'. As Wetherell (1996: 11) puts it:

> I want to argue for a 'critical social psychology' which takes the term 'social' very seriously indeed. We are not isolated individuals but social beings. Our dreams, hopes, fears and expectations may be the products of solitary reflection but they also tell us a great deal about the ways in which we are inserted into society. Social psychology should be a social science, not an imitation natural science. We belong with disciplines such as sociology, politics and cultural studies rather than physics, chemistry and astronomy. Our methods, research aims and theories should reflect the particular nature of social action, difficult though this is. We should work with and study the ambiguities, fluidity and openness of social life rather than try to repress these in a fruitless chase for experimental control and scientific respectability.

But critical social psychology does not seek to replace one form of social psychology with another – it seeks to undo, un-define, deconstruct those (powerful) presentations of nature, fact and essence within social psychology and wider culture. In the chapters which follow, we hope to illustrate and develop the critique of experimental-cognitive social psychology as applied to a number of relevant topics and to show how critical concepts such as discourse, ideology and power can be brought to bear on such material.

Summary

In this chapter we have situated mainstream social psychology within a modern Western philosophical context where values of science, progress and individualism are embraced. We then described how the social psychological preoccupation with scientific measurement which subsequently developed came to be criticized during the late 1960s and early 1970s in what is often referred to as a time of 'crisis' for the discipline. The drive for increased relevance led some social psychologists towards humanistic approaches while many in Europe articulated a more group-centred focus to counter the perceived dominance of North American individualistic approaches. But, as we stressed, such 'alternative' directions have not made a huge impact on social psychology; in fact, the 'cognitive revolution', which has overtaken psychology in the past thirty years, has dictated the agenda so that mental phenomena are given priority, even within apparently social perspectives such as Social Identity Theory. We then discussed more fundamental critiques offered by a range of theorists both within and outside social psychology which highlighted the role of the discipline in perpetuating 'knowledge' in the service of social inequalities. The turn towards examining the social functions of theory – and discourse in general – is one of the key features of Critical Social Psychology, an approach which concentrates on power relations, difference, ideology and the social construction of meaning.

Key references

Armistead, N. (1974) Introduction, *Reconstructing Social Psychology* (Harmondsworth: Penguin). This introductory chapter gives a flavour of the disillusionment felt by many social psychologists with the discipline at the beginning of the 1970s.

Sapsford, R. (ed.) (1996) chapters 10 and 11, *Issues for Social Psychology* (Buckingham: Open University Press). The two final chapters present a range of objections to the theories and applications of cognitive-experimental social psychology.

Doing Critical Social Psychology

3

This chapter will highlight:

- The turn to language in critical social psychology
- Forms of discourse analysis
- Relevant 'texts' (e.g. interview transcripts)
- Ongoing debates within discourse analysis (e.g. realism–relativism)
- Action research
- Reflexivity

Introduction

The methods and practices of critical social psychologists differ widely from those of mainstream or 'scientific' social psychologists. As the last chapter argued, there are many problems associated with experimental-cognitive social psychological research. To reiterate, conventional quantitative methods have been criticized for:

- reducing complex human phenomena to measurable variables and simplistic categories;
- presenting 'subjects' as naive stimulus-response machines and 'society' as invisible or constant;
- providing 'knowledge' which is technical, mystifying and uncritical;
- helping to perpetuate social relations of inequality;
- obscuring significant personal and contextual features of the research;
- facilitating a myth of social psychology as science.

Critical social psychology, in contrast, has been influenced by a range of critical traditions such as Marxism and feminism and follows markedly different assumptions and practices about research. The focus is very much on language, in line with a general shift in social theory towards an analysis of 'discourse' (e.g. Burman and Parker, 1993; Potter and Wetherell, 1987; Wilkinson and Kitzinger, 1995). This critical focus on discourse incorporates the meanings people negotiate in social interaction (the interpersonal level) and, more broadly, the ways in which everyday talk is structured or framed by prevailing cultural norms or discourses (the socio-cultural level). These two levels of analysis are interrelated – people use language to communicate but the terms and assumptions they draw upon are provided by the surrounding culture. So, two men having a conversation about football might work to preserve a joint identity as 'football fans' but they will also be reproducing cultural norms about gender and sport (masculinity–football–sexism, etc.). Although language is spoken or written, there is an emphasis on the latter, a turn to 'text', since speech tends to be transcribed for ease of analysis. So, an infinite variety of 'texts' can be studied, such as interview transcripts, newspaper reports, field notes from observations, diaries, magazine articles, recordings of actual conversations, film scripts, etc.

Such texts may be analysed in a quantitative fashion using 'content analysis' (e.g. Stratton, 1997), for example, whereby superficial features can be identified and frequency counts conducted. For instance, a content analysis of a wrestling magazine might categorize units into different types (advertisements, interviews, features, etc.) and produce a table displaying the relative frequency of key terms such as 'strength', 'reputation', 'aggression'. Whilst such analyses can present a useful indication of important themes in the text, critical social psychology tends to favour qualitative forms of data analysis, although there are examples of quantitative methods being re-worked and used 'critically' within critical social psychology (see Lubek, 1997; Unger, 1996) and, of course, a summary of quantitative data can provide a helpful reason for further qualitative analysis. In light of the preoccupation with language, however, most forms of 'critical' research involve linguistic or 'discourse' analysis.

In contrast to traditional scientific models of research, discourse analysis and critical research in general is informed by social constructionism, a contemporary school of thought which presents 'knowledge' as a social product, the outcome of specific relationships and practices within the research context (see Chapter 1). Theoretical orientation and research practice are regarded as interconnected, as mutually influential, which is why some critical writers resist the practice of separating out theory from method in journal articles and books. The fact that we are here presenting a visibly distinct chapter on methods is somewhat ironic of course, but we see this as a useful resource for students of social psychology who may already be familiar with reading about and writing discrete methods sections. Nonetheless, we continually link form of method with theoretical positions throughout this chapter and urge students to bear in mind the ways in which the whole research process is framed by researcher (and participant) ideals and values.

Indeed, the researcher's ideas and feelings about the research topic dismissed as 'bias' from the perspective of conventional 'scientific' research is re-viewed as an inevitable occurrence within qualitative research and, moreover, is often considered a positive resource in informing the research process. As a result, any research report is considered a construction, i.e. an account from one perspective of the study in question, one which is always open to alternative interpretations. For this reason one has to strive to provide persuasive arguments and supporting textual evidence to bolster one's analysis, otherwise the quality of the analysis will be called into question. Hence critical researchers tend to be as 'transparent' and 'reflexive' as possible concerning the steps taken in the research and the part they played in conceiving, conducting and re-presenting it. As you would expect by now, the aims of critical research revolve around highlighting and challenging discourse/s and practice implicated in the oppression of individuals and groups. In short, compared to the above features of mainstream research, 'critical' research usually sets out to:

- emphasize the variation, complexity and often contradictory qualities in human experience;
- situate individuals/research participants within wider social contexts;
- offer knowledge which is partial, incomplete and critical;
- challenge aspects of existing inequalities in society;
- make visible pertinent personal and contextual elements within the research;
- deconstruct the myth of (social) psychology as science.

These features will be discussed below as this chapter highlights forms of discourse analysis and critical research generally in relation to a variety of texts. This is not a (qualitative) methods chapter which describes in detail how to collect data and analyse it; rather, the emphasis here is on illustrating forms of critical enquiry, although guidance on critical discourse analysis is provided at the end. For more thorough advice on methods of qualitative data collection and analysis you are referred to other texts, such as Banister *et al.* (1994) and Hayes (1997). In this chapter, we will firstly introduce forms of critical discourse analysis and then illustrate their application with reference to studies using interview transcripts, taped conversations and media excerpts. It is difficult to state precisely where discourse analysis begins and ends and this point is most vividly emphasized by researchers using 'Q-sorts', whereby lots of material on the subject in question is gathered and distilled into a range of discourses. These discourses are then presented to participants in the form of specific statements and participants' comments on these then subjected to further analysis, and so on. After discussing discourse analysis, this approach will then be evaluated and other important critical themes and debates discussed, such as reflexivity and action research.

Discourse analysis

There is no one or definitive brand of discourse analysis to which all 'critical' social psychologists subscribe and, to make matters worse, a variety of terms are used often interchangeably with little or no consensus on meaning – discourse; text; narrative; theme; story; repertoire, etc. For students (and researchers), concepts and debates can appear rather abstract, which may inhibit or discourage attempts at understanding. At the same time, efforts such as this to simplify the literature are open to charges of reductionism. Nonetheless, a key aim of this chapter is to clarify and illustrate forms of discourse analysis to facilitate critical awareness and stimulate research practice. An important point to make from the outset is that discourse analysis is not an automatically critical endeavour – some researchers who present themselves as discourse analysts could not be said to be doing critical research (see Burman, 1991). However, the analysis of discourse is the dominant activity within critical social psychology and although many different strands exist, two broad approaches are normally distinguished.

Subjects as discourse users

One tradition influenced by post-structuralism, microsociology (e.g. ethnomethodology – Garfinkel, 1967) and the sociology of science emphasizes the 'performative' qualities and 'action orientation' of conversational and linguistic activities (e.g. Billig *et al.*, 1988; Potter and Wetherell, 1987). This 'bottom-up' approach attends to the rich and varied use of language as it is produced in interactions, and highlights the rhetorical strategies people use to achieve particular ends such as justifying one's position or defending a friend from perceived slander. In order to present self, others and the world in specific ways, people are said to draw upon 'linguistic (or interpretative) repertoires', which 'consist of sets of recurrent and coherently related stylistic, grammatical and lexical features, including seminal metaphors and tropes or figures of speech' (Wetherell, 1997: 162). For any given 'object' ('men'; 'parenthood'; 'football' ...) there will be a range of repertoires from which people draw, and the same person may well use different, even conflicting, repertoires at different points, depending on the conversational context and the (inter)personal goals. For example, members of a sports team or street gang might variously describe the group in terms of:

- family – everyone is a 'brother'/'sister';
- army – defending perceived group rights against designated enemies;
- body – where each member is an integral part/arm of the central figure/whole;
- religion – when faith in and devotion to the group's abilities is expressed;
- sanctuary – shelter/escape from everyday existence/hassle, etc.

The three key features of talk emphasized within this tradition are variability, construction and function (Potter and Wetherell, 1987). Discourse analyses of texts often highlight the multiple and conflicting ways in which people account for something. For example, a child speaking about family might present it as supportive at one point (e.g. talking about pocket money received) and prohibitive at another (e.g. talking about family rules). The second feature, construction, refers to the use of language to produce a given account in conversation. The categories and strategies used by people to create meaning are drawn from those existing in surrounding culture. The concept of 'family', for example, will have a number of understandings or representations in a given society at a given time, some of which will be negative (e.g. 'family as controlling') and some positive (e.g. 'family as nourishing'). Finally, the third feature of function refers to the social effects of such 'speech acts' (Austin, 1962). Continuing with the example, a 'family as controlling' repertoire used by a child or adolescent might serve to position the child as a victim of unreasonable family restrictions and help justify some 'rebellion', whilst employing a 'family as nourishing' repertoire would emphasize a more positive family image and perhaps work towards attracting favours or concessions from parents. The repertoires chosen and functions served would of course be understood in relation to the context in which they were used, whether as part of a family discussion at home, an interview with a researcher, or talk at school with friends, and so on.

Some work within this approach has attempted to create a 'discursive psychology' which is primarily concerned with using discourse analysis for understanding (social) psychological phenomena, such as attitudes and memory (e.g. Edwards and Potter, 1992). Such work contributes to the critique of mainstream (social) psychology by arguing convincingly that 'cognitive' structures and processes are better understood as having a public rather than private reality, i.e. in the language used to construct such phenomena. But, according to Parker (1992), this form of analysis is rarely extended to comment on the political implications of individualistic and mentalistic discourse within (social) psychology and wider culture generally, although Potter (1997) suggests that studies of discourse and rhetoric should not always or exclusively deal with social critique. Despite these debates, however, much research in this tradition has investigated the ideological dimensions to everyday talk. Indeed, Wetherell *et al.* (1987) use the term 'practical ideologies' to convey how people deploy various rhetorical methods in order to present a particular view as factual or natural – and other views as incorrect or unnatural: 'the often contradictory and fragmentary complexes of notions, norms and models which guide conduct and allow for its (inequality) justification and rationalisation' (1987: 60).

Presenting a personal view as factual or 'the way things are' helps resolve what Edwards and Potter (1993) call the 'dilemma of stake'. For example, a government politician would be expected to defend policies, but to make the defence more credible and deflect potential criticisms of stake or interest ('you would say that'), the speaker might refer to statistics ('facts') or demonstrate a 'bias' on the part of opposition politicians in order to authorize or reinforce the account. Of course, 'scientific' psychologists are faced with the same dilemma and are often at pains to stress the 'objectivity' of the research and sophistication of the statistical analysis. And efforts to protect statements or actions from being undermined are to be found frequently in everyday conversations, with the speaker presenting self as rational and the other as emotionally involved, for example ('I did what was logical, but you overreacted').

Box 3.1   Ideology as common sense: talking of the Royal Family (Billig, 1992)

According to Billig, everyday understandings of the British monarchy present an important opportunity to study 'ideological thinking in practice', since an uncritical acceptance of monarchy amounts to an acceptance of social inequality based on class/status differences. Although written texts tend to be favoured by discourse analysts, Billig emphasizes the value of studying actual conversations in naturalistic settings. Consequently, the project on the monarchy involved a researcher visiting sixty-three families from a range of socio-economic backgrounds in order to record their conversations on this topic.

Billig also argues that perspectives on the Royal Family (or any topic) will be varied and often contradictory, indicating a 'dilemmatic' quality to common sense – and ideology (see Billig *et al.*, 1988). For example, in the family discussions, the 'royals' were frequently urged not to be too 'ordinary' ('they're quite different, really they have to set standards') – nor to be too 'royal' ('they're just human, after all'). Similarly, the institution of the monarchy was presented both as the 'priceless' heritage of the nation and as a significant source of revenue from tourists.

The examples above perhaps relate to a broader 'ideological dilemma' between 'history as national progress' and 'history as national decline'. According to the former account, old differences in power and prestige between individuals and groups (e.g. between 'ordinary' people and the 'royals') had largely been eroded such that people enjoyed a better quality of life today. In contrast, another story drawn upon presented a conflicting picture, one where respect for valued traditions such as the Royal Family had diminished, to the detriment of society. This oscillation between two positions between speakers – and often with the same speaker – supports the contention of ideology as fragmented, negotiated and fluid.

To sum up so far, the above approach to discourse analysis attends closely to the 'repertoires' deployed in everyday conversation. It is assumed and frequently illustrated that speakers will draw upon a wide range of (sometimes competing) metaphors, images, and idioms in different conversational contexts; indeed, the same speaker may well use conflicting repertoires during one social encounter. Although discourse analysis in this vein is not always or necessarily used for 'critical' ends, there are many examples of research projects which examine links between common sense and the ideological maintenance of inequalities. Such analyses are often sophisticated expositions of the complex and contradictory workings of discourse/ideology as reproduced in everyday talk.

Subjects as structured by discourse

Another distinct but related form of discourse analysis is more explicitly concerned with discourse/s as producing and maintaining people ('subjects') within particular positions and relationships (e.g. Burman and Parker, 1993). This is a more 'top-down' approach as it concentrates mainly on broad historical and cultural representations advertised within dominant institutions (medicine, law, government) and the ways in which people are constrained within and/or resist these frameworks. This work has a more macro-sociological flavour and is influenced by social theorists such as Althusser and Foucault who were interested in language, power and subjectivity. Foucault's work became familiar to (social) psychology in the late 1970s and reflects concerns with the historical representations and practices around madness, punishment, confession and the self used to contain and control populations (see Parker, 1992). Following Foucault (1972), who characterized discourses as 'practices that systematically form the objects of which they speak' (1972: 49), Parker (1992: 5) defines a 'discourse' as 'a set of statements which construct an object'. For example, a 'medical' discourse will produce representations of unusual behaviours in terms of illness or disease.

An important conceptual framework utilized by discourse analysts within this tradition is the 'psy-complex' (Rose 1985; 1989). This refers to the contemporary preoccupation with and promotion of psychological or individualistic 'objects' (attitudes, personalities, etc.) and explanations embedded in a range of cultural texts and practices (soap operas, government policies, sport, etc.). But these and other discourses can be resisted and there is a particular interest here in developing and articulating alternative 'counter-discourses', after Foucault (e.g. 1980). In line with the three features outlined by Potter and Wetherell (1987) – variability, construction and function – Parker (1994) suggests the Foucauldian triad of contradiction–constitution–power. Although sympathetic to the former system, he argues that these latter three concepts attached to discourse analysis signal a more explicitly critical endeavour. As opposed to variability, the first concept of contradiction between discourses is said to imply struggle, fragmentation and social conflict. The notion of constitution rather than construction is presented as emphasizing structural constraints on individual activity – 'our ideas are constituted within patterns of discourse that we cannot control' (1994: 290), although meaning as contestable remains a theme. Finally, the preference for power over function stresses the force of discourses in positioning individuals in complex and often constraining ways.

Box 3.2   A discourse analysis of instructions for using children's toothpaste (Parker, 1994)

Parker considers the text presented on a tube of children's toothpaste to highlight the versatility of discourse analysis as well as the cultural structuring of such 'innocent' material. The 'MAWS PUNCH & JUDY TOOTHPASTE' is accompanied by pictures of Punch and Judy and provides the following directions:

> Choose a children's brush that has a small head and add a pea-sized amount of Punch & Judy toothpaste. To teach your child to clean teeth stand behind and place your hand under the child's chin to tilt head back and see mouth. Brush both sides of teeth as well as tops. Brush after breakfast and last thing at night. Supervise the brushing of your child's teeth until the age of eight. If your child is taking fluoride treatment, seek professional advice concerning daily intake. Contains 0.8% Sodium Monofluorophosphate.

After explaining the steps in and assumptions of his analysis in some detail, Parker goes on to identify four discourses in the Foucauldian tradition: 'rationalist' – implying an ability to follow procedures, make judgements, etc.; 'familial' – where children are 'owned' and supervised by parents; 'developmental–educational' – which stresses teaching the child until a developmental milestone is reached; 'medical' – linking the use of toothpaste to hygiene, professional supervision and chemical composition.

He proceeds to argue that such discourses function to reinforce the institutions of the family and of medicine, which are interconnected; medical authorities have often sought to advise parents on best practices (Donzelot, 1979). The image of Punch and Judy, on the other hand, provides a conflicting symbol of family in that it represents bad parents but also suggests revolt against the forces of discipline and order. In sum, parents and medics are positioned as powerful subjects whilst children are their subordinates, under their surveillance and control. Parker goes into much more detail in presenting and arguing for this form of analysis and acknowledges potential criticisms (e.g. implying that discourses are constructed, external and static) and mentions some general issues for discourse analysts, but we will discuss these towards the end of the chapter.

Common practices

In practice, many discourse analysts draw on both broad approaches in their work (Willott and Griffin, 1997) and there have been recent calls for more eclectic, integrationist methods (Wetherell, 1998). Since there are many different practices and disagreements within this broad area, it is difficult to produce a formal set of procedures for conducting discourse analysis. However, several authors have provided useful guidelines in this respect (e.g. Billig, 1997a; Parker, 1994; Potter and Wetherell, 1987; Willott and Griffin, 1997).

As you might expect, discourse analysis requires close, careful reading of the texts in question. Next, the coding of relevant material is undertaken, with care taken not to be too selective or exclude too much text. This process is complex and the identification of discourses fraught with uncertainty and revision. The important point is that your interpretations must be grounded in textual evidence, but there must also be an openness to and acknowledgement of potential alternative interpretations. Once fairly confident that you have identified the main discourses employed in the text, it might be fruitful then to discern the functions which these serve. Discursive functions can be understood or read in terms of the interpersonal context (justifications, accusations, etc.) as well as the wider socio-cultural climate (how the phenomenon is constructed in society). For example, if 'men as victims' has been identified as a common discourse, this could be related to the research context (e.g. a gathering of unemployed men) and/or wider social trends (e.g. a backlash against feminism) (see e.g. Gough and Peace, 2000). Throughout this process it is important to consider the variability as well as consistency in talk, as even short extracts can yield complex and contradictory positions (see the appendix to this chapter for further details).

As mentioned, discourse analysis may be applied to a wide range of 'texts', and various journals provide excellent examples of critical discourse analytic work, including *Discourse and Society*, *Feminism and Psychology* and *The Sociological Review*. The following section briefly summarises some recent studies which interrogate a variety of texts, although it should be borne in mind that discourse analyses are typically grounded in close scrutiny of often large data sets.

Discourse and text/s

Interview transcripts

Perhaps the most common application of discourse analysis is with interview transcripts based on interviews conducted between the researcher and one or more participants, although those influenced by conversation analysis are more inclined to examine actual conversations between people in natural settings (see Kleiner, 1998, below). Semi-structured interviews are popular and provide opportunities for both researcher and participant/s to explore areas of interest. Let us consider an example.

Doctoral research conducted by Reavey (1999), some of which has been published (see Reavey and Gough, 2000), was in part based on interviews conducted with ten professional counsellors, therapists and psychiatrists on the subject of childhood sexual abuse (CSA). One of the aims of the study was to critically examine the discourses reproduced by participants around femininity and sexuality – and how female abuse survivors were positioned within these discourses. The research was informed by feminist criticisms of psychology, therapy and medicine wherein women were subordinated and pathologized with reference to dominant norms around heterosexuality (see Hare-Mustin, 1991; Kitzinger, 1987). Some evidence for these claims was found in the texts, for example with a clinical psychologist (Oliver) and a sex therapist (Marg) (Box 3.3).

Box 3.3   Professional constructions of women survivors of childhood sexual abuse (Reavey and Gough, 2000)

Oliver   I think always, think the choice of partners often fascinating.

Paula   Right, why?

Oliver   So often they choose a partner who will in turn abuse them in some form.

Paula   Right.

Oliver   Cos it's like, it's almost like ( ) kids build up some kind of internal working model of um the environment still being abusive in some way, and I think in some unwitting way also [women] seek that out, it's like that's what you know ... [Extract 1]

Marg.   They may be very much more needing to control, not let themselves go, making sure that there's a safe... longing quite unrealistically, a man without any force, when in fact what they do need is a man with force, because they end up getting a man without any power, and then that isn't going to work for them because they need a powerful man, one with authority, but it needs to be a good authority, not a manipulative or abusing one. If that makes any sense? [Extract 2]

( )   Unintelligible material

In the first extract women survivors of CSA are constructed as making irrational choices of partner, thereby reproducing aspects of the original abusive situation, i.e. involvement with a male aggressor. This theme is continued in the second extract, this time with non-abusive partners representing an abnormal choice. So, a woman survivor is damned for selecting both violent and passive men, both taken as signs of a pathological behaviour from a victim of childhood trauma. Further, Marg suggests a route to recovery via a 'powerful' man – ironically returning women to a relationship based on strong men and weak women which may well have characterized prior interactions with male perpetrators. In these ways, women survivors are positioned within discourses of deviance, victimhood and heterosexual masculinity.

'Natural' conversation

Conversation analytic approaches which tend to concentrate on studying micro-linguistic features of 'natural' talk are not normally associated with critical social psychology, but this need not be the case. For example, Kitzinger and Frith (1999) have used conversation analysis to study sexual refusals to show that young women can and do draw on various culturally available techniques to clearly indicate unwillingness for sexual intercourse (with silences, compliments, deferred acceptance, and so on). Rather than regard such responses as weak, they argue that young women are displaying skill in communication and that it is their male partners, in claiming not to understand the refusals, who are behaving like 'cultural dopes'. Clearly, such uses of conversation analytic approaches can contribute to feminist readings of (hetero-)sexual interactions. However, the data used to support these arguments are drawn from focus group interviews with young women, whereas conversation analysts normally prefer to focus on 'natural' conversation.

A study by Kleiner (1998) published in *Discourse & Society* explored conversations between undergraduate students discussing issues of race at university (see Box 3.4). Instead of standard individual or group interviews, 76 student volunteers were asked to get together with two or three friends in a relaxed setting to initiate and record a discussion on race, thereby resembling 'ordinary' or 'natural' talk. Several interesting patterns of racist discourse emerged within all-white conversations, as Box 3.4 suggests.

Box 3.4   Racist discourse (Kleiner, 1998)

1   *B*: They totally have this– y – Exactly. And – You
2   know with Asians, you don't see Asians like =
3   *K*:   ( )
4   *B*: = pulling an attitude, and I don't think I – I
5   have like Asian friends and--I – I don't think I've
6   ever seen an Asian--pull– you know and like – Black
7   people bring up like 'Well-- you owe it to us
8   because--you know--you had us as slaves--=
9   *K*:
10   how long:
11   *B*: = thousands of years ago, and blah blah blah:,
12   and you OWE it to us. Blah Blah' Well what about--
13   what about when we took like during what was it
14   World War Two, when we took all the Japanese, and

```
15      stuck them in prison camps in California. I mean
16      What about THAT? You don't see Asian people still
17      all fired up about THAT,--I mean it is totally =
18  K:                          Yeah and if that IS the
19      case
20  B: =Wrong but-Just-I mean it was a mistake in
21      the PAST, and it shouldn't--like--I don't know,
22      it- it- YEAH it does affect us, and YEAH it was
23      WRONG, but--it wasn't ME, it wasn't even my DAD.
24      It wasn't even my GRANDpa. It was like-
25  C:                                And they're-
26      now they're STILL--you know basically treated =
27  B:                    (                    ) ago.
28  C: =not just equal, but they get a- the advantage
29      of--you know in a lot of situations so they can't
30      complain they're not treated equal now.
```

Transcription conventions:

--	pause
!	exclamation
CAPS	emphatic stress
:	lengthening
=	unbroken continuity on speaker's talk
[	starting point of some overlap
]	ending point of some overlap
( )	unintelligible material
(text)	text in parentheses [uncertain transcription]

To reinforce their arguments, the speakers import into their talk the presumed arguments of an absent antagonist (in this case 'black people') and proceed to undermine these other views. Such talk is cited as an example of modern racist ideology, whereby prejudice is located 'in the past' and minority groups are presented as receiving unfairly privileged and protected treatment ('advantages'). In addition the speakers construct themselves as reasonable and liberal ('yeah, it was wrong, but ...') to further authorize their arguments and divert potential accusations of racism (see also Van Dijk, 1984; Wetherell and Potter, 1992).

Media features

Critical discourse analysis can also be performed on already existing texts, such as film scripts, newspaper articles, and magazine features. In another article featured recently in *Discourse & Society*, Santa Ana (1999) studies 107 articles in the *Los Angeles Times* on the controversial subject of immigration policy. The newspaper reports reflect the 1994 political debate around the 'Proposition 187' anti-immigrant referendum which, if passed, would have denied various services and benefits to undocumented immigrants in California. The specific analytic focus of the paper is on metaphor, whereby language users seek to understand something unfamiliar or conceptual with reference to convenient or accessible material (see Lakoff, 1987). The dominant metaphor which Santa Ana discerned from the media reports was 'Immigrants are animals' (see Box 3.5), with other less common examples appearing such as 'Immigrants as debased people/weeds/commodities'. We will focus on the dominant metaphor, where immigrants are presented as animals to be lured, pitted or hunted, even when anti-immigration positions are taken. Several examples are provided (see Box 3.5). Santa-Ana discusses this and related language in terms of racism, where immigrants are represented as sub-human and subordinate to the white majority in California. The power of metaphors such as 'Immigrants as animals' lies in their subtle construction and common usage – they are rarely announced crudely and tend not to attract too much attention.

Box 3.5   Immigrants as animals (Santa Ana, 1999)

[Governor] Wilson said he believed public benefits are a lure to immigrants and his intent was to discourage illegal immigration by denying them access to health care, education and welfare programmes (22 August 1993: A-1)

Democrat Kathleen Brown branded Republican Pete Wilson a cynical career politician who will do anything to get re-elected: 'We're not going to play into those games of pitting workers against each other' (3 November 1994: D-1).

Beaten-down [Immigration and Nationalization Service] agents, given only enough resources to catch a third of their quarry, sense the objective in this campaign is something less that total victory (5 July 1992: A-3)

Q-sorts

Q-sorts are not a 'text' as such but a method of examining texts which draws heavily on discourse analysis. This technique has been enthusiastically adopted by a few feminist and critical researchers as a way of examining variation in subject positions and experiences (Kitzinger, 1986; Senn, 1996; Stainton-Rogers *et al.*, 1995). Typically, the researcher will have collected lots of material on the topic in question in the hope that most or all possible perspectives on that topic are represented. The participant is presented with the range of items and required to sort them into a continuum on the basis of how much/ little they agree with the stance projected by a given item. The extent of similarity/difference between participants can then be neatly displayed on a grid or matrix, as each person will have a score for each item depending on where they placed it on their continuum. Analysis can then move into a more interpretative mode, with findings related to research context, participants' lives and previous work in the area. An example of this method is taken from Senn (1996) (see Box 3.6).

Box 3.6   Q-methodology and women's constructions of pornography (Senn, 1996)

In order to sample a range of views on pornography, interviews were firstly conducted with 30 women from diverse backgrounds. After transcribing all interviews, three co-researchers were then asked to study the texts to identify a spectrum of views on pornography. This exercise yielded 98 items! Sixteen participants were then recruited to perform Q-sorts, half from the original interview group and half from another population of students and academics accessed via a university college. The participants were invited to place each item on a continuum ranging from +5 (strongly agree) to −5 (strongly disagree), and to attempt to produce a normal distribution of scores. This data was then factor analysed and five factors were produced, including the 'radical feminist' perspective', the 'conservative' perspective, the 'humanist, child-centred' perspective and the 'ambivalent but mildly pro-pornography' perspective. To illustrate, the 'humanist, child-centred' perspective places special emphasis on harm done to children, as women espousing this view tended to especially endorse items pertaining to children, e.g. item 85: 'Pornography using children is the worst kind of pornography'.

Other dimensions of this factor include pornography as demeaning to women and male-centred. Also, women employing this factor who had experience of partners using pornography suggested that these men consumed the material away from the gaze of partner and children, and without resorting to sexual violence. Other dimensions to this factor and comparisons with other factors are discussed by the author and she concludes that Q-sort analysis deriving from and combined with textual material (e.g. interview transcripts) allow the most important features of women's perceptions and experiences of pornography to be elicited. Factors can then be linked to existing feminist literature on the topic (emphasizing power, ideology, etc.) in order to forge a sophisticated critical analysis.

Q-sort techniques obviously involve some quantitative aspects and come under the heading of 'using numbers differently'. Other tech niques used by critical social psychologists also combine quantitative and qualitative features. For example, Shields and Crowley (1996) argue a case for using questionnaires 'critically' in feminist research as part of a broader multi-method project. They suggest that questionnaires and rating scales can help refine research questions and may even challenge the researcher's own assumptions.

Evaluating discourse analysis

Is discourse analysis always critical?

As noted earlier, discourse analysis is understood and practised in different ways by critical social scientists (e.g. 'bottom-up' v. 'top-down' approaches) and there are some issues concerning whether discourse analysis can be considered inherently or unproblematically 'critical'. Indeed, the literature on discourse analysis, and critical social psychology more generally, is peppered with debates on a range of key issues (see Burman and Parker, 1993). One such issue pertains to the focus of discourse analysis, as emphasis varies between those who prioritize language use in its rhetorical/conversational context (e.g. Potter, 1996) and those who favour a more structural or Foucauldian analysis of the cultural discourses and the subject positions these inscribe (e.g. Parker, 1992). Both approaches have been criticized. For example, the image of speakers manipulating discourses in strategic interactions informs the former approach, an image which may promote overly individualistic or psychological understandings of human action (Burman and Parker, 1993). Conversely, the Foucauldian approach could be criticized for presenting an over-deterministic view by which individuals are structured or entrapped within prevailing discourses (see Potter *et al.*, 1990). Although both types can produce critical contributions, the latter approach is more often associated with a more explicitly critical agenda, although this has been disputed (Potter, 1997). In practice, however, most discourse analysis work is influenced by both traditions (e.g. Willott and Griffin, 1997) although debates continue (e.g. Schegloff, 1998; Wetherell, 1998).

In any case, it is how discourse analysis is applied in practice which determines its critical (or otherwise) quality. It is not difficult to imagine sanitized forms of discourse analysis interested only in the technical aspects of language use (grammatical rules, etc.) or instances of discourse analysis performed in the interests of dominant groups (e.g. applying discourses of victimhood to middle-class, heterosexual, white majorities). Even if a 'critical' position is adopted in discourse analysis, it is difficult to avoid a sense in which the analyst is imposing her/his interpretation upon the text. This power and control over other people's words is ironic in light of the desire to conduct critical or democratic research where the participants are empowered. A related issue here is the tendency to disrespect what is presented in the text in the attempt to get at the more abstract discourses 'beyond' or 'behind' the words. In this way participants' voices and words are subjected to a suspicious reading which may devalue or undermine their perspectives, a stance which has been labelled 'anti-humanist'.

The problem of 'reality'

Another, not unconnected, issue surrounds the relationship between discourse and reality. Many researchers using discourse analysis and working within critical social psychology are interested in contextualizing their work with respect to prevailing social structures (such as capitalism; patriarchy) and subjective experiences (abuse, violence). Yet the turn to language within contemporary social theory and signalled by the popularity of discourse analysis emphasizes an 'anti-foundational' stance: i.e. language does not refer to some reality or foundation beyond the text, but only to itself. In other words, our talk and texts *create* or *construct* a reality rather than reflect what is 'out there', so that for any given topic there will be a wide range of (sometimes conflicting) voices and perspectives (see Burr, 1995). This relativist position has been proved a useful tool in deconstructing (social) psychological assumptions about internal objects (attitudes, personalities, etc.) as possessing some kind of reality discoverable by 'scientific' methods (see Parker, 1992; Potter and Wetherell, 1987; Stainton-Rogers *et al.*, 1995) but poses problems for engaged, critical research interested in the materiality of power.

Box 3.7   The realism–relativism debate

A recent book by Parker (ed.) (1998) raises issues concerning the appropriateness of discourse analysis for critical social psychology. A note of caution is sounded by several contributors in championing discourse analysis as a critical framework since it entails a relativist epistemology. In other words, the method of discourse analysis tends to be informed by post-structuralist or constructionist ideas which stress the language-based or 'textual' nature of the social world. Whilst such ideas have proved invaluable in destabilizing various truth-claims (e.g. women are maternal, men are rational, etc.), the absence of any agreed or neutral version of reality beyond discourse can inhibit critical commitments to the specific causes or groups. For example, a critical project on male homophobia might seek to identify those discourses of gender and sexuality which construct gay men as subordinate, but cannot claim that gay men are 'really' oppressed, or all equally oppressed (white, middle-class gay men might feel quite privileged, for example). So, the constructionist focus on diversity can discourage researchers from making claims about the collective situation of a specific group.

Also, the exclusive focus on language can overlook social practices and structures which may be implicated in oppression, such as physical violence and capitalist economics. For this reason 'critical realists' such as Parker attempt to preserve some sense of the real whilst acknowledging social diversity and the role of language in constructing reality. A relation between discourse and reality is proposed where reality informs the language we use to define the world and where our capacity to act on and construct things is constrained by material and discursive forces. Willig (1998) argues that discourse analysts should move from deconstructing discourse/s towards reconstructing particular versions of the world based on one's personal and political values. This 'critical realist' stance is promoted by several feminist writers (see Wilkinson and Kitzinger, 1995).

For critical work implies a commitment to a particular position/s. To adopt a feminist stance in research, for example, is generally to suggest that women are oppressed in some form (e.g. in the workplace), but it is not difficult to imagine alternative constructions of reality ('white women are privileged in the workplace'; 'men are the real victims in the modern workplace') (see Gough and Peace, 2000). Action or resistance based on shared or collective positions then becomes a difficult project, although recognition of diversity and conflict within a group may assist a critical endeavour (e.g. Walkerdine, 1981). There is no clear solution to this dilemma, but many critical researchers work with 'problems' identified by those participants and client groups generally assumed to be 'oppressed' or with whom the researcher feels some affinity, as the next section suggests.

Action research

Action research typically involves the researcher/s working in partnership with a particular group or community in order to facilitate positive changes in social position and experience. As such, it is especially attractive to critical researchers committed to raising awareness of inequalities and attempting to bring about social change. Indeed, it is a form of research which has been used by academics associated with feminism, socialism, gay rights and anti-racism, although it does not necessarily involve discourse analysis. Rheinarz (1992) refers to 'action-in-research' and helpfully specifies five relevant tasks/goals:

Action research	the obvious but nonetheless crucial requirement of a research project working towards desirable change;
Participatory/collaborative research	a democratic research process is favoured where participants have an equal say in decisions concerning data collection and analysis – the term 'co-researchers' is often used in this context;

Prevalence and needs assessment	instead of being defined in advance by researchers, participant needs and issues are identified during the initial stages of the research through open discussions, etc.;
Evaluation research	to assess the effectiveness of actions instituted within the research process and decide between competing strategies for further use;
Demystification	refers to knowledge gained during action research as prompting change – the greater the awareness of the situation, the greater the capacity for action.

So, the key theme of action research is intervention in a situation perceived to be 'problematic' in some way/s. An action research 'spiral' is summarized by Elliott (1980):

- select the general area; discuss, observe, read and decide on your first action
- take your action (and monitor the action)
- examine the information you have collected
- evaluate processes and outcomes
- plan next action
- take next action
- continue

Banister *et al.* (1994) describe an hypothetical example of action research. The 'problem' a youth worker identifies upon firstly arriving at a new centre concerns the relative lack of young women using the centre. The next step is then to gather information and develop research questions by engaging with the relevant research literature, discussing the issues with colleagues and centre-users and studying local documents regarding that particular centre. Having completed these tasks, a course of action might be devised, such as organizing women-only activities and discussions. In the midst of such action male domination and sexual harassment might well arise as a deterrent to the women's attendance at the centre. Further action here might be to continue the women-only sessions if desired by the users, observe if this support group is having any demonstrable effects on participation in centre activities and perhaps take formal action to ensure equal access to facilities, such as the pool table. All the while the effects of in/action would be monitored and further actions planned and initiated, depending on the time constraints of the project. The action research should then be written up, preferably in conjunction with users, and written for lay as well as academic audiences. All stages in the research process should be documented (a reflexive diary is useful here, see below) and the final analysis should be returned to participants for further comment and possible revision. Critical qualitative research in general tends to emphasize 'critical subjectivity', or reflexivity, in order to interrogate the values and interactions which have created the research and its outputs.

Reflexivity

Reflexivity is signalled by the researcher's incorporation of information relating to the research context and to relevant 'personal' thoughts and feelings into the research report. In contrast to 'scientific' psychology, where researcher detachment and neutrality are cherished, it is thought inevitable that the perspectives of researcher and participants and their interrelationship will impact on the research and, moreover, that such influences should be documented to further contextualize the research. In feminist work, for example, the suppression of the human researcher is viewed as a particularly masculine practice, rather than some universal or necessary scientific norm, and a more participative and open stance is advocated (Wilkinson, 1988). Making public one's interpretative resources and processes renders the researcher more accountable for the analysis and places the reader of the research report in a better informed position from which to situate and assess the research as a whole.

In a much-cited piece, Wilkinson (1988) notes three distinct but interrelated forms of reflexivity: personal, functional and disciplinary:

- *Personal reflexivity* requires that the researcher make visible their individuality and its effects on the research process. There is an attempt to make visible those motivations, interests, attitudes, etc. which the researcher has imported to the research process and to reflect on how these have impacted on the research. Such subjective factors are typically construed as 'bias' or 'interference' within 'scientific' research, but recognition of the (inter-)personal dimension to research is heralded as enriching and informative by qualitative researchers.

- *Functional reflexivity* relates to one's role as a researcher and the effect this might have on the research process. It focuses attention on the different identities presented within the research and the interactions between researcher and participants. In this case a key issue concerns the distribution of power and status within the research process; although many qualitative researchers are committed to democratic forms of inquiry where the voices of participants are encouraged and respected, it is virtually impossible to escape researcher–participant relationships structured by inequalities (see Parker, 1992). After all, it is the researcher who principally develops an idea, formulates the research questions and organizes the format of the research.

- Finally, *disciplinary reflexivity* involves a critical stance towards the place and function of the particular research project within broader debates about theory and method. It suggests outlining those existing concepts and traditions which have been important in shaping the research and requires some discussion of the potential contribution of the research to a particular literature. This dimension of reflexivity is enthusiastically endorsed by feminist and critical researchers interested in challenging the findings of conventional (usually quantitative) social science research (see Stainton-Rogers *et al.*, 1995).

A common way of tracking the impact of the researcher and research context is to keep a diary or journal which documents the researcher's thoughts and experiences before, during and after data collection and analysis (Banister *et al.*, 1994). Notes concerning why certain choices and decisions were made, about changing directions, personal reactions, etc. can be used to inform a 'reflexive account' which in turn will inform the research report. The question of how to incorporate this narrative into one's writing-up is indeed difficult, with many authors preferring to simply provide information about researcher and participant subject positions (gender, age, social class, race) and perhaps hazarding some speculation towards the end of the paper on the effects of these factors on the research outcomes. But there are examples of more ambitious forms of reflexive writing which entail disrupting the narrative flow of the text, for example with commentaries at the end of each section contrasting the academic analysis with more personal reporting, thereby highlighting the fragmented positions of the researcher and the status of the text as constructed (see Lather, 1992). But even when engaging in such adventurous and creative forms of writing up research, certain problems plague the notion of reflexivity, as discussed below.

The observation and reporting of subjective thoughts and feelings germane to the research rests on some dubious assumptions. Prevailing definitions and practices around reflexivity do tend to presume a conscious subject with unproblematic access to their 'intentions', 'motivations', and 'feelings': a reflexive stance implies 'honesty' about presenting one's position. But can we be sure that we know what prompts us to choose a particular research project, to ask certain questions, to respond in specific ways? To accomplish such an onerous task would require a 'superhuman self-consciousness', which may only be attainable (if at all) through an intensive programme of psychoanalysis, according to Seale (1999). Compounding this problem of self-awareness is the post-modern deconstruction of subjectivity as socially constructed, fragmented and contradictory (e.g. Shotter and Gergen, 1988; see also Chapter 4). How can we pin down a self which is multifaceted, dynamic and embedded in language and social relationships? Indeed, there is an emerging consensus that our identities are dispersed across time and place, subject to negotiations within sets of relationships at home, at work, and at leisure (Wetherell and Maybin, 1996). Consequently, reflexivity must be re-viewed as similarly complex and tenuous.

A fruitful way of exploring the complexity of positions and relationships within the research process is to turn to the text, whether this constitutes interview transcripts, field notes, or diary entries and so on. Close reading of the text will highlight the multiple and shifting positions of the researcher during the data collection phase and perhaps enhance reflexivity through identifying positions not consciously adopted at the time. For example, the researcher could describe themselves as 'feminist', presenting details about self and existing theory which justify this self-identification, whereas a study of the interview transcripts could throw up instances where anti-feminist talk was ignored or even encouraged by the researcher. The point is, it is impossible and simplistic to presume a fixed, knowable researcher-subject in advance when diverse and conflicting positions may well become apparent upon retrospective analysis. Therefore, it is important for qualitative researchers to acknowledge a potentially numerous range of possibly competing interests and to return to the transcripts a number of times in order to achieve this end. And the reader of the research report will similarly be in a position to relate claims about subjectivities and relationships between researcher and researched to the textual evidence and to make judgements about the persuasiveness of the reflexive analysis. So, it is important to sustain an openness to the possibility that one's research aims and stated orientation may be complicated or compromised during interactions with participants and in the subsequent presentation of the research 'findings'. But it should be borne in mind that reflexivity can slide into self-referential analysis if the focus shifts from the account/s and potential critical analyses to the researcher's construction of the account/s (Burman and Parker, 1993).

Summary

Critical social psychological research follows from concerns to highlight and challenge forms of oppression in contemporary society, a concern which often entails critical discourse analysis, although it is acknowledged that other modes of enquiry can be adopted by critical researchers, even quantitative methods. As discussed, discourse analysis can be useful in interrogating a range of texts for evidence of language used in the service of power, although complex and difficult issues attend discourse analysis and critical social psychology in general. Practices involving reflexivity and action research are also emphasized. On a final note, it must also be stressed that critical activities need not be confined to research. As Nightingale and Neilands (1997) suggest, a 'critical' attitude can be usefully deployed in the services of charitable organizations (telephone counselling, befriending schemes, etc.) and political groups (anti-sexist, environmental campaigns, etc.). Similarly, many critical writers stress the importance of resisting ab/uses of psychology in practice – in the areas of therapy, health and education, for example (see Parker, 1999). The boundaries between critical research and practical activities are of course blurred in forms of 'action research'.

Appendix: guidelines for discourse analysis

To reiterate, discourse analysis does not lend itself to a rigid step-by-step instructions manual, but attempts have been made to summarize key activities.

Billig (1997) emphasizes technical linguistic analysis and offers helpful guidelines, which we reproduce below:

1. Read background material about discursive psychology and about the topic you want to study;
2. Read some more;
3. Decide on the type of data you want to study;
4. Collect data. If the data are printed materials, proceed to 9;
5. If you are collecting speech data, then collect your tape recordings;
6. Listen to tape recordings;
7. Transcribe the recordings;
8. Check the transcription against the tapes;
9. Read the transcriptions/data;
10. Keep reading them; start looking for interesting features and developing 'intuitive hunches';
11. Start indexing for themes and discursive features;
12. Read, read and read, especially to check out intuitive hunches against the data; always try to look for counter examples;
13. Start writing preliminary analyses, testing your hunches against details of the data; always be critical;
14. Keep drafting and re-drafting analyses, comparing different extracts, looking in detail at extracts and being aware of counter examples;
15. Keep writing, reading, thinking and analysing until you produce a version with which you are not totally dissatisfied;
16. Be prepared to return to stage 1.

Parker (1994) emphasizes a Foucauldian or socio-historical reading and offers detailed advice, which we summarize below:

[a] turn the text into a written form;
[b] free associate to the text (i.e. play around with potential meanings with colleagues);
[c] systematically itemize 'objects' that appear in this text (e.g. nouns);
[d] identify the ways of speaking used in relation to the objects (the 'discourses');
[e] systematically itemize 'subjects' (the categories of person who appear in the text);
[f] identify the rights and responsibilities attached to each subject;
[g] map the different versions of the social world which coexist in the text;
[h] speculate as to how each of these versions would contest each other's claims;
[i] identify contrasts between ways of speaking;
[j] identify points where these ways of speaking overlap;

[k]   compare these with other relevant texts;

[l]   choose appropriate terminology to label the discourses;

[m] examine when and where these discourses developed;

[n]   describe how the discourses have operated to naturalize the things
      they refer to;

[o]   examine the role of the discourses in reproducing institutions;

[p]   explore discourses which subvert those institutions;

[q]   consider the beneficiaries and those disadvantaged within the
      discourses;

[r]   imagine who would support and discredit such discourses;

[s]   link together discourses which enjoy power;

[t]   show how these can reproduce or challenge ideas about social
      change and future possibilities.

Key references

Burman, E. and Parker, I. (eds) (1993) Introduction, *Discourse Analytic Research: Repertoires and Readings of Texts in Action* (London: Sage). A useful text in which contributions define, apply and discuss different forms of discourse analysis.

Gavey, N. (1997) 'Feminist Poststructuralism and Discourse Analysis', in M. Gergen and S. Davis (eds), *Toward A New Psychology of Gender: A Reader*. (London: Routledge). A helpful discussion of issues pertaining to the use of discourse analysis for feminist/critical practice.

Deconstructing
the Self

4

This chapter will highlight:

- The psychological concept of 'personality'
- Social roles
- The impact of culture on the self
- The self as fragmented and de-centred
- Societal and discursive constraints on identity
- The problem of subjective experience

Introduction

In most Western societies, we are used to thinking about ourselves as unique, as different from other people. We may admit some family resemblances ('I'm a bit like my dad') and make generalizations about members of a particular group ('all men are pathetic'), but we tend to emphasize individual differences above all. We are fascinated by the latest surveys on personality which categorize the self into different types ('which type of lover/boss/driver/parent are you?'). Our language provides us with many terms for differentiating between people – assertive/passive; anxious/calm; lazy/productive – which we may also use to predict an individual's behaviour. After all, if we label Linda as 'quiet' then this implies that she will normally be quiet, and this is 'knowledge' which is helpful when we anticipate encountering her in the future (we will not be surprised by Linda's quietness and will 'know' to direct the conversation, for example). In other words, the term 'personality' is used to suggest those 'core' characteristics thought to 'capture' a person's being. Of course, such ideas have been present(ed) in psychology for much of this century, where it is proposed that personality can be clearly defined and measured; most people are familiar with Eysenck's Personality Inventory (1952) which is used to calculate extroversion–introversion and stability–neuroticism.

However, this assumption that personality is fixed and amenable to measurement has been questioned both within and beyond (social) psychology. Within sociology and sociological social psychology, for example, the psychological focus on the individual is, predictably, criticized for ignoring how society shapes people in various ways (e.g. Shotter and Gergen, 1988). Role theory is used to highlight the impact of social expectations and situations on the self: interviewees will hardly appear in casual clothes and refuse to answer questions nor will mourners at a funeral tend to dress colourfully or speak disrespectfully of the deceased in public. There is a sense, then, in which the self must be managed, at least in certain situations, in order to fulfil social norms and obligations (see Goffman, 1959). Such an analysis points to a self which is flexible and dynamic, adopting and discarding 'multiple roles' as the situation demands – a fragmented rather than a unitary self. The argument that people are responsive to local rules and conventions has been extended to cultures, where different values related to the individual have been noted between nations and societies. For example, Eastern countries such as Japan tend to encourage self-effacement, in that individual needs and desires are secondary compared to the requirements of the family, the organization, the club, etc., in contrast to the Western promotion of self-expression and self-interest (see Smith and Bond, 1993).

With the emergence critical social psychology, this latter sociological–pluralistic view of selfhood is favoured over the psychological–unified stance, although there are many debates concerning the extent to which an individual is moulded by societal and cultural forces (see Parker, 1992; Potter and Wetherell, 1987). Critical social psychology considers the various representations of self on offer in a given culture and examines how these are taken up, re-worked or even resisted by people in the way they talk about themselves (Burman and Parker, 1993; Potter and Wetherell, 1987). For example, a gay man might wish to refuse an effeminate identity in favour of more traditionally 'masculine' positions (strong, rational, etc.), thereby challenging the discourse which associates male homosexuality with femininity and weakness. Moreover, as critical social psychology is concerned also with issues of power and inequalities, questions about the functions which certain ideals are pushed to serve would be asked. For example, it has been argued that the Western capitalist spotlight on individuals rather than societies facilitates a politics where individuals are blamed for problems which might otherwise be conceived in terms of social factors (see Parker, 1992; Sampson, 1993). The murder of a black teenager in London,

Stephen Lawrence, and the subsequent bungled police inquiry which has prompted a debate within the UK about whether racism is 'institutional' or located within a few extreme minds, is a case in point.

So, this chapter presents a critical view of the traditional psychological (and 'commonsense') position which presents the self as a stable, measurable essence or object set apart from social relationships. Instead, critical social psychology uses terms such as 'subjectivity' and 'identities' to suggest a fluid, multiple process embedded in social practices; but not completely determined by social practices – identity is constructed, negotiated and defended in relation to other people and in the light of prevailing values and conventions. Such ideas are developed below.

CRITICAL THINKING ON PERSONALITY

Psychologists have popularized the concept of personality, which assumes a stable and consistent self. But how do different people you know describe your 'personality'? Do their assessments agree? What factors influence how *you* think about yourself?

Deconstructing the psychological self

As mentioned above, individualist societies like most Western societies promote a culture where the self is visible, distinctive and personally responsible. We talk constantly about 'personality', debating those 'types' of person most likely to engage in 'road rage', collect stamps, obsess about football, take drugs, surf the net, and so on. We assume that the cause or one of the main causes of such behaviours reside within the person, in their personality, so that only those predisposed towards aggression will submit to road rage and that only certain weak or pathological individuals will seek narcotic stimulation. When we resort to such explanations we echo personality theorists and assume that personality is:

- identifiable (and measurable);
- stable over time (i.e. fixed);
- internally consistent (all characteristics fit together);
- the (main) cause of behaviour.

Let us take a closer look at these assumptions. Firstly, we take it for granted that people possess a unique set of personal characteristics, or 'traits', which corresponds to their 'core' or 'essence', their personality. In psychology, much time and effort has been invested in producing thousands of personality tests which claim to measure such traits as 'authoritarianism', 'need for achievement', 'androgyny', 'emotional stability' and 'attributional style' – the list is endless!

To give you a flavour of such instruments, the form of the 'Attributional Style Questionnaire' (ASQ) is detailed below (Box 4.1). The theory behind the scale proposes that individuals differ in their

---

Box 4.1 'Attributional style questionnaire' (Peterson *et al.*, 1993: 156)

Instructions:

Please try to vividly imagine yourself in the situations that follow. If such a situation happened to you, what would you feel would have caused it? While events may have many causes, we want you to pick only one – the cause if this event happened to you. Please write this cause in the blank provided after each event. Next we want to ask you some questions about the cause. To summarize, we want you to:

1 Read each situation and imagine it happening to you.
2 Decide what you feel would be the major cause of the situation if it happened to you.
3 Write one cause in the blank provided.
4 Answer three questions about the cause.

At this point the subjects are presented with six 'bad' events (your friend is hostile; you can't make a work deadline, etc.) and six 'good' events (a success at work, in a relationship, etc.). The task is to discern the cause of each event on 7-point scales according to internality/externality, stability/instability and globality/specificity. And for each cause, the subjects respond to three questions:

1 Is this cause due to something about you or something about other people or circumstances?
2 In the future will the cause again be present?
3 Is the cause something that influences this situation or does it also influence other areas of your life?

Scores for the three dimensions – internality, stability and globality – are collated for the good and bad events separately. Often an overall, composite score for 'explanatory style' is calculated.

---

attributional or explanatory style. Attributions refer to our accounts or 'causal explanations' pertaining to particular situations. For example, in considering why you were late for work your boss might focus on the personal (an internal cause, such as 'laziness'; 'lack of responsibility') whereas you might point to an external cause (e.g. the train was cancelled). You might also suggest it was a one-off event (unstable cause) whereas your boss might suspect future tardiness (stable cause). You might console yourself with thinking that at least you are not late for other events, such as a 'date' or a doctor's appointment (a specific cause) while the boss might wonder if you are late for everything (a global cause). The ASQ attempts to assess how you think in terms of these three attributional dimensions: internality/externality, stability/instability and globality/specificity.

In general, two main explanatory styles have been identified. On the one hand there are people who explain positive outcomes in terms of internal, stable and global factors ('my success in the exams is down to me, I am wonderful') and negative outcomes as external, unstable and specific to the situation ('my failed exam was down to a bad paper, I did well in other exams'). On the other hand, some people are said to exhibit a reverse pattern where positive events are construed as external, unstable and specific and negative events viewed as internal, stable and global: in short, people who show signs of depression (Peterson *et al.*, 1993).

However, the problem with such questionnaires is that they oblige you to select a limited option (in this case, the major 'cause') when, in fact, your response to the item might have otherwise been much more complex. There is just no room for responses like: 'Well, I'm not quite sure, I did well on that paper because I worked hard, although it was a pretty fair exam and I did buy the recommended texts whereas others didn't.' Similarly, when thinking about the selected cause in terms of the three dimensions it might well be difficult to select numbers on a scale because of the potential number of competing explanations for an outcome (as above). Moreover, the exercise feels not a little artificial: you are asked to respond in a limited way to a set of predetermined items and scenarios and the 'causes' you select for the experiment might well reflect the situation and your status within it. There is little scope for the subject bringing his or her own interpretations to bear on the material – definitions of 'good' and 'bad' events are likely to vary between people. Indeed, there has been much work on 'demand characteristics' and 'social desirability' (Orne, 1962) which suggests that subjects' responses are sensitive to the dynamics of the test situation.

In avoiding or dismissing such influences, the complexity in people's social interactions is foreclosed and the portrait of the individual based on overall score surely simplistic and one-dimensional.

When we categorize someone as, say, neurotic we imply that they have always been this way and always will; in other words, a person's character remains stable throughout life – the second assumption. After all, if we thought that someone fluctuated a lot in their behaviour then personality terms which suggest stability would become meaningless. In psychological and popular parlance it is sometimes further assumed that personality is at least partially preordained by biology. Body shape itself was originally linked to personality (Kretschmer, 1925) although more modern theories point to neural wiring (Eysenck, 1952). Commonsense ideas frequently focus on family resemblances ('like father like son', etc.) with a typical claim that such similarities are due to genetic inheritance. Hormonal systems are highlighted to suggest personality differences between men and women, with the former identified as more aggressive by virtue of greater testosterone levels (e.g. Goldberg, 1977) and the latter deemed more nurturing because of oestrogen effects (Rossi, 1977).

CRITICAL THINKING ON BIOLOGY AND 'PERSONALITY'

A range of biological 'causes' have been used by psychologists to explain 'personality' (e.g. genetics, hormones, neurochemistry). Do you believe biology plays a role in fixing 'the way you are'? How far can biological influences be overcome?

But such theories do not seem to recognize that people change, that quiet children may become loud adults, that sullen adolescents may develop into contented grown-ups. Apart from changes brought about by life stage, people may also vary their behaviour according to the situation, as in a teacher being efficient and disciplined at work but getting drunk and dancing at weekends, or a therapist prone to excitability when not being professionally detached.

The third assumption of personality-talk is that the different aspects of someone's self necessarily fit together into a neat, consistent package. For example, if we describe a person as outgoing, we may also guess that she or he is talkative, has a good sense of humour, enjoys novel situations and challenges, and that traits such as passivity and neuroticism do not feature. The notion of personality, then, implies that a person cannot be both extroverted and introverted at the same time, as this would be inconsistent – the categories are mutually exclusive. Again, this way of thinking does not do justice to the variation in behaviour witnessed in daily interaction. A friend or partner can be sensitive and caring one day and cold and aloof the next, depending on mood, context, or events (see Burr, 1995).

Finally, personality is commonly used as a means of accounting for someone's behaviour, held up as the reason or cause. Hence, criminal activity is explained in terms of violent or antisocial personalities, good performance at school is attributed to intelligence, watching lots of television is construed as laziness, etc. The problem here is one of circularity, where both the alleged cause and the outcome amount to much the same thing (criminal behaviour is due to a criminal personality; academic excellence is due to academic qualities; lazy behaviour is due to lazy people). So, much the same terms are used to describe the behaviour and its cause (personality), a case of tautology (see Potter and Wetherell, 1987).

So, the main problem with personality theories is that a whole host of factors outside (but connected to) the individual are not considered as valid explanations for behaviour, such as the social situation, cultural and historical forces, interpersonal relationships. This point has been emphasized in social psychology by social learning theory (e.g. Bandura, 1977; Mischel, 1966) in which the 'situation specificity' of behaviour is the key assumption. How we present ourselves in a given set of circumstances will depend on what we have learned from previous comparable situations. For example, if a child has been rewarded ('reinforced') in the past for asking permission to leave the dining table then this behaviour is likely to be repeated; rather than some personality trait accounting for this behaviour ('politeness'? 'respect for authority'?), the 'cause' is located in the particular context. If a person carries out a criminal act, for example, it could be because they have been forced to by other people, because they need money to feed a family, because they have ingested alcohol or drugs, because it may earn some respect from peers, and so on. Moreover, those making judgements on the case will inevitably vary in the weight they grant to the different accounts so that the 'real' reason for the criminal act will likely not be found, only competing versions of the 'truth'. It is clear, then, that a number of problematic issues are raised when the definitions and uses of the concept of personality are probed. The principal objection here relates to the simplistic categorization of a person in terms of a few broad traits, a practice which neglects the dynamic and complex ways in which people present themselves across different contexts.

In considering how personality is deployed within (social) psychology, it has been proposed that the focus on the measurement of the individual acts as a form of social control. According to Stainton-Rogers *et al.* (1995), the emergence of psychology as the scientific study of the individual served to define and 'treat' persons in the interests of securing a stable and successful society. That is, (social) psychology sets out to market the discipline as the only proper and effective technology for selecting staff to do particular jobs, screening out dangerous parents, identifying which children will benefit from academic education, and so on (see Hollway, 1989). The use of personality tests therefore functioned to define, explain, predict and, if necessary, control 'problematic' subjects (see Chapter 2). Nonetheless, there has always been a branch of (sociological) psychology which has preferred to understand the self as embedded within society, as subject to various roles.

CRITICAL THINKING ON SITUATIONAL SELVES

The critique of 'personality' suggests that people are actually difficult to categorize once and for all, that different selves are presented for different occasions. One self or many selves – what do you think? To what extent do you present different 'faces' in different environments?

The sociological self

Not surprisingly, sociological social psychologists have been more inclined to locate the individual within social structures and processes. This idea is expressed in role theories (e.g. Dahrendorf, 1973) where people are said to conform to expectations placed on them by various social forces, such as family, work, gender, age, etc. Roles which may be relevant could relate to marital status, profession, political affiliation, sport team/s supported, nationality, voluntary work, etc. Within this perspective, then, the self is distributed across different social arenas rather than limited to a space within the person and is connected to multiple roles rather than one central core.

As traditionally conceived, roles were thought to be enacted in a largely mechanical, conformist fashion – the individual as fixed into place by social institutions (Parsons, 1954). But theorists such as Goffman (1959) allowed the individual more agency with the idea that roles were performed, sometimes in a conscious, strategic way. The 'presentation of self' could be manipulated to achieve particular ends, such as avoiding embarrassment or blame, or attracting praise or material rewards. For example, a child might resort to tears upon falling down ('playing the victim') in the hope that chocolate might be forthcoming from father or mother; a lecturer might attempt a few references to youth culture to dispel the stereotype of the ivory tower academic, and so forth. The language of theatre is used by Goffman – the 'dramaturgical metaphor' – to suggest a social actor rehearsing and reproducing the various scripts provided by society.

But objections to this public, superficial view of self have been raised, mainly by humanistic or experiential psychologists (e.g. Stevens, 1996). They argue that 'behind' the facade of the social roles played out by an individual lies the 'real' or 'true' self, much in the same way as a director shapes the action in a film off screen. In other words, a distinction between public and private selves is set up, with the latter deemed more 'authentic' and significant. Consequently, therapeutic activities informed by such humanistic conceptions of self attempt to 'uncover' and develop this true self, as characterized by notions like 'self-actualization'. However, as with the concept of 'personality', the construct of an authentic self marks a separation of the individual (self) from society (roles) and privileges psychological explanations of (social) phenomena. Instead of looking at the self-in-society, causes of action are framed in terms of internal motivations or cognitive processes (see Potter and Wetherell, 1987).

The concept of social roles, then, provides us with one explanation for variability in behaviour, but rather than see the roles we play as merely superficial or even false (although some may not be that central for us), it is perhaps more useful to regard our main roles as important for identity (Burr, 1995). It is likely, for example, that the role of 'bread-winner' is taken seriously by many men (and, increasingly, women) and the same goes for other key roles (parent, Anglican, school governor, team manager). But when the demands of one role compete with those of another, especially those roles we regard as major, then experiences of tension and conflict often ensue. For example, playing for the local pub football team on a Wednesday night might become difficult during half-term when you are faced with childcare obligations, and difficult decisions have to be made (do you let the team down or leave the children with friends promising future treats?). Managing such incompatible expectations and desires is part of most people's lives which the notion of a coherent, unified personality cannot accommodate; instead, we must locate identity within the social arena with concepts such as roles in order to account for the complex negotiations which characterize the making of identities.

CRITICAL THINKING ON SOCIAL ROLES

Clearly there are many roles which people play in everyday life. Think about the many roles which you perform. Which ones are most fulfilling? Give examples of conflicting roles and discuss with a partner how you might reconcile these.

The cultural self

CRITICAL THINKING ON MY SELF

Write down 20 responses to the question 'Who am I'? as quickly as possible (i.e. 1. 'I am ...; 2. 'I am ...' etc.). There are no 'correct' answers – include whatever responses you think are relevant. This exercise is called the 'Twenty Statements Test' (see Bond and Cheung, 1983).

We have commented on the multiple roles available in a given society. But if we compare different societies, as recent research has done, it becomes apparent that cultural norms and practices also have a bearing on how the self is presented and understood. Indeed, in some 'collectivist' cultures (Asia, Africa, Latin America) the very notion of a self-contained individual so dominant in the West does not figure prominently. Instead, identity is defined in terms of relationship with other people, such as family members, work colleagues, friends, acquaintances. What this cultural variation means, of course, is that the Western ideal of personality, where people are seen to possess a natural, essential, unique self, is but one (perhaps limited) way of conceptualizing person-hood. This contrast between individualist/independent and collectivist/interdependent models of the self is illustrated below.

These broad cultural differences are reflected in everyday practice, in the ways that people perceive and relate to self and others. For example, rather than resort to a vocabulary of abstract personality traits, Asian cultures tend to favour concrete descriptions of people embedded in the surrounding community. According to research cited in Shweder and Bourne (1982), Indian subjects prefer more 'holistic' accounts of behaviour, such as 'she brings cakes to my family on festival days' (as opposed to simply generalizing to 'she is generous') or 'he has trouble giving things to his family' (instead of 'he is mean'). So, such descriptions function to situate the behaviour in a specific context and do not suggest any consistency or stability beyond the particular instance – an individual who does something nice one day may well do something nasty the next. Also, collectivist cultures do not restrict the focus to individuals, a point vividly reinforced by some interesting research by Semin and Rubini (1990) on the variation in favourite insults used between Northern Italy (characterized as individualist) and Southern Italy (deemed more collectivist) (Box 4.2).

Clearly, it is not damning enough to slight the target individual in collectivist cultures; the reputation of the family (or other group) must be undermined for the insult to achieve maximum impact. The importance in choosing the culturally appropriate type of insult is supported

---

Box 4.2   Insulting differences between cultures (Semin and Rubini, 1990)

Semin and Rubini (1990) asked students from Sicily (South) and Bologna and Trieste (North) to give examples of the types of insults they had experienced or used. Whereas insults in the North targeted the perceived offender, Southern people extended the insult to include relations:

Individualist insults (Northern Italy)
You are stupid;
You are a cretin;
Swear words referring to religious figures;
Swear words referring to sexual nouns.

Collectivist insults (Southern Italy)
I wish cancer on you and all your relatives;
You are queer and so is your father;
You are a Communist;
Insults relating to incest.

by Bond and Cheung (1983), who noted that Hong Kong students reacted more to slights directed at their group than those directed at them as individuals.

Another difference concerns the importance attached to self-expression as opposed to self-discipline. Whilst US therapists encourage open communication about self as a way to psychological health, Japanese therapists advocate suppression of emotions and impulses as beneficial. Similarly, Hindu men realized their identity more through fulfilment of social roles than emotional expression. This cultural obligation to subordinate individual desire in favour of group roles and responsibilities is reflected in the common sense of collectivist societies, as the following proverbs illustrate:

'If a nail sticks up, hammer it down' (Japan);
'If one finger is sore, the whole hand will hurt' (China).

Such thinking extends even to the realm of emotions. US subjects tend to select personal events as provoking anger (indicating independence) whereas Chinese subjects indicate events which had happened to other people (suggesting engagement with others) (see Smith and Bond, 1993).

Of course, we must be careful not to categorize cultures simplistically in terms of the individualist–collectivist dimension, as most contemporary societies boast both individualist and collectivist aspects. It is not difficult to produce examples of collectivist behaviours in Western societies, such as patriotism during times of war and loyalty to a sports team, when individual needs often become secondary. Moreover, examples of interdependence are often located within subcultures, ethnic minorities and assorted marginalized groups. In the UK, for example, the importance of connectedness with family and others is stressed especially by Asian and Afro-Carribean communities whereas notions of group belongingness and even sacrifice are present in religious, sports and even criminal settings. It is also pertinent to note that past historical periods have witnessed more communal social organization in Western societies, as in pre-capitalist agricultural communities characterized by the sharing of resources such as food, space, etc. Conversely, there is evidence of individualistic pursuits in collectivist cultures. In an interesting study by Bond and Cheung (1983), Hong Kong students came out as less collectivist than Japanese peers and less individualist than North Americans in their self-descriptions. Obviously Hong Kong society has been influenced by both Chinese and British ideologies.

> ### CRITICAL THINKING ON CULTURE AND SELFHOOD
> Consider your responses to the Twenty Statements Test above. How many of your responses can be labelled 'individualist'? How many 'collectivist'? Compare your results with peers and discuss reasons for similarities and differences.

Multicultural identities

When we consider those people/s who have migrated from one country or community to another, complexities and ambiguities in identity are vividly illustrated. The concept of 'diaspora' conveys identities which are framed by and situated in different locations and highlights the increasing multiculturalism of many cities and communities. Immigrants to the UK from Asia, for example, may recruit aspects of both their original and adopted country to forge an identity; indeed, it has become popular to mix aspects of different cultures to produce eclectic and innovative styles in music, fashion, cinema, etc. But this fusing of two (or more) cultural traditions is by no means a straightforward process, as a recent newspaper profile of Anglo-Indian musician Nitin Sawhney suggests:

Beyond Skin (his acclaimed third album) is Nitin Sawhney's attempt to come to terms with the fact that, while he was raised as an outsider in England, the motherland of his parents is no longer available to him as an innocent spiritual alternative, because it no longer exists. As such, it is about the identity of an individual and the becoming of two cultures, two nations: 'I'd love to be able to gain back what my parents left in terms of their heritage, but you can't', he is saying, 'I go back to India, and I'm a stranger, and I accept that. But I'm still a stranger here too' (in the UK). (Andrew Smith in *The Guardian*, 19 September 1999: 13–17)

This sense of being 'homeless' or not belonging in any particular community is perhaps something you have experienced upon moving to another country or region, whether for work or university or family commitments. For example, 'working-class' individuals may well encounter difficulties in the face of predominantly middle-class institutions such as higher education where the culture and values may mitigate against academic success. In such circumstances, any sense of self as coherent and unified will most certainly be undermined as the 'homeland' is left behind and a new location taken up. In a recent piece by Joseph O'Connor, contemporary Irish novelist and journalist, he reflects on the meaning of 'home' and identity from the perspective of an Irish 'exile' in London, capturing the contradictions, difficulties and advantages of a dichotomous existence (see Box 4.3). You may recall that critical social psychologists are content to

---

Box 4.3   Ireland in exile (Joseph O'Connor, 1996: 150–9)

'You might be coming home for a family celebration or a funeral. Or to see a friend. Or you might be coming home for Christmas. You would meet your friends the night you got home, the people who stayed behind in Ireland to tough it out. You pretended you knew what your friends were talking about, because you still wanted to belong. And . . . your friends resented you a little for going, and if the truth be told you resented them a little for staying, although you could never really put your finger on why. When you used the word "home", for instance, or "at home", your friends sometimes didn't know where exactly you meant. Sometimes you didn't know yourself.'

'Suddenly, about half an hour before closing time, you find yourself looking around the pub and becoming frantically uptight. It's weird. You're feeling completely out of place, you don't know why. You don't get it. Somehow, despite the crack, something is wrong. You're home in Ireland but you're not home really. Your heart is in London or New York or Paris. But the rest of you is in Ireland. How did this happen to you? It's not that you're unhappy exactly. It's Christmas after all. You wanted to be here, didn't you? But it's just not right.'

'In the old days, emigrants went forever when they went, or came back once in forty years. So different now. Air travel is cheap, you could come back really soon, and you'd say you would, although you probably wouldn't .... You'd be thinking: run. You'd be thinking: Christmas is over now. You'd be thinking: Go. Run. Don't stop. Get out. Just get on that plane and vanish. Before you change your mind.

'Still, being Irish abroad – half-invader and half-native – is a fine thing for a writer to be. It means you probably won't get shot in the event of an airplane hijack, and it certainly helps you understand just how very Irish you are. Indeed, it sometimes seems to me that you almost have to get out of Ireland to be Irish at all, in some important sense, that those who stay sometimes turn out to be the real exiles, whereas those who go are the natives. We have gone about the world like wind, Yeats said. Wish you were here. Wish I was there. Well, sometimes anyway.'

consider accounts from already existing texts, for example from journalism or literature, instead of or in conjunction with accounts from research participants. This practice is consistent with the view that social psychological texts, as with texts from other disciplines and sources, may be regarded as constructed, partial or even fictional (see Kvale, 1992).

CRITICAL THINKING ON MULTICULTURAL IDENTITIES

Have you had any experience of inhabiting two (or more) different, perhaps conflicting, cultures? Have you felt 'out of place'? How have you managed to negotiate such diverse influences on identity?

The 'death of the subject'

Evidence of cultural (and historical) diversity and complexity in conceptions of selfhood poses problems for deciding which model/s of self provide better or more useful insights. The growing consensus amongst researchers and theorists of identity is that the Western individualist view is somehow inferior, as the anthropologist Clifford Geertz stressed: 'The Western conception of the person as a bounded, unique, integrated motivational and cognitive universe ... is a rather peculiar idea within the context of the world's cultures' (1974: 229).

The critique of dominant Western conventions governing the self has gathered pace in recent years. Markus and Kitayama (1991) agree that the Western de-socialized notion of the self is not an adequate description of selfhood. The charge here that the Western view is misleading suggests that identity is often bound up in relationships with others and is framed by broader cultural constraints. Some critics (Parker, 1989; Sampson, 1993) go even further to suggest that an ideology of individualism originates from and serves to promote the interests of elites which typically comprise white middle-class males. Within capitalist patriarchal structures the fostering of competition between individuals obscures differences in power and prestige whilst subjecting people to personality tests in order to differentiate between the chosen/healthy/successful and the subordinated others.

The resistance of oppressed groups (women, gay and lesbian people, ethnic minorities, etc.) has contributed to the critique of the dominant Western view of self as independent and detached from society. The emergence of 'identity politics' from the 1960s counter-culture zeitgeist made visible a range of diverse positions previously regarded as secondary or 'other' by mainstream society. Feminism, for example, has provided a platform where women's voices are presented and respected, often arguing for forms of identity which are inclusive and communal as opposed to self-centred and separated from society (e.g. Gilligan, 1982). Indeed, it is argued that individualism has flourished precisely because alternative ideologies of selfhood have been suppressed.

This point highlights the connection between identity and difference – that any particular form of identity is defined in relation to, or against, other competing forms. Some 'essentialist' feminists, for example, opted to reclaim a repressed unique female identity which was nurturing and maternal in opposition to a dominant male identity perceived as destructive (Daly, 1978). Indeed, masculinity and femininity are often understood as opposing tendencies (cold/warm; hard/soft; rational/emotional; strong/weak). But such 'binary oppositions' do not usually contain two equal-status terms, for the 'masculine' term is usually more culturally valued: head over heart, culture over nature, etc. (Cixous, 1975). The same goes for classifications of race (white over black), sexuality (straight over gay), social class ('higher' over 'lower') and so on, all cultural constructions which have been undermined by various social movements. In the last thirty years or more, the 'otherness' of marginalized identities has been celebrated. But if we accept a dispersed, interdependent view of identity, does this mean that we abandon our cherished concept of self as unique and personal?

CRITICAL THINKING ON OTHERNESS

Think about the social categories that you occupy (e.g. heterosexual, Asian, middle-class). How are these identities defined in relation to 'others' (e.g. homosexual, white, working-class)? Which identities are privileged/subordinated?

De-centred selves

To reiterate, the position expressed above that identity is tied to social and cultural ideals suggests that the self as a discrete object that is owned and treasured by the individual is nothing but a fantasy, a myth brought about by a set of institutions (including psychology) which has been shattered by contemporary theory. In other words, 'personality' is regarded as a cultural construct which, although persistently popular in Western societies, amounts to a rather strange and flawed way of thinking about selfhood. As expressed by Freeman (1993: 8): 'how are we to escape the conclusion that we ourselves are ultimately fictions? The self, after all, is not a thing: it is not a substance, a material entity that we can somehow grab hold of and place before our very eyes.'

To claim that we possess knowledge and control over our 'selves' is merely to reproduce a dominant cultural myth founded on a rather arrogant, detached individualism. The gathering consensus, meanwhile, proposes a decentralized version of identity where the individual is dispersed amidst a variety of social relationships and cultural expectations. The metaphor is one of distribution, destabilization, a disrupted, fragmented being-in-the-world. Gergen (1991) suggests a 'saturated' self, a subject bombarded with images, ideas and values from the surrounding culture which are absorbed and debated. The spotlight is on the surface, on the language of a sign-obsessed society and its processing by individuals, rather than on some deep core self nestled somewhere within the person. By virtue of contemporary technology, Gergen argues that the voices and representations of others assail us from every direction, via mobile phones, e-mail, fax, newspapers, magazines, film, television, radio, video, and contribute to the fragmentation and mutability of self. In other words, the relationships we have with others are framed and derive from many, often transitory, disembodied interactions and emphasize the immersion of self in the surrounding social world. Although Gergen's argument has been criticized for depicting the experiences of middle-class elites (see Smith,

1994), the emphasis on the deconstruction of (the unified, stable) self in the contemporary world is shared by many other theorists of identity (e.g. Giddens, 1991).

CRITICAL THINKING ON CONTEMPORARY SELFHOOD

Think of the interactions you have in a typical day/week. To what extent are these mediated by technology? Describe instances where you have experienced social saturation.

Self as process

It is difficult, admittedly, to stop thinking of the self as just that, a real object. The concept of roles is useful for exploding this 'object' into fragments, but there is perhaps a sense that roles are preordained slots which have a certain order or logic to be grasped with little or no room for manoeuvre on the part of the individual. After all, people can and do rebel against or re-work the way they have been presented in a situation. However, in his later work, Goffman (1959) abandons a description of self in terms of differing substances in favour of a more flexible notion of self as social process, a changeable formula for managing oneself during events. Perhaps it is helpful to think about identity in terms of projects, ongoing negotiations within a complex web of relationships and practices, to regard the self as emergent, as always in the process of construction during social interaction. To this end many discursive psychologists examine the ways in which identity is produced in talk in social encounters. Shotter (1993a/b), for example, speaks of 'joint action' to indicate the co-production of identities in the course of an interaction, a process which is open, incomplete and given to misunderstandings (Box 4.4). From this example the complex and often fraught nature of social interaction can be witnessed as both parties struggle to construct meaning from words and action and, by extension, to fashion identities for self and other (and both, as a couple).

The work of Potter and Wetherell (1987) using a discourse analytic approach has explored the dynamic and at times difficult (re)working of identities which frequently features in everyday social interaction. The image of the person as 'discourse-user' is prominent here, whereby speakers draw upon a range of strategies and 'interpretative repertoires' to achieve particular goals in conversation (see Chapter 3). If a

> **Box 4.4   Self as emergent, negotiated, incomplete**
> **(Shotter, 1987: 228, cited in Radley, 1996)**
>
> Witness the making of sexual approaches. 'I'm just off to the cinema', says a woman in the vicinity of a man she is attracted to, in the hope that he will respond as she desires. The significance of her utterance is not yet complete, however. If he says 'Oh, can I come too?' then he has completed its significance as an invitation, and she is of course happy to accept it as having been as such. If he just says, however, 'Oh, I hope you enjoy the film', then he completes it simply as an 'informative statement'. Embarrassment has been avoided by her not having to issue a direct invitation, which might risk a direct refusal.
>
> But if he did turn her down, was it because to go to a film at that time was truly impossible for him, or because he truly did not want to be with her? Clearly, the situation between them is still somewhat vague, and thus requires further practical investigation between them if they are to clarify it further. Let us imagine that he did accept her invitation, and as they walk out of the cinema after the film, she then says 'Would you like to come back for a coffee?' He says, 'Oh, yes please!' and goes to put his arm around her. But she draws back and says, 'Whatever gave you that idea?' He is taken aback. He knows what gave him the idea. It was the whole way she offered the original 'invitation': it seemed to imply an invitation to greater intimacy, but at the same time, as both he and she were aware, it did not explicitly request it. The character so far of the relationship they are in is 'open' to such reversals as these; while perhaps unexpected they are not unintelligible.

couple are having an argument, for example, there is often a struggle towards presenting the other as transgressor and self as victim and the person who manages to manoeuvre into a morally virtuous position (thus constructing the other as blameworthy) will indeed be satisfied. Such discourse dynamics are frequently on show in political debates where there are constant attempts to defend positions and construe another party as misguided, irresponsible or even ridiculous. For example, arguments for greater government expenditure on defence could be framed in terms of protecting the nation, with those against this policy projected as jeopardizing the future of the nation, whereas a call to divert defence monies to health and education could be presented as more ethical, with those against cast as irresponsible hawks sacrificing improved services for the population.

As Billig *et al.* (1988) have suggested, a position or argument is always voiced in opposition to another 'inferior' counter-stance: there is usually an eye fixed on potential criticisms of your position and a move on your part to undermine the other position. For example, a claim by Sue that Jack watches too much sport on television could be seen to position Jack as lazy and uninteresting, which he could attempt to resist by recasting this activity as a form of relaxation or release from the pressures of work, thereby regaining a more morally positive position for himself. In turn, Sue may suggest an alternative, more active or healthy stress-relieving pursuit, such as jogging or using the local gym, a move which undermines Jack's former justification and returns him to his previous (negative) position of slob. Of course, he could defend his sport-watching further by framing the alternatives in a critical light ('jogging is boring'; 'the gym is full of preening air-heads'), and the debate could go on until some mutually satisfactory resolution is achieved or one party capitulates or storms off so that this particular language game is postponed until another time. Negotiating subject positions with another need not be so conscious, strategic or hostile, but the example serves to illustrate the dynamic, interconnected and often combative qualities which such activities involve.

Power and subjectivity

But Potter and Wetherell (1987) also accept that the form and content of self-construction will inevitably be subject to local language; how we may speak of ourselves is constrained by the linguistic norms of the relevant community. Prevailing discourses will make available a limited number of 'subject positions' from which individuals forge identities (see Davies and Harre, 1990; Henriques *et al.*, 1984; Parker, 1992). In the words of Shotter and Gergen (1989: ix): 'persons are largely ascribed identities according to the manner of their embedding within a discourse – in their own or in the discourse of others'. This means that the possibilities for self-formulation are far from infinite, as various constraints may operate to oppress particular identities. Many examples spring immediately to mind: Jewish identities in Nazi Germany, Black identities in apartheid South Africa, homosexual identities in the military, female identities in Moslem cultures. This focus on how individuals are positioned within discourse/s is most commonly associated with the work of Foucault (e.g. Foucault, 1972 – see Chapter 3; Parker, 1992).

The oppression of particular groups and individuals is engendered by the use of discourses which re-present certain categories of person as somehow inferior, abnormal, illegitimate or dangerous. For example, historical constructions of the Irish in UK culture as unintelligent, feckless and prone to violence and drunkenness can be linked to instances of discrimination and hostility in this society. Indeed, the construction of immigrants as uncivilized, work-shy and alien has pre-cipitated restrictive legislation and even violence against foreign visi-tors, as witnessed in California, USA (see Santa Ana, 1999 – Chapter 3, p. 59 this text). So, discourses within which we are inscribed or in which we define ourselves will shape relationships with others and produce concrete consequences. Research on the discursive representation of others and the connection to prejudice is covered in detail in Chapter 9.

Other examples based on gender, sexuality, employment status, appearance, social class, regional background, etc., are not difficult to produce. You can imagine or may have experienced situations in which women, gay men, street cleaners, obese individuals and working-class people have been discriminated against on the basis of conventional stereotypes or discourses. The way motherhood is culturally presented as the pinnacle of femininity has been used to criticize women who work or who do not find parenting pleasurable or easy (see Woodward, 1997). The associations between 'fat' and ill-health and gluttony offer a means of judging people who are overweight when medical rather than 'personality' factors may well account for this situation. Of course, there is often more than one representation of a particular 'object' in circulation, so that 'career women' and 'women as consumers' may co-exist with 'women as mothers' (to which many 'women's' magazines testify) and alternative discourses can be drawn upon to resist domi-nant positionings – a decision not to have children or to place them in a nursery at an early stage can be justified from a 'career woman' position. But how this action will be perceived will depend on which discourses are currently more powerful in a given culture. The con-tinued promotion of motherhood for women by various institutions (church, state, soap opera, etc.) may well cause difficulties and tensions for women attempting to pursue a career as well as bring up children. Moreover, other discourses, such as those around fatherhood, work, etc., will impinge upon the positions adopted and how these are experienced.

CRITICAL THINKING ON SUBJECT POSITIONS

Think about a time when you have been judged because of some social category you inhabit. What were the ideas reinforcing this assessment? How did/could you resist the position in which you were cast?

The problem of subjective experience

Whilst this view of the self as a collection of subject positions within discourse has enabled a critical relocation of the individual within the social realm, there is a danger that the psychological or personal dimension to identity is overlooked (Burr, 1995). Indeed, several theorists sympathetic to social constructionism have nonetheless lamented the absence of ideas on 'subjectivity', or the actual experience of selfhood. There is little work on how individuals feel about the various subject positions they inhabit or the personal meanings attached to these. To adopt the position of 'househusband' within a discourse of 'the new man' is perhaps to be marginalized in a society still obsessed with the ideal of a nuclear family, but how does this feel for a man in the twenty-first century? Similarly, how does it feel for a women to positioned as a single mother in contemporary society, or to be positioned as unemployed, elderly or disabled? Although these various positions can be analysed in terms of their relative status and historical production, a discourse analysis cannot convincingly get at the experience of identifying with (or resisting) a given position. To be fair, the whole notion of experience is called into question by social constructionism (something which is mediated or framed by language and convention) but this does not satisfy many critics who believe in some connection between language and 'reality' (see Chapters 3 and 10). This critique is summed up by Henriques *et al.* (1984: 204):

> In this [post-structuralist] view the subject is composed of, or exists as, a set of multiple and contradictory positionings or subjectivities. But how are such fragments held together? Are we to assume, as some applications of post-structuralism have implied, that the individual subject is simply the sum total of all positions in discourses since birth? If this is the case, what accounts for the continuity of the

subject and the subjective experience of identity? What accounts for the predictability of people's actions, as they repeatedly position themselves within particular discourses? Can people's wishes and desires be encompassed in an account of discursive relations?

As a result of this critique, some contemporary feminist and critical social psychologists have returned to psychoanalysis in order to complement discourse analysis. Social psychologists such as Walkerdine (1987), Hollway (1983; 1989) and Frosh (1993) focus on the (unconscious) desires and anxieties which people invest in particular speaking positions. Of course, much ('unacceptable') desire is routinely repressed in social interaction, so it becomes important to consider what is repressed and how it is defended in talk. Thus, discourse analysts are encouraged to use psychoanalytic concepts such as repression, splitting and projection in addition to the more familiar tools (multiplicity, construction, contradiction, power) in their work. In contrast to Freud, however, these psychoanalytic concepts are applied *between*, rather than within, individuals – a form of 'relational dynamics'. According to Hollway (1989), one of the key tasks in social interaction is to present oneself in ways which protect and/or enhance the ego, a task which (following Klein) is often accompanied by anxiety and which will typically involve defensive moves.

As feminist social psychologists have been prominent in interrogating the preoccupation with language in discourse analysis and social constructionism, psychoanalytically informed analyses have concentrated mainly on gendered subjectivity (a key focus for psychoanalysis also). For example, psychoanalysis as well as discourse analysis can be applied to the study of masculinities. The conventional discourse which constructs men as rational and dispassionate (i.e. not feminine or irrational) ensures that feelings of vulnerability experienced by men will produce anxiety which then pushes the emotion out of awareness – and often projected on to women (hence the prevalence of sexism, misogyny and anti-feminism in much male discourse and practice). Indeed, this is further evidenced by reports that in certain discreet situations, such as visiting a prostitute or during fantasy, men will gladly relinquish prevailing expectations (see Friday, 1980). Accounts that are presented in talk, then, will depend on those discourses which are culturally available but also on the relationship with other/s, the context of interaction and the power to present preferred alternatives (see Jefferson, 1994). Although there are difficulties associated with attempts to integrate psychoanalytic theory (often seen as essentialist) and social constructionism, the turn to psychoanalysis is interesting and could be developed fruitfully to complement the broader discourse analytic approach to subjectivities.

Summary

The Western individualist concept of 'personality' or the 'self-contained' individual or the 'unitary, rational subject', has been subjected to a wide-ranging critique in this chapter. This psychological focus, which presents selfhood as stable and consistent, is rejected by sociological approaches such as role theories where the person is construed as taking on different roles according to what is expected in particular situations. Such approaches promote an image of the self as multi-faceted and decentred. These social roles are largely determined by social norms and practices, a point emphasized by research cited on cultural variation which shows markedly different self-conceptions, notably between Western (individualist) and Eastern (collectivist) societies. As most societies today could be understood as multicultural and technological, a huge range of 'identities' are potentially on offer, a situation which can be both liberating and difficult to manage. Critical social psychologists would, however, stress constraints on identity 'choices', as it can be difficult to take on subject positions within discourses which define you as 'other' (e.g. for a woman to assume 'masculine' positions or a man to assume 'feminine' positions). The critical focus on subjectivity as determined by discourse, however, has recently been challenged by social psychologists influenced by psychodynamic theory. In analysing subjectivity in terms of the investments which individuals make to specific discourses within social contexts, an (inter-)personal dimension to subjectivity is recovered.

Key references

Burr, V. (1995) 'Where Do You Get Your Personality From?', chapter 1 in V. Burr, *An Introduction to Social Constructionism* (London: Routledge). A clearly written chapter which presents a critique of 'personality' from a social constructionist perspective.

Wetherell, M. and Maybin, J. (1996) 'The Distributed Self: A Social Constructionist Perspective', in R. Stevens (ed.), *Understanding the Self* (London: Sage/ Open University Press). A comprehensive chapter which explores the role of culture and language in shaping selfhood.

Social Influence

5

Introduction

In crowds, do we disintegrate into untamed animals, or function as passive recipients of others' knowledge, even when that knowledge defies our perceptions? These are two images of what happens to the individual in the presence of other people that have, until recently, enjoyed currency in social psychology. Many people continue to draw on these accounts today, citing examples of the seemingly mindless violence of football hooligans or instances of ethnic cleansing which litter recent history. This chapter reviews the classic studies and theoretical explanations of social influence processes, including the work of Le Bon (1895) and Asch (1952). By raising questions about the theoretical framework and the content of this work, alternative insights into how and why people behave in the presence of others are offered from the perspective of critical social psychology.

Historical context

The pursuit of answers to the question of whether the presence of others enhances or inhibits individual performance dates back to the nineteenth century. Early work by Triplett (1898) investigating the effect of others on the racing times of cyclists suggested that the presence of others enhanced individual performance, with those cycling in groups achieving faster times than those cycling alone or against pacers. Later researchers such as Zajonc *et al.* (1965) pursued and consolidated this idea, incorporating it in a theory of social facilitation. Historically, though, the bulk of experimental work conducted on social influence processes has concentrated on the negative impact that the presence of others has on the activities of the individual. Primary among such studies is Le Bon's (1895) work on crowd behaviour. His observations were based on events he witnessed during the French Revolution in 1872 when, as a member of the ruling classes, he was dismayed at what he perceived as the erosion of traditional standards accompanying 'modernity' (briefly defined as a socio-political project emerging around 1770 with the triple aims of replacing irrational thought with reason, replacing superstition with scientific truths, and promoting human betterment: see Chapter 2). The lower classes were viewed as the source of decay, endangering civilized society. The keystone of this work was that in crowds people lose their rational, human capacities and regress to savage activities. The work of Le Bon (1895) sowed the seeds of later work in social psychology on conformity by suggesting that when in crowds, people suffer 'collective hallucinations which are distortions of the external world suffered by people in crowds as a result of processes of "contagion" and "suggestibility" ' (Stainton Rogers *et al.*, 1995: 79).

'Classic' experiments

Sherif's (1935) autokinetic effect

Sherif (1935) set out to investigate the nature of 'distortions' that individuals experienced in the presence of others. To do so, he employed the autokinetic effect, a perceptual illusion whereby in a darkened room a stationary point of light appears to move. Firstly, individuals in isolation were asked to estimate how far the light moved. Despite wide individual variation, when individuals came together in a group, estimates of movement converged to produce a 'group norm'. Conversely, Sherif found that when people firstly estimated the movement of light in groups and were then asked in subsequent trials to estimate movement individually, in the second instances estimates made as part of the group seemed to influence those made when alone.

Asch (1952) and conformity

One of the major concerns with Sherif's experimental design was that he had effectively based it around an illusion, and thus many argued that the inherent ambiguity weakened any conclusions that could be drawn about the impact of others on the performance of the individual. This was addressed in the work of Asch, who used objective stimuli, the lengths of different lines, to assess if individuals experienced distortions in the presence of others. This experiment went as follows. Subjects were asked to compare sets of two or three lines and to judge which of the lines was most similar in length to a comparison line. An easy enough task we hear you say! However, unknown to the 'naive' subject, the others present (usually up to seven) had been employed by Asch (as confederates) to perform the task of deliberately choosing lines that were not the most similar to the comparison line. So, we have a naive subject participating in what has been described as a study on perceptual judgement, sitting at the end of a table with people providing verbal responses to the comparison task. On the first two trials all 'subjects' agreed on the appropriate line as they called out their choice. However, on the next and subsequent trials, the seven confederates called out what was clearly the wrong choice. And what did the subject do? Asch found that 5 per cent of subjects conformed to obviously wrong estimates of line size on all trials, 33 per cent conformed on half or more of the trials, and 25 per cent did not conform on any trials.

Throughout the trials the disbelief and discomfort of the naive subjects was visible, and in interviews following the experiments many of those who according to Asch had conformed to the incorrect majority view, talked about not wanting to be different or believing that the others in the group had a clearer view of the lines. Theoretical explanations for the activities witnessed in the above studies centre around the dual concepts of normative and informational pressure, coined by Deutsch and Gerrard (1955). In the Asch (1952) studies, naive subjects who answered incorrectly on trials are believed to have done so from a need for social approval and acceptance: that is, out of a desire to be liked. In contrast, Deutsch and Gerrard (1955) suggest that those converging towards a group norm in the Sherif (1935) experiments did so as a result of informational pressure: that is, on uncertain territory subjects used other people as sources of objective information about the situation and so conformed from a desire to be right.

The Milgram experiment: obedience

Events witnessed during the Second World War instigated new questions into how others can influence the behaviour of the individual. In particular, the concept of obedience took centre-stage, embodied in Milgram's (1974) empirical studies into the psychological mechanisms underlying obedience. Milgram advertised for volunteers to participate in a study at Yale University on the effects of punishment on learning. Over one thousand volunteers were to perform either as teacher or pupil, roles that were assigned randomly. 'Teachers' were to aid learning by giving electric shocks of increasing voltage each time 'pupils', situated in a separate room, answered incorrectly. Voltage levers were labelled from mild up to 450 volts (Danger: Severe shock), and teachers were instructed to progress with shocks by the experimenter standing beside them. The disturbing findings showed 62 per cent of the teachers inflicting shocks to the maximum, despite their own discomfort and the cries of pain coming from pupils

Explanations for why people were prepared to unexpectedly shock other people to 450 volts centred on the pervasiveness of social power and status; that, in the presence of authority figures, individuals lose their capacity for rational, moral thinking and succumb to the authority of the powerful 'other'. Milgram illustrated that obedience is related to situational pressure, a finding that was extremely novel for psychology in the 1960s, as previous explanations of destructive obedience had centred on character traits and certain types of people (e.g. 'The Germans are different' hypothesis).

Common themes in classic
social psychology

Although Le Bon's (1895) work could be described as a naturalistic enquiry, and that of Sherif, Asch and Milgram as experiments, they share a number of common themes. Firstly, the focus of this work was on the power of one or more persons to change and shape individual behaviour. For Le Bon, observations made during the French Revolution, and for Milgram the events of the Second World War, narrowed the focus further to concentrate on the presumed negative influence that others could have on the behaviour of the individual. Secondly, each shared a vision of the individual in his (or her) natural state of existence, that of the rational moral being existing separately from an objective social world. Finally, each shared similar epistemological origins: the classic works are, as Stainton Rogers *et al.* (1995) describe, products of an historical force, 'modernity', whereby social science sought to provide universal truths relating to human behaviour in the belief that such knowledge would ultimately promote human betterment. It is through unpacking these common themes and assessing their influence on the knowledge derived from the classic works, that many authors are increasingly sceptical about what experimental social psychology has actually told us about social influence processes (see Brown, 1996; Harré and Secord, 1972: 79).

The individual and the social

Understandings of social behaviour offered by classic experimental studies on conformity and obedience are based on a particular mechanistic formula regarding the origins of people's activities:

behaviour = the sum of individual + the situation

However, for the formula to be of use to social psychologists, certain givens are assumed about the nature of each of the components in the equation. Firstly, behaviour is presented as an outcome or response by the individual to a specified situation. It is assumed that human behaviour is observable and measurable and can be explained using knowledge of the individual and specified stimuli he or she has been exposed to. Secondly, the individual is defined as *self-contained*, an entity existing independently of social contexts and circumstances. All individuals are viewed as possessing states that are internal and stable – attitudes, cognitions, personalities, to name a few. These have become the bread-and-butter of psychology, with human activities explained in relation to how these states are influenced by and affect social contexts and situations. The third part of the equation, situational influences, is also viewed as objective and malleable. It is assumed that a singular reality, *a real world,* exists which all humans experience and react to universally. In the work of Sherif and Asch, the social is defined as the presence of others, and their impact on the activities of individuals explored in isolation from the other issues, such as the identity of participants, historical practices, cultural contexts, differences in power and social status. Yet the influence of such factors was ever present in Asch's later work and that of subsequent researchers. In the various permutations of his original experimental design, Asch illustrated that the presence of even one ally who went against the majority view reduced conformity among the 'real' participants (as opposed to confederates). Furthermore the influence of historical–cultural contexts was highlighted in later replications of Asch's studies by Larsen (1974) and Perrin and Spencer (1981) and others (see Box 5.1).

Box 5.1 Replications of Asch studies

Larsen (1974) replicated Asch's experimental design with American students and found significantly lower rates of conformity than Asch found. Perrin and Spencer (1981) draw attention to differences in the historical climate when this work was conducted: that is, the post-hippie era, when independence and freedom of expression were vehemently guarded, in contrast to the 1950s McCarthite America of Asch, where deviance from norms and values was tinged with accusations of Communism.

Perrin and Spencer (1981) replicated Asch's design using British engineering, mathematics and chemistry students, and found that across trials these students remained independent, reporting correct line comparison even in the face of a majority who repeatedly gave incorrect answers. As Brown (1996) notes, the academic culture of these individuals and the nature of the task may have combined to encourage confidence in their ability to judge lines correctly.

Experiments/groups

Following on from the above equation of human behaviour, the assumed certainties that it enshrines about an objective reality and the nature of the individual promote the experiment as the logical method to explore the impact of certain social stimuli on the behaviour of the individual. However, one of the most resounding criticisms of the work of Sherif, Asch and Milgram is their use of the experimental paradigm to explore conformity and obedience. Many question the ecological validity of the autokinetic effect, the comparison of lines and the learning paradigm used. Take for example the events of the Second World War, with Germany, a previously economically and politically unstable country, steeped in the propaganda of a dictator promising worldwide domination through the extermination of Jewish populations and other marginalized groups. Does administering (fake) electric shocks to volunteers in the safety of Yale University, with its academic kudos, equate with the gross acts of inhumanity witnessed in Germany in the 1930s and 40s? In arguing against such comparisons, many critical social psychologists point out that Milgram's work was conducted in surroundings unfamiliar to participants, where individuals responded in isolation, and was also a short-term activity. In contrast, the inhumanity witnessed in camps such as Auschwitz and Belsen occurred on the longer term, in contexts that were familiar, and where many carrying out such acts believed that the fate of Germany in the 1930s and 1940s was due directly to the subversive influence of Jews, a belief fed to them in daily Nazi propaganda (Housden, 1997). Harré (1989), among others, suggests that the omission of the wider, more complex social fabric in experiments is a fundamental flaw in experimental paradigms of human social activity. Like others, he berates experimental social psychology for ignoring that which is fundamental to understanding human social behaviour – the humanness – people's identities, cultural structures and practices. Wetherell (1996b: 11–12) sums this up as follows: 'Social relationships are complex and multilayered. The lines of influence from one person to another are intertwined and difficult to disentangle. The controlled experiment has never been adequate to this task. The patterns involved are much more complex than the linear laws of experimental (*cause and effect*) social psychology suggest.'

Further questions relating to the design of social influence experiments arise from assumptions embodied in the work of Sherif (1935) and Asch (1952). Sherif and Asch talk of the collections of people participating in their work as groups, but is this a legitimate perception? Many, including Wetherell (1996b), would suggest not, as collections of people with no shared history or experience does not constitute a group. The impact of established group membership is further highlighted in Williams and Sogon's (1984) replication of the Asch study, where among Japanese participants a higher error rate was recorded for intact groups (sports club members), and a lower rate for unacquainted students.

Social influence as negative

As a starting point, let us remind ourselves of what Sherif, Asch and Milgram were attempting to uncover about human social behaviour. If we think back to the paradigm of human behaviour extolled by Le Bon (1895), two strands emerge: firstly the assumption that in the presence of others the 'normally rational civilized' behaviour of the individual in some way changes, and secondly that the nature of this change is negative (Le Bon talked of how in crowds the rational and moral basis of individuality is shattered, exposing the savage beneath). In this sense the expectations of Sherif, Asch and Milgram about what they would find were pre-formed by the Western doctrine of individuality and the way this had historically been enshrined as a truth within the discipline of psychology.

So, what was it that these experiments showed us about human social activity? Firstly, the Sherif, Asch and Milgram studies did indicate that in certain situations social influence occurs. However, where many contemporary psychologists diverge from the historical narrative embodied in this work is in relation to the ways these findings have been reported and the implications about human social activity that have been drawn. Let us take Asch's findings for example. Asch illustrated that 5 per cent of subjects conformed to obviously wrong estimates of line size on all trials, 33 per cent conformed on half or more of the trials, and 25 per cent did not conform on any trials. But what do these statistics really tell us if, say, people were asked to choose between X, Y and Z washing powders and that over a period of forty washes 33 per cent of consumers used X for half or more washes. Would you accept this as a basis for believing that a preference for X was a universal behaviour and be happy to conclude that we are a nation of X users? We think not, yet Asch's work instilled beliefs that in the presence of others, people regardless of class, age, background or situation, conform to perceived pressure from others; that they are prepared to change their beliefs due to a desire to be right (informational influence) or to be liked (normative influence). In addition, as Brown (1996: 19) comments, later replications of Asch's work reported in Box 5.1 indicate 'that there is no universal way in which individuals respond to group pressure when there is a discrepancy between their own perceptions and those of other group members. They show that participants will be affected by the *meaning* a situation has for them which itself may be influenced by *cultural* variables which have a bearing on how we relate to groups.'

So how do we explain the widespread currency of Asch's work in psychological explanations of human social activity? To do so, again we must return to the historical basis of psychology as a scientific discipline and the ingrained assumptions about the nature of the individual, the social and behaviour. Social psychology, since the nineteenth century, has been, as Stainton-Rogers *et al.* (1995) describe, on a *humaneering mission* (see Chapter 2). In response to the shifting intellectual and social structures of Western societies in the nineteenth century and the subsequent anxieties relating to the position of the lower classes and, ultimately, the social and moral fabric of civilised existence, psychology has historically positioned itself as the procurer of objective truths about the nature of human social activity. This knowledge is offered as something that can contribute to the protection and indeed enhancement of the moral and social underpinnings of civilized society (as defined in nineteenth-century rhetoric). In order to produce such knowledge, concrete definitions of the nature of the individual, society and behaviour are essential, as from such foundations universal codes relating to human activity may be formulated and actions taken to make improvements. In many ways, Asch's studies did not rock the theoretical boat, so to speak, as he produced concise experimentally-based evidence that reinforced the existing narrative about the negative influence of groups on individual performance and placed explanations for such phenomena solely at the feet of the individual – as a result of her or his desire to be liked or right. In doing so, there was no need for psychology to ask any messy questions about either the social mechanisms through which conformity and obedience are secured or the political purpose of such mechanisms. Conformity and obedience remained firmly within the psyche of the individual.

Rethinking social influence

Within critical social psychology, insights into social influence (conformity, compliance to requests, obedience) are based on understandings of the *individual situated within society*. Conformity and obedience are understood as discursive practices (representations of social ideas and codes of practice in language and everyday talk), in contrast to mainstream (social) psychology, where such practices are analysed at the level of the individual, as internal desires or motivations resulting in specific behaviours (think back to Asch's work – 'the desire to be liked and the desire to be right'). Consequently, the theoretical assumptions framing the work of experimental social psychologists such as Asch and Milgram are revised. This section maps out these revisions.

Social influence processes are not viewed as behaviours which people do (or do not) perform but rather, as Burr (1995) points out, are viewed from the social practices that people engage in and the interactions that take place between people. Activities acquire meaning in the social processes that people participate in and, as such, give rise to social phenomena such as conformity and obedience. For example, consider the interactions between people during a social psychology lecture in a university. I (Majella) as the lecturer prepare my lecture in advance, produce overhead slides, lecture notes and relevant reading materials. The students indulge (I hope!) in active listening and make relevant additional notes, and opportunities to ask questions are created by me at certain intervals throughout the process. These weekly classes are shaped by the wider academic context in which we are situated and produce knowledge relating to the legitimate conduct of such sessions (as well as the penalties incurred should this not take place). From my position as the lecturer these penalties include negative appraisals from my employers and/or the students, while students who do not participate in an acceptable manner may face disciplining from the lecturer or, even worse, from their fellow students. As such, the practices of the lecturer and/or students are not dictated by individuals who desire to be 'liked' or 'right', but rather by the wider social interactions, norms and identities.

Box 5.2 Group anorexia: The deadly way women bond
(*Cosmopolitan*, September 1993: 33–5)

The article in *Cosmopolitan* describes the way in which groups of women influence each other's eating behaviours. The main theme to run through the article is the pressure on women to achieve and maintain the ideal size-10 body and the dangerous activities (vomiting, laxatives, excessive dieting and exercise) many women indulge in to attain such a body. One of the case studies presented is that of Emily, a final-year student at university, who vomits to 'stay a neat size 10, just like all her flatmates' (p. 33). The article describes how Emily had a normal attitude towards food and no hang-ups about her body before leaving home for university.

'But, life in a shared house changed all that. Just weeks into her first term at university, she and her new friends were comparing their bodies, swapping slimming tips and sharing paranoias. The subject of food loomed over them constantly and, soon, it was a common enemy. Eating disorders were not far behind. "Leaving home had a lot to do with it," admits Emily now, "Suddenly food mattered. Sizes were *so* important. We'd try on each other's clothes and notice which bits were too big and which were too small, and say do I look fat in this? The cruellest thing you could do was try on someone else's outfit and say it was too big. In the supermarket, we'd look in each other's trolleys and count the calories. You couldn't even eat a bar of chocolate without the others focusing on it, making comments like, oh you're so brave"' (pp. 33–4).

CRITICAL THINKING ON COLLECTIVE IDENTITIES

Read Box 5.2, and in small groups, discuss the explanations offered for the development of communal eating patterns. Then consider the following questions: Do friends influence how you relate to food? If so, how? Why do you think this happens? Are there other activities where you conform to group ideals (e.g. dress, social or sexual activities)? Why might this be? Can group influences be resisted?

The social theorist Michel Foucault (1978; 1988) provides insights into the construction of the socially legitimate person and the practices this person could indulge in. Through his consideration of the progressive regulation of what are traditionally thought personal properties or activities (e.g. the body, sexuality, reproduction), Foucault (1978) illustrates the construction of norms relating to a wide range of human activity and explicates the mechanisms through which conformity and obedience among people is achieved. For Foucault, human social activities such as obedience and conformity are not situated either in the desires of individuals or the authority of powerful figures. Rather, Foucault suggests conformity and obedience are produced by, and are products of, evolving social organizations and the interactions of people within these. Foucault tracks the evolution of social organizations from religious dictates to state regulation, through to a multiple network of sites of social control, new forms of knowledge about the human activity. Primary among these mechanisms producing a more disciplined society are the social sciences – psychology, sociology, criminology, etc. The function of this discipline according to Foucault (1988: 59), 'is to create useful subjects, men and women, who conform to a standard, who are certifiably sane or healthy or docile or competent, not free agents who invent their own standards' (1988: 59).

Power relations are the key concept in this organization and in particular how these function in different historical, political and social contexts to generate frameworks of norms. Foucault points to the rise of science in the nineteenth century whereby, historically, bodies such as psychology through its scientific knowledge and investigation generated social norms and codes relating to normal/abnormal/healthy, etc. In Foucault's work, the production and generation of the self and activities prescribed for the care and maintenance of this self situates the body and soul at the centre of a diverse collection of philosophical, religious and (later) scientific discourses. For example, the Greek philosopher Epictetus describes man's (*sic*) care of the self as a moral duty, the activity that separates man from animal. In his writings, man is presented as

> the being who was destined to care for himself. This is where the difference between him and other creatures resides. The animals find 'ready prepared' that which they need in order to live, for nature has so arranged things that animals are at our disposal without them having to look after themselves, and without our having to look after them. Man, on the other hand, must attend to himself: not however as a consequence of some defect that would put him in a situation of need and make him in this respect inferior to animals, but because the god (Zeus) deemed it right that he be able to make free use of himself; and it was for this purpose he endowed him with reason. (Foucault, 1988: 49)

Foucault underlines the complex regimes that have accompanied the care of the self, including abstinence, health regimes, physical exercise, and so forth, and the continued embodiment of these activities in a range of nineteenth- and twentieth-century medical and religious discourses. He emphasizes the complex nature of such regulation and the collusion of individuals in their own subjection when he concludes: 'Now there is a new subjection, which creates and legitimises new subjects – not the carriers of rights but of norms, the agents and also the products of moral, medical, sexual, psychological (rather than legal) regulation. Our interest shifts, because the action shifts, from the singular state to a pluralist society' (1988: 54). That is, in accepting the authority of specialized bodies of knowledge, by seeking counselling, or treatment, people submit themselves to scrutiny and regulation. It is this active role for the individual, the seeking and legitimizing of authority, that is interesting in Foucault's work as it conceptualizes the individual as inseparable from the social context. In Foucault's vision, the person is simultaneously shaped by and shapes the social context. Consequently, simplistic notions of the exercise of power as a top-down process are challenged, and Foucault presents a more diffuse and fluid view of power relations. Power is not something that is held by one set of people, but rather, 'power is exercised from innumerable points. Power is employed and exercised through a netlike organisation ... individuals circulate between its threads; they are always in a position of simultaneously undergoing and exercising power. They are not only its inert or consenting targets; they are also elements of its articulation' (1988: 54–5).

Box 5.3   Alternative reading of conformity and obedience

In contrast to the work of Sherif (1935) or Milgram (1974), Foucault (1978: 88) emphasizes the socio-political context of conformity and obedience. These activities are not situated within individuals but, rather, are the products of macro and micro social interactions. Conformity and obedience are not universal behaviours: they fluctuate in different historical, cultural and social contexts. Thus, Foucault provides an important rationale for exploring the meaning and status of knowledge and the importance of the socio-political context in which such knowledge is produced. Explanations for the popularity and power of experimental studies on social influence must then surely also include an understanding of the scientific status and values underlying such research as well as the impact of the over-arching socio-political contexts on the researcher's expectations of human social activity.

It is such influences that Brown (1996) highlights when she argues that the very language psychologists use reveal underlying value judgements: 'Asch certainly viewed conformity as deplorable and perhaps did not emphasise enough that in his experiments it was a minority response. ... Asch describes conforming subjects as "yielding" when he might have referred to these subjects as trusting other people. Those who did not succumb to group pressure he refers to, approvingly, as independent' (Brown, 1996: 25)

In her work with young adolescent women, Sue Lees (1993: 98) describes how women's conformity to specific understandings of femininity is achieved through a collection of linguistic and social practices subscribed to by both men and women. Terms such as 'slag', 'slut' and 'bitch' are highlighted as key mechanisms through which young women's activities and social reputations are controlled to the advantage of men: 'The term "slag" can be seen as part of a discourse about behaviour as a departure, or potential departure from, in this case, male conceptions of female sexuality which run deep in the culture' (1993: 23). Lees (1998) points out that the term 'slag' is used in a multitude of ways, not only in relation to young women's sexual activities but to their appearance, how they talk, how they relate to boys and even their future aspirations. In addition, Lees (1993: 98) notes that despite an awareness among her young female participants of the unfairness of these controls on women's sexual and social behaviour, many of the young women conformed to socially prescribed behaviours rather than incur the negative social penalties of being called a slut or slag. As Lees (1998: 22) states: 'The crucial point about the label slag is that it is used by both girls and boys as a deterrent to non-conformity. No girl wants to be labelled bad and slag is something to frighten any girl with. The effect of the term is to force girls to submit voluntarily to a very unfair set of gender relations.'

What is a 'slag'?

As discussed, Lees (1993) suggests that the term 'slag' is used in a variety of ways to control identities and activities of many young women. Women can earn the label of 'slag' by virtue of the way they dress; wearing too much make-up or not being interested in their appearance and thereby appearing dirty and unkempt; wearing clothes that are too tight or tops that are too low, and so on. Yet as Lees (1993) notes, there are no definitive guidelines on what constitutes too much make-up or how low a top can acceptably be. Rather, this is something that young women learn through their negotiations with others, and for many this can be a risky and painful learning curve.

The power and pervasiveness of the term 'slag' in ensuring young women's conformity to socially constructed and frequently contradictory representations of femininity also emerged in interviews conducted with a group of thirty heterosexual women in Northern Ireland (McFadden, 1995). As these women talked about their sexuality, the image of a tightrope walker came to mind as, in their everyday activities, they negotiated the thin line between appearing as a slag or a drag (i.e. frigid). These young women presented a range of complex strategies (see Box 5.4) including self-surveillance and censorship of and by others, which they used to get it (femininity) right.

Box 5.4   How nice girls behave (McFadden, 1995)

Lesson one: Nice girls don't talk about sex

From the interviews conducted with the thirty women, norms relatng to how young women talked and behaved in mixed company emerged. These women indicated that talking about sex or even commenting on someone's appearance in the company of men was a no-go area. Zoe described the reactions of male friends when she strayed outside the boundaries and commented on a passing male: '... like men are really funny. For example I was walking down the road with male friends and I saw this really nice guy and I said "He's nice", and they were all, "What are you talking about?", "Don't be such a slapper", and things like that. They got really annoyed. They're really funny. Girls aren't expected to do things like that.'

Similarly Stephanie describes the negative consequences if a woman was to talk about sex in front of men: '... like I think a lot of fellas would be put off by a girl who talked about sex, probably think that she was some kind of slut or something'.

Lesson two: Nice girls don't carry condoms

Nice women definitely do not carry condoms unless in a steady relationship. Of the 30 women, 25 described in derogatory terms women who carried condoms and who they knew were not in a relationship. For example, while in principle Marilynne thought it was OK for women in light of AIDS to carry condoms, she goes on to say, '... but if I saw a girl with condoms in her handbag and I knew she wasn't in a steady relationship I'd think she was a bit of a slag. I know it's an awful way to think but ... that's what I think.'

Jenny voiced similar opinions: 'If they're in a steady relationship ... that's fair enough, but if they're [women] just going out for the night with a packet of condoms in their pocket, I don't think that's on. It's really low.'

The social penalties that single women who carry condoms may face was further elaborated on by Tess, who suggested that '... if a woman was to do that [sleep around, using condoms] people would talk about her and say that she was dirty and that she'd probably got all types of diseases'.

Lesson three: Nice girls don't do it on a first date

'Women aren't supposed to have sex on the first night, like even if a girl really liked a boy, if she wanted to go with him again she wouldn't sleep with him on the first night because he might get the wrong idea' (Dot, aged 17).

'... a girl would get called a slut for doing it [having sex] on the first night and a fella doesn't get called anything. I think that's why a lot of girls would prefer to wait until a steady relationship ... they're afraid of getting a bad name' (Emma, aged 18).

Lesson four: Nice girls don't have too much of a sexual history

These young women's narratives about femininity in the 1990s related to how much information you disclose about sexual activity. For most of the women interviewed this was a task that had to be carefully negotiated. Among female friends, talk of sex did take place, but disclose too much and you risk being labelled as a slut, even by close friends. This was a risk Marilynne was well aware of: 'Well women do talk about sex but I suppose there are some of my friends that it would bo hard to lot know that I had sexual experience, they'd probably talk about me ... think that I was a bit of a slag or loose or something. I suppose you do have to be careful who you tell whereas among men when they talk about who they've slept with it's all boasting.'

Daisy described how there were clear rules about how much sexual experience was alright and when you were in danger of being passed over by men or thought of as low. Although these rules had not been formally recognized, women are aware of the conse-quences of transgressing them; to the extent that according to Daisy women lie about their sexual histories: 'It [denying sexual experi-ence] would be because of social pressure ... you know all men want to marry a virgin ... so it's easier to let on that you're sexually inexperienced. ... I know a lot of people [women] who have lied about their experience for fear of what their friends might say. Like no one wants their friends distancing themselves because they think you've got a bad name or calling you a slut or something behind your back.'

Experimental social psychology has traditionally been concerned with identifying how internal and external processes influence the behaviour of the individual. Within this paradigm both the 'individual' and the 'social' are understood in specific ways. It is assumed that in his or her 'natural' state the individual exists separately from his or her social world, and that all individuals share internal states (motiva-tions, desires, drives, instincts) which are impacted upon by external factors in stable and predictable ways (McGhee, 1996). Similarly certain assumptions are made about the structural nature of the social world in experimental social psychology. It is assumed that a single objective reality exists, that social forces can be isolated and their effects on the individual monitored and understood. Think back to the work of Asch and his explanations for the conformity witnessed among those participating in his experiments.

CRITICAL THINKING ON CONFORMITY AND GENDER

To what extent do the above discourses on femininity still constrain women's behaviour in the twenty-first century?

In experimental studies of social influence, it is suggested that the subjects involved conformed as a result of the 'desire to be right' among fellow subjects or the 'desire to be liked'. The social world is understood simply in terms of the 'presence of others' without any recognition of the cultural and social contexts in which the experiments are undertaken or the characteristics of the participants (e.g. age, ethnic background, status). In contrast, critical social psychology views the person as product of, and enmeshed within, diverse social, historical and cultural contexts. Take for example the baby in its mother's womb. Prior to its birth it is recognized within the social order as a foetus; this term elicits different understandings of its status depending on the viewpoint of the speaker (e.g. a collection of cells, or a human being from the moment of conception). After birth, the child's experiences may differ from others depending on its gender, ethnic background, current parenting philosophies, and so on. Within critical social psychology, rather than being viewed as being born in the possession of a set number of personality traits the person is understood as being gradually constructed through her or his social interactions and actions. This doesn't mean, as Wetherell (1996) points out, that we do not have our own dreams, expectations and hopes but rather challenges understandings of how these are shaped as well as assumptions that these are universal and stable.

Similarly, critical social psychology challenges the taken-for-granted notion of the social that is embedded in experimental social psychology. Rather than understanding the social as, for example, the presence of others and exploring the impact that the presence of one or more persons has on an individual's behaviour, a broader definition of the social is developed. In critical social psychology the structure and content of a person's social world is central to understanding human behaviour. The social world of the individual is viewed as complex and dynamic, influenced by their physical environment, economic structures, language, representations and ideologies. New questions then emerge about human behaviour, such as where and how the person is placed within the existing social order, the factors that contribute to this positioning (e.g. gender, ethnicity, class), and how social positioning can change during and as a result of social interactions.

CRITICAL THINKING ON CONFORMITY

Think about an experience you have had when you feel you may have conformed. Why did you do this? Look at your reasons and compare them with the explanations offered by mainstream social psychology and by critical social psychology. Which fits most comfortably with your understanding?

Critical social psychology does not offer a neat, universal explanation of why people conform or obey based on internal states, nor even a grand theory on social influence. Rather it reintroduces what Harré (1979) described as the 'humanness' in explanations of social activity, focusing on the meaning of a situation for those involved and how this meaning may be mediated in relation to a variety of influences including identity, class, race, gender, and culture. As such, explanations centring on socially constructed norms and the contexts in which these are produced and reproduced become more complex and diverse than those traditionally offered. In particular, power relations and ideologies become central to understandings of why people 'conform to' or 'obey' social dictates. For example, Wilkinson and Kitzinger (1994) trace the psychological creation of heterosexuality as a normative identity. They highlight the dominant view of heterosexuality as 'natural' and as detrimental to other identities, which are then seen as 'deviant' or 'abnormal'. An exploration of the ways in which heterosexuality is constructed through established relations of power within many Western societies is, the above authors suggest, central to an understanding of the ways in which people are produced as, and reproduce, heterosexuality. As well as exploring the construction of heterosexuality as the norm in a variety of powerful nineteenth-century historical, psychological and political discourses, Wilkinson and Kitzinger (1994: 309) highlight a number of social sites where the privileged position of heterosexuality continues to be preserved:

> men and especially women are coerced through a variety of forces including rape, child-marriage, sexual harassment, pornography and economic sanctions. For most of those who are not heterosexual the coercive nature of heterosexuality is everywhere apparent. But for many heterosexuals, their heterosexuality feels 'natural' and 'innate' or freely chosen and often – in both cases – enjoyed as a pleasurable experience. Others feel *excluded* from heterosexuality because of their failure to conform to sex-role stereotypes or to conventional ideas of able-bodied attractiveness.

In the above quotation the discursive production of heterosexual identities is made explicit, and consequently researchers are required to deal with multiple influences to explain how and why people are produced as, and reproduce, heterosexuality. The historical, social and political contexts for heterosexuality require examination as well as differences in experience mediated through class, gender, race, and age. Consequently the meaning of this social phenomenon becomes more diverse and complex.

In addition, setting activities such as conformity and obedience within such contexts introduces to a further level of analysis absent from traditional accounts – the function of conformity and obedience. Many writers within the social constructionist traditions explicitly talk about such activities in the language of social control. In his writings on the care of the self, introduced earlier in this chapter, Foucault concludes that the regimes prescribed relating to the maintenance of the body and mind are exercised with a series of aims and objectives, in particular to establish sophisticated sets of social regulations that structure relations between the individual and his or her body as well as generate channels of communication with others, e.g. medical profession, psychology, legal bodies, etc.

Critical social psychologists explicitly identify as problematic the view of the person as a passive recipient of her or his experiences inscribed in much traditional social psychological theorizing. Rather, the individual is represented as actively negotiating her or his social activities. It is recognized that such negotiations are not, strictly speaking 'free choices', but may be constrained by various social and cultural processes, including gender, class, historical context and ethnicity (Smith, 1988). Viewing the person as an agent demands that

psychologists explore the ways that people resist dominant representations and understandings, and so provides additional information
for piecing together the complex picture of human social activity.
Again, the social theorist Foucault (1978: 95) stressed the centrality of
resistance for accounting for the diverse and changing social positions
individuals occupy and the social actions they perform: 'Where there is
power, there is resistance, and yet or rather consequently, this resistance is never in a position of exteriority of power.' As an example
Foucault (1978) cites the resistance of many homosexual men earlier
this century to representations of themselves as biological deviants
in the writings of sexologists such as Freud (1908) and Ellis (1913).
In challenging such perceptions, homosexual men not only gained
public visibility but also began to articulate alternative representations of homosexuality. Yet, while at the same time gaining a recog-
nizable identity, the activities of homosexual men came under the
scrutiny of many kinds of specialized knowledge, including medicine,
psychology and law.

To return to the examples of femininity mentioned earlier in this
chapter (see Box 5.4), although the activities and identities of the
young women in both Lees (1993) and McFadden (1995) were regulated
by a variety of punitive linguistic and social processes, this is not
the end of the story. Understanding these young women's attempts
at resisting notions of how they should dress, behave, etc. provides
important insights into the changing and diverse nature of feminine
identities and practices and highlights the emergence of new understandings regarding how young women negotiate socially constructed
ideas of what 'woman' means. Many of the young women interviewed
used diverse ways to challenge others' expectations of how they should
act or behave (see Box 5.5).

Box 5.5   Strategies of resistance

Strategy one: Inverting the term 'slag'
In response to the question Is it more acceptable for men to have sex
outside of a steady relationships?

'I personally don't think it is but it seems so because they can't get
pregnant or anything so it's just easy for them to do it [have sex]
quickly and walk away. I don't think its acceptable though, like girls

---

get called sluts and I would still call a man a slut if he was doing it . . . Like it's unusual but I would still say he's a slut.'

In this extract, Jenny makes visible the double standards that exist around the sexual behaviours of women and men. However, she challenges such differences by turning the socially constructed notion of a slag on its head and applying it to men who behave in particular ways.

Strategy two: Subverting the term 'slag'
'I mean some people look down on women who carry condoms. In fact among my friends I'm the only one who carries condoms, yet most nights my female friends come up to me and ask for a condom . . . I have come across people, both men and women, who have thought of me as a bit of a slag, but if being a slag means you have sex when you want and you can protect yourself, then fine, I'm a slag.'

In this extract Gillian redefines the term 'slag', from someone who does not follow social regulations to someone who is satisfying her own desires and taking responsibility for her own sexual safety.

CRITICAL THINKING ON AGENCY

Using Boxes 5.4 and 5.5 as examples, can you think of any times that you have behaved in ways other than were expected. If so, what did you do and why did you do this? What were the consequences for you of doing this?

Summary

Theories of social influence based on the classic studies are critiqued in relation to definition of the individual and social, methodologies employed and the universal status of analysis undertaken. In addition, the influence of socio-political context on psychological research is highlighted. Critical social psychological understandings of social influence processes, such as conformity and obedience, as social actions produced and reproduced in a variety of discourses, are introduced. Consequently, the need to extend the parameters of explanations for conformity and obedience to include a consideration of the meaning and function of social influence processes within historical, social and political contexts is argued. Finally, the concept of agency, absent from traditional explanations of social influence, is introduced.

Key references

Brown, H. (1996) 'Themes in Experimental Research on Groups from 1930s to the 1990s', in M. Wetherell (ed.), *Identities, Groups and Social Issues* (London: The Open University). This chapter provides a detailed outline of experimental research on groups and discusses the limitations associated with these approaches for understanding human social practices in their full complexity.

Lees, S. (1998) 'The Policing of Girls in Everyday Life: Sexual Reputation and the Social Control of Girls', in S. Lees, *Ruling Passions: Sexual Violence, Reputation and the Law* (Milton Keynes: The Open University Press). This chapter is based on the finding from a three-year research study with young women (aged 15–16). It highlights the complex ways in which women's sexualities are produced and constrained within varying social and cultural contexts.

Re-viewing Sex Difference

6

This chapter will highlight:

- Biological accounts of gender
- Sex roles
- Cognition and gender
- Discourse, power and gender
- Recent feminist work on men and masculinities
- Reflections on feminism and discourse

Introduction

The common sense view that men and women are different is deeply embedded in contemporary culture; as the title of a popular book suggests: *Men are from Mars, Women are from Venus* (Gray, 1993). Perceived sex differences cover a range of dispositions, abilities and activities which conform to conventional stereotypes: men are rational, women are emotional; men are assertive, women are passive; men do, women talk. Such assumptions have been enshrined in, and informed by, many social psychological approaches to gender, ranging from psychoanalytic theory (Freud, 1931) to cognitive perspectives (Maccoby and Jacklin, 1974), and there has been considerable debate concerning the extent to which sex differences are produced by nature or nurture (see Burr, 1998; Trew and Kremer, 1998). Feminists have long pointed out, however, that the acceptance and promotion of gender stereotypes within society and social psychology tend to construct men as superior to women, revealing a profound male-centred bias (e.g. Cixous, 1975; Wilkinson, 1986).

This chapter begins with a critical review of strands of social psychology and 'essentialist' feminism which have drawn upon biological concepts (e.g. hormones) and processes (e.g. reproduction) to account for perceived sex differences (e.g. Daly, 1978; Wilson, 1975). Yet, despite continued public fascination with the notion that men and women possess different 'natures', and although bio-psychological research on sex differences continues (see Kimura, 1987), most feminist and social psychological work concentrates on social or 'environmental' factors, and this work is scrutinized next (e.g. Bem, 1974). This focus on sex roles, however, has been given a cognitive twist in that much recent research considers the ways in which socially defined roles and scripts are processed by individuals and groups in various situations (e.g. Bem, 1985; Halpern, 1992). This cognitive approach is in turn criticized for endorsing stereotypical accounts of gender and neglecting social/discursive practices which define femininities and masculinities (e.g. Wetherell, 1997).

The remainder of the chapter is dedicated to developing an understanding of gender along the lines of contemporary feminist social psychology, which situates gender in social, cultural and historical contexts in critical and complex ways. Here, the focus is on social interaction (the meanings that people negotiate between themselves) and social construction (the meanings that are made available by the local culture and which people use to define themselves and others) rather than individual cognitive processes. This feminist social psychology approach is illustrated with regard to some pertinent research examples on the subject of men and masculinities (e.g. Gough, 1998; Willott and Griffin, 1997). Finally, some critical reflections on feminist social psychology perspectives on gender will be provided.

Before exploring the social psychology of gender, however, it is worth stressing from the outset that feminist theory and research within and outside social psychology has greatly enriched understandings of gender. It is also important to point out that feminism has offered a range of insights and arguments from different perspectives and that debates continue concerning key issues. Some significant feminist schools of thought are presented in Box 6.1 and will be encountered again throughout the chapter.

Box 6.1 Feminisms (see Burr, 1998; Percy, 1998)

Essentialist feminism	regards women as 'essentially' different from men and emphasizes women's distinct (and often 'superior') psychology;

Psychoanalytic feminism	stresses the unconscious as an important force in producing gender identity, difference and conflict, and highlights both biological and social influences;
Liberal feminism	based on a humanistic philosophy of individual rights and equality for all, this perspective has been useful in countering sexism and discrimination against women;
Marxist feminism	locates women's (and men's) suffering within capitalism and class oppression and suggests resistance to prevailing economic structures and relations;
Radical feminism	focuses on patriarchy as a source of men's power and women's subordination and advocates gender separatism;
Black feminism	criticizes academic feminism for its white middle-class bias and highlights race relations as a key site for struggle;
Socialist feminism	recognizes a role for relations of gender and class (and other systems, e.g. race) in the oppression of women and men;
Post-modern feminism	is suspicious of grand theories (e.g. Marxism) and notions of 'truth' and highlights gender as fragmented, constructed and amenable to change.

CRITICAL THINKING ON GENDER STEREOTYPES

Clearly the notion that men and women are fundamentally different is very popular. Why do you think gender stereotypes hold great appeal?

Biological sex differences

The nature–nurture debate within (social) psychology and feminism has structured much of the literature on sex/gender differences. The weight attributed to biological and/or social factors in accounting for variation in behaviour and 'personality' between men and women has fluctuated, but nowadays most social psychologists agree on a compromise position. Indeed, many social and cognitive understandings of gender tend to rely on the notion of natural and fixed differences between the sexes (see Muldoon and Reilly, 1998). Nonetheless, the essentialist view that men and women are fundamentally different continues to frame much bio-psychological research.

To this end, studies of sex differences have invoked a range of anatomical and physiological factors, including hormones, genetics, brain lateralization and even brain size. For the most part, research has studied the effects of biological processes on female activity and, moreover, has tended to emphasize negative consequences. For example, much research has focused on the influence of reproductive hormones (e.g. oestrogen) on women's performance and behaviour, often emphasizing detrimental outcomes, such as mood swings, irritability and unreliability (see Choi, 1994). Such research continues despite evidence that the relationship between hormones and mood is complex (e.g. Ussher, 1991) and feminist analyses which point to the absence of premenstrual 'symptoms' in non-Western cultures (e.g. Johnson, 1987).

Where male biology has been investigated, much work has relied on animal studies, making generalizations to humans problematic. Such research has tended to find a correlation between testosterone levels (which are higher in males) and aggression, but this conclusion has been challenged by studies involving humans, where the evidence is mixed (see Archer and Lloyd, 1985). Other studies have considered cases where opposite sex hormones have impacted on the foetus. For example, Imperato-McGinley *et al.* (1979) studied a group of individuals with 'five alpha-reductase deficiency', whereby the penis and scrotum remain underdeveloped until puberty, and found that all individuals in the study, most of whom were raised as female, pursued a male identity when the external sex organs became visible. The fact that 'biological' men may pass as women suggests that social definitions of gender have a great impact on identities ascribed to individuals from birth. Such evidence also undermines the biological view that gender is fixed from birth.

Within sociobiology (e.g. Wilson, 1975), sex differences in various behaviours such as aggression and promiscuity are asserted and interpreted in terms of evolutionary advantage. For example, men are 'naturally' more aggressive because it enables them to go out and hunt/work in order to provide for their families, whilst women are regarded as biologically suited to nurturance and hence childcare. Although this argument is often used to justify sexism ('women are not *naturally*

Box 6.2   Essentialist feminism

Although not a common feminist stance in the twenty-first century, several feminist writers during the 1980s especially promoted an analysis of sex difference as embedded in 'nature'. In these accounts men are associated with vices such as violence and war whilst women are accorded virtues such as greater humanism, nurturance and spirituality. A classic text here is Mary Daly's (1978) *Gyn/Ecology*, which claims that '[women] are rooted, as are animals and trees, wind and seas, in the Earth's substance. Our origins are in her elements', whereas men 'are the life blockers, radically separated from the natural harmony of the universe' (1978: 4, 363). Although such work importantly underlines the prevalence of men's abuses of women and nature, the explanation for such oppression within a discourse of biological determinism creates problems, as such discourses have been used by right-wing groups to maintain the subordination of women by men (e.g. religious institutions which promote femininity as maternal and domestic). As Segal (1987: 37) comments: 'A feminism which emphasises only the dangers to women from men, which insists upon the essential differences between women's and men's inner being, between women's and men's natural urges and experience of the world, leaves little or no scope for transforming the relations between men and women ... [this form of feminism] denies all the contradictions and tensions in existing relations between the sexes, both in and between different social groups.'

---

suited to work', etc.), some feminist theorists have drawn upon biological 'essentialism' in order to promote women's 'superior' nature. In contrast to 'malestream' psychobiological theories, women and femininity are associated with protecting children and nature, with peace rather than 'male' aggression and war (e.g. Daly, 1978) (see Box 6.2).

Essentialist biological perspectives are discussed in more detail in the next chapter on sexualities, but we can point to criticisms by feminist social constructionists who reject the notion that sex differences and inequalities are somehow fixed by nature and therefore unchangeable (see Kitzinger, 1994; Oyama, 1997).

Much the same point can be made in relation to research which attempts to discover differences in brain size and function between men and women. For example, Gray (1981) points to left/right hemisphere specialization as a way of explaining reputed sex differences in visuo-spatial ability: 'women do worse at science because their brains have not developed to favour such skills because ... men needed those skills for hunting and protecting the family unit'. Such use of biological discourses to reinforce or justify gendered inequalities against women has been effectively criticized by feminist social psychologists (see Box 6.3). In any respect, the social cognitive literature on sex differences discussed below has failed to clearly or consistently demonstrate significant sex differences in cognitive abilities (see Segal, 1990).

Box 6.3 Challenging 'natural' differences/inequalities between men and women (Wilkinson, 1996)

Wilkinson cites work by a psychologist (Wilson, 1994) which argues that men occupy the majority of high-status positions in the professions (managers, professors, judges, etc.) because of men's greater competitiveness and 'dominance [which] is a personality characteristic determined by male hormones' (1994: 62–3). To reinforce this claim, the author draws on the 'scientific' evidence from psychology which has consistently offered 'proof' of women's inadequacies, such as poor mathematical ability (Benbow and Stanley, 1980), spatial ability (Masters and Sanders, 1993) and impaired performance on a range of tasks during parts of the menstrual cycle (Hampson, 1990). But such work fails to acknowledge feminist psychological research on 'sex differences' which has found little evidence of significant differences and which has exposed psychology's disciplinary male bias in conducting and presenting such research (see Parlee, 1975; Weisstein, 1993; Wilkinson, 1991).

However, most feminists and social psychologists prefer accounts of gender which include the concept of socialization and which tend to suggest an interaction between nature and nurture. Despite having been rejected by cognitive-experimental social psychology, psychoanalytic accounts of gender provide interesting and provocative analyses and do emphasize an interplay between biological and social forces. Although Freud's writing can be said to be more directly concerned with sexuality and is therefore reviewed in more detail in the next chapter, psychoanalytic concepts have influenced subsequent theories of sex role socialization (see below). For now a brief synopsis will be offered.

CRITICAL THINKING ON BIOLOGY

Describing men and women as 'naturally' different can serve both feminist and anti-feminist goals. Discuss the ways in which feminists and non-feminists may use biology to support their views.

Psychoanalysis and gender

Since Freud's account of early childhood experience and development is well known we will focus here on those elements directly relating to gender. The first point to make is that psychoanalytic theory is fundamentally premised on the power of the unconscious to shape individual identity and interpersonal relationships. The source of unconscious desires is located both in biology (instincts, emotion) and society (reality, reason) – and the conflict between the two. The emergence of gender identities is said to begin with the child's recognition of anatomical sex differences during the 'phallic' stage – the realization that males have a penis and females do not – and is reinforced by gendered social norms and practices as promoted by the parents (e.g. encouraging boys' activity and girls' passivity).

During the phallic stage, which occurs age 3–4, the Oedipal complex operates, whereby the child unconsciously desires the opposite-sex parent and resents the same-sex parent for their access to the love object. For boys, the father is initially a love rival, provoking feelings of hostility and envy, but the boy's desire for the mother, who represents femininity in general, is soon compromised by a rising fear that he will attract punishment from the father for his secret impulses. This 'castration anxiety' is enhanced by the boy's observation that females (mother, sister/s, etc.) have apparently been 'deprived' of the male organ, a fate which the boy desperately wishes to escape. Thus, boys will attempt to redirect their erotic energies into identifying with the all-powerful father and developing paternal or 'masculine' attributes such as work, discipline and obedience – and rejecting 'feminine' practices such as emotional expression. It is through repressing sexual desire in this way that young boys develop into men. However, this progression towards a stable gender identity is far from smooth, since the desire for the mother and 'feminine' values persists and will emerge at different points in the individual's life. In other words, masculinity is achieved through a constant effort to deny and repress the feminine, which is one explanation for 'projecting' feminine weakness on to women and 'un-masculine' men (see Edley and Wetherell, 1995).

The process by which young girls become 'feminine' is less clearly presented in Freud's account. Having already been 'castrated', there is no great anxiety about being punished for expressing desire. Instead, Freud claimed, controversially, that the young girl suffered from 'penis envy' whereby the lost organ is prized and sought after, initially by desiring the father. However, and somewhat less convincingly, the girl reputedly realizes that the father does not reciprocate her affections since his erotic love is directed towards the mother. Consequently, the girl (unconsciously) decides to become like the mother (i.e. 'feminine') in order that she attract her father's attentions. Ultimately, it is asserted, a woman's decision to give birth represents an unconscious wish to satisfy the father by displaying the baby – a surrogate penis. So, as with boys, gender identity for girls is never complete, as identification with the mother and femininity is undermined by continued desire for the father and masculine values. Since masculine ideals are highly valued in society, it is asserted that girls will be more attracted to these and will find it especially difficult to form a coherent feminine identity.

Obviously, Freud provides an original and intriguing theory of gender development which has largely been rejected within mainstream social psychology. Psychoanalytic concepts have been criticized from a scientific perspective for offering a host of untestable, even fantastical, concepts whilst many feminists have lamented the male-centred bias in Freud's work which subordinates women as castrated men (e.g. Tavris and Wade, 1984). However, some 'psychoanalytic feminists' stress the merits of this approach, arguing that theorists such as Freud and Lacan provided a compelling account of the processes of female oppression within the patriarchal family and male-centred society in general (e.g. Mitchell, 1974). Also, there are elements of psychoanalytic theory which have proved influential in subsequent accounts of gender socialization within sociology (e.g. Parsons, 1954) and social psychology (e.g. Bandura, 1977) which drew upon notions of identification with same-sex 'role-models', to which we now turn.

CRITICAL THINKING ON PSYCHOANALYSIS

Freud argues that gender socialization is basically problematic, especially for girls. Do you agree?

Sex role theories

Most commentators agree that Talcott Parsons, an influential sociologist writing in the 1940s and 50s, was responsible for originally developing the concept of sex role. Based on his studies with small groups, he came up with the terms 'instrumental' and 'expressive' to classify the two orientations thought necessary for social cohesion (Parsons, 1954). The former category neatly maps on to 'masculine' capacities such as reason and physical labour, whereas the latter connotes 'feminine' domains of emotion and nurturance, etc. The two forms of orientation were deemed complementary, working together in order to ensure the smooth functioning of society (hence 'functionalism', the name given to the broader theory).

Parsons also drew on elements of Freudian theory to help explain how people became socialized into sex roles, notably the Oedipus complex wherein young boys and girls come to identify with the same-sex parent and hence internalize 'sex-appropriate' attributes (see above). This focus on early family dynamics qualifies Parson's account as genuinely social, although the reliance on unobservable, untestable Freudian constructs gradually attracted much criticism from sociological and psychological quarters which were increasingly concerned to flag their 'scientific' status. This drive towards quantification in the pursuit of scientific respectability culminated in a widespread rejection of psychoanalysis and, with it, Parson's functionalism.

Social learning theory

Consequently, within (social) psychology in the 1960s and 1970s, social learning theory (Bandura, 1977; Mischel, 1966) became the dominant approach to sex role socialization. Deriving from basic behaviourist principles propounded earlier by theorists such as Watson and Skinner, the focus here is on overt, measurable behaviour and how it is learned by a combination of observation, imitation and reinforcement. Also drawing on psychoanalytic principles, individuals are said

to be encouraged to behave in 'sex-appropriate' ways through identifying with significant others of the same sex (parent, athlete, cartoon
character, etc.) and by virtue of social rewards and punishments issued
by appropriate socializing agents.

There is a wealth of evidence documenting how a range of agents,
popularly known as 'role models' (parent, teachers, peers, media figures), reinforce traditional sex roles. For example, Fagot (1974) found
that parents typically promote assertiveness in boys by responding to
their demands whilst ignoring and therefore discouraging equivalent
behaviour from girls. Similarly, many studies indicate that in the class-
room boys attract more praise for the intellectual quality of their work
whereas girls receive more attention for the neatness of their work (see
Renzetti and Curran, 1992). Conversely, children are frequently repri-
manded – and indeed caution their peers – for engaging in activities
deemed to be 'inappropriate' or 'deviant' for one's sex (boys playing
with dolls, girls climbing trees) (e.g. Garvey, 1977). From a very early
age, then, many children are proficient at recognizing, realizing and
regulating norms around masculinity and femininity.

CRITICAL THINKING ON SEX ROLES

Reflecting on your own experience, list those people who have had
an impact on your personal development and identity. Which figures
have been the most influential? Are there more examples of same-
sex 'models'?

This modelling explanation has recently become popular with mass
media and the general public. It can be witnessed in a recent debate
in the UK around the 'Spice Girls', an all-female pop group that
was considered by many to be setting a 'bad example' to young girls
(e.g. through wearing revealing clothes, becoming pregnant, behaving assertively) but at the same time was credited with inspiring confidence and assertiveness in their female fans. The theme of 'inappropriate' role models has also been generated to account for increasing
juvenile violence, most notoriously in the UK with the Bulger case,
where a specific video-movie was cited as a key influence in the murder
of a young boy by two others. Interestingly, evidence concerning the
impact of media violence on boys and girls has found little or no gender
difference (e.g. Huesmann and Eron, 1986).

'search literature on sex differences in general has
much convincing evidence of sex role socialization.
'ehensive review of sex difference research in the 1970s sug-
⸱ests that only small differences could be claimed on a few variables,
such as visual–spatial ability and mathematical ability, which have
since disappeared (see Baumeister, 1988; Maccoby and Jacklin, 1974).
Tellingly, feminist writers have pointed out that this literature only
tends to publish research where significant differences are demon-
strated, thus failing to take into account many studies which show
little or no variation between the sexes (see Segal, 1990). Moreover,
recent research suggests that the gap is narrowing and even that girls
outperform boys in traditionally male areas such as mathematics (see
Kimball, 1994). The notion that gender stereotypes need not impinge
upon an individual's identity or behaviour has been actively pursued
since the 1970s when Sandra Bem, a liberal feminist social psychologist, introduced the concept of 'androgyny'.

Androgyny

It was only in the 1970s that social psychologists recognised that
'masculinity' and 'femininity' were social constructs that did not have
to equate with biological sex. This assumption is inherent, for example,
in Terman and Miles's (1936) Masculinity–Femininity scale, which
assessed the degree to which men and women embodied their 'natural'
roles, that is, to be a task-oriented breadwinner (men) or a domesti-
cated carer (women). Bem (1974) rejects the idea propounded by
sex role theories and related research that individuals automatically
and unproblematically assume gender identities consistent with traditional expectations. Rather, masculinity and femininity could be
viewed as independent orientations such that any individual could dis-
play aspects of both. Of course, an individual could just as well embody
traditional ideals ('sex-typed') but the focus switched to 'androgynous'
people, those who scored highly on both masculinity and femininity;
those with low scores on masculinity and femininity attracted the
dubious label of 'undifferentiated' (see Bem, 1974; and Box 6.4).
Bem's hypothesis is consistent with Jungian psychology which suggests the presence of two complementary archetypes within the
individual psyche – the anima (feminine) and the animus (masculine)
(see Johnson, 1976). Characterizations of these archetypes corres-
pond closely to gender conventions: the animus is defined by 'active

Box 6.4 Bem sex-role inventory (Bem, 1974)

From an initial list of 200 attributes, Bem asked groups of under-graduate students to rate the items according to how 'desirable' they were for a man or woman in order to elicit gender norms or stereotypes. Based on the results, twenty items were identified as more appropriate for men, twenty for women and a further twenty which did not differentiate between the sexes. 'Masculine' and 'feminine' items are listed below.

Masculine items	Feminine items
acts as a leader	affectionate
aggressive	cheerful
ambitious	childlike
analytical	compassionate
assertive	does not use harsh language
athletic	eager to soothe hurt feelings
competitive	feminine
defends own beliefs	flatterable
dominant	gentle
forceful	gullible
has leadership abilities	loves children
independent	loyal
individualistic	sensitive to the needs of others
makes decisions	easily shy
masculine	soft-spoken
self-reliant	sympathetic
strong personality	tender
willing to take a stand	understanding
willing to take risks	warm
	yielding

College students were then asked to specify the degree to which each trait described themselves. Low correlations were found between masculinity and femininity scores, thus confirming Bem's hypothesis that these dimensions referred to independent traits rather than a continuum. Also, the results suggested that rigid gender stereotypes were not necessarily or automatically internalized by the 'appropriate' sex. Using a slightly different test, the Personal Attributes Questionnaire, Spence, Helmreich and Stapp (1974) confirmed these findings.

achievement, cool reasonableness, mastery, penetration.' whilst the anima comprises the 'primeval and oceanic, instinct, unity, relationship and relatedness..' (see de Castillejo, 1973: 57). Both approaches claim that a combination of the masculine and the feminine within the individual make for a more advanced, psychologically healthy subject (see Bem *et al.*, 1976), although feminists argue that possessing 'masculine' characteristics is more important for both sexes because these tend to be more highly valued in society (see Wilkinson, 1986).

– Bem's work was undoubtedly valuable for questioning the rigid equation between biological sex and gender identity promoted by social psychology and widely accepted in the general public, and it therefore contributed to the feminist challenge to existing gender norms. However, Bem's approach has been criticized for locating gender at the level of the individual and ignoring societal factors such as power and ideology. In other words, it is up to individuals to decide which 'sex-role orientation' to adopt, as if free choice were possible and not constrained by differential access to power due to social positions of class, race, education, etc. (see Wetherell, 1997). According to Hollway (1989: 99), Bem's 'feminist intentions were subverted by the methods and assumptions she reproduced uncritically as a result of her training as a social psychologist [within] the atheoretical, empiricist tradition of Anglo-American psychology'. This liberal, idealistic and individualistic approach continues to inform much apparently feminist social psychology in the United States, as embodied by journals such as *Sex Roles* (see Connell, 1987). From a critical social psychology perspective, the ideals and approaches of mainstream social psychology – which do not theorize societal relations of gender – remain intact.

This psychological approach to gender has continued within the cognitive revolution which has defined the discipline over the last twenty years.

CRITICAL THINKING ON ANDROGYNY

Select 10 items from Box 6.4 which you think best describe your 'personality'. Using the Bem sex-role inventory (BSRI) system, categorize your choices as 'masculine' or 'feminine'. How androgynous do you appear? Are there specific situations when your more 'masculine' traits emerge? How about 'feminine' traits?

Social cognition

Emerging from the work of Piaget, Kohlberg and others, this perspective favours an analysis of 'internal' phenomena (thought processes, mental representations) as opposed to 'external' stimuli (rewards, punishments, role models) in order to account for the internalization and endurance of gender stereotypes. Consequently, the concept of 'role' in social psychology has largely been displaced in favour of cognitive processes such as categorization. Gender awareness and identity is seen as a product of the child's cognitive development rather than 'environmental' factors. There is little concern here with the social origins and content of stereotypes (regarded as the province of sociology or politics); their existence is simply accepted and the emphasis is on how – and to what extent – people use these in social perception and identity formation.

Feminist social psychologists working within this tradition have made important contributions. Notable here is the work of Carol Gilligan during the 1970s and 1980s which produced an influential critique of Kohlberg's (1969) theory of moral development. This theory outlined six stages of moral reasoning through which individuals may develop, although very few people reach the highest level and, significantly, fewer people from working-class, non-white and female samples were found to master the advanced stages. But Gilligan (1982) criticized Kohlberg's model for its male-centred values and assumptions, arguing that its emphasis on justice over social care was biased against women and in favour of white middle-class men who were Kohlberg's subjects. Gilligan suggests that women have a different and arguably superior way of thinking about moral issues, another form of essentialism which emphasizes sex differences and which prioritizes women's distinct nature.

On the other hand, later work by the liberal feminist Bem moved away from notions of distinct gender roles and sex differences towards a theory of individual differences based on cognitive processing known as 'gender schema theory' (Bem, 1985; 1987). This approach assumes that individuals will vary according to the importance they ascribe to the category of gender, with 'strongly sex-typed' people (highly masculine or feminine) prone to classifying information about themselves and the world in terms of gender, and vice versa. A 'gender schematic' might decompose fitness activities into 'feminine' aerobics and 'masculine' weightlifting; likewise 'masculine' may be used to denote certain supermarket products, such as red meat and beer, whereas baby food and shampoo could be labelled 'feminine'. Experimental support for this hypothesis has been generated (e.g. Bem, 1981), although there are some criticisms of Bem's analysis (see Spence and Helmreich, 1978).

However, the focus on individual cognitive tendencies which informs much North American work on gender has been criticized for neglecting the cognitive consequences which ensue from membership of social groups and categories such as gender. In European social psychology especially, the emphasis of theory and research is on *social* identities, that is, the impact that belonging to a group has on individual and group behaviour. Most of the work in this area is framed by Social Identity Theory (e.g. Tajfel, 1981).

Social Identity theory (SIT)

This theory has already been described (see Chapter 4), but we will briefly summarize the key concepts and discuss how they apply to gender. The approach is principally concerned with inter-group conflict and change, and assumes that 'individuals define themselves in terms of their social group memberships and that group-defined self-perception produces psychologically distinctive effects in social behaviour' (Hogg and Abrams, 1988: xi). The theory suggests that, regardless of emotional investment in any group identity, the cognitive process of categorization of itself will inevitably tend towards maximizing similarity within categories and maximizing difference between categories. In terms of gender, for example, all women will be viewed as similar, as will all men, and the differences between the two groups will be exaggerated. The theory also moves beyond cognition to suggest that people will be motivated to maximize the attractiveness of groups to which they belong ('in-groups') and, conversely, will be concerned to downplay or ignore the positive qualities of other groups ('out-groups'). It is assumed that enhancing the status of one's in-groups provides a boost to one's own identity, at least that component of one's identity associated with group memberships – termed 'social identity'.

SIT regards gender as one of a range of relevant social groups or categories (others being race, nationality, etc.) which are drawn on by individuals for self-definition. Hence, members of the same sex category (i.e. male or female) will tend to minimize differences within the in-group (e.g. 'all blokes like football') and exaggerate differences between in-group and out-group along favourable or 'biased' dimensions (e.g. 'men can park the car properly, women can't'). Such critical comparison processes will come into play when gender identity becomes 'salient', i.e. more visible – for example a 'women's night out' or 'men playing/watching sport together'. Thus, the SIT perspective offers a cognitive account of gender which also appears to locate gender in the social realm. In addition, the theory considers the dimension of power between groups, highlighting strategies for maintaining and/or promoting social identity which differentiate dominant from subordinated social groups (see Hogg and Abrams, 1988).

However, SIT has been criticized for assuming that all members of a particular group perceive or experience the group – and other groups – in the same way. In the case of gender, this analysis suggests that all men see themselves as similar to each other and that they share common perceptions of women (and similarly for women). Clearly this perspective overlooks differences and tensions within any one group such as men or women which may be related to social class, sexuality, race, ethnicity and so on. As such, the theory implies a non-existent homogeneity within groups thereby presenting an oversimplified analysis of gender relations. In addition, SIT has been criticized for its claim that inter-group phenomena such as in-group bias derive from 'basic' or 'hard wired' processes of categorization – with the implication that prejudice between groups is rather inevitable. This view of cognitive processes as innate and universal presents an image of individuals as passive information processors incapable of challenging stereotypes or treating members of other groups in positive ways (see Billig, 1985 for an extended critique). Critical social psychology approaches, however, have acknowledged that categories of gender can be subjected to multiple and sometimes contradictory meanings.

CRITICAL THINKING ON SOCIAL IDENTITY

In what ways do you behave in the company of same-sex friends? How do you view the other sex on these occasions? To what extent does 'social identity' overtake the self at these times?

Towards a critical/feminist social psychology of gender

Contemporary critical and feminist analyses of gender typically deploy terms such as diversity, conflict, ideology and power. Within this broad perspective, the social construction of gender is emphasized, where representations of masculinities and femininities are regarded as cultural, multiple, dynamic, interrelated and influential on self-definition. As feminists have pointed out, meanings around masculinity have been traditionally privileged over all things feminine. For example, the common social practice of favouring 'masculine' over 'feminine' activities and characteristics is referred to as the 'plus male, minus female' by Spender (1980). This phenomenon extends to instances where the same behaviour performed by men and women is differentially evaluated (men are assertive, women are pushy, etc.).

CRITICAL THINKING ON GENDER INEQUALITIES

Consider again the list of BSRI items above. On a scale of 1–5, rate each attribute on its social importance, i.e. the value placed on possessing the characteristic in society (1 = not important; 2 = limited importance; 3 = neutral; 4 = fairly important; 5 = very important). Now compare the mean ratings for 'masculine' and 'feminine' items. Did you rate 'masculine' items as more important? Why (not)?

This point has been used to criticize theory and research propounded by liberal feminist social psychologists such as Bem, who point to the damaging effects of gender stereotypes and emphasize personal choice and development in the formulation of one's gender identity, with a preference towards androgynous identities. Concepts such as choice and internalization, however, do not address social relations of difference and inequality between men and women and between constructs of masculinity and femininity. For example, the capacity for a woman to play football or drink lots of beer will be constrained and framed by wider social understandings of gender which define femininity outside particular sports and leisure pursuits. Similarly, the capacity for a man to take an interest in sewing or nursing will be mediated by prevailing ideals of masculinity which identify such activities as unmanly, effeminate, soft, etc. Women who aspire or attempt to move into 'non-traditional' arenas (e.g. driving a bus, playing football, displaying sexual assertiveness) are often subjected to ridicule and abuse (verbal and physical attacks, lower pay, harsher conditions, etc.). Research consistently uncovers deep resentment and a multitude of barriers which act to preserve male dominance, typically warranted by claims that 'it isn't natural for women to demand equality' or 'women have gone too far' (see Faludi, 1992; Ford, 1985). Women are thus caught in a double bind: to adhere to the norms of femininity is to remain a second-class citizen (excluded from public life, etc.) whereas to struggle for equal rights often means enduring much psychological and physical suffering. Within radical, Marxist and socialist schools of feminist theory, sex roles are situated in 'patriarchal' society where established social structures and relationships favour men. Instead of concentrating on encouraging individuals to become more androgynous, a strategy which ignores the deep structural constraints which inhibit free movement, the concern here is to challenge the wider (patriarchal) social, economic and historical structures which conspire to cement traditional gender relations (see Segal, 1987).

The gender picture is more complicated still when other systems of difference are acknowledged. It is relatively easy to imagine various limitations on number and type of roles practised depending on social class, sexual orientation, ethnic background and occupational choice. For example, it is often difficult for gay and lesbian individuals to 'come out' and fulfil this role in a heterosexist society. Similarly, a working-class single mother may well find it difficult to hold down a full-time job or register for a course because of childcare responsibilities and/or lack of transport. Conversely, those individuals defined as heterosexual or middle class will probably encounter fewer obstacles and will have more opportunities to take on and enjoy a range of roles. Socialist and post-modern (or social constructionist) forms of feminism highlight issues of diversity, conflict and fluidity in relation to gendered identities. A feminist social psychological analysis would seek to identify the range of gendered roles or positions available, examine any difference and/or conflicts between these representations and highlight their implications for gender relations. Indeed, special editions of the journal *Feminism & Psychology* have featured debates on social diversity and politics in relation to (hetero)sexuality (Kitzinger *et al.*, 1992), race (Bhavnani and Phoenix, 1994) and social class (Walkerdine, 1996).

CRITICAL THINKING ON SEXISM

Considering the examples below, identify relevant popular images/ representations:

female footballers;
male nurses;
single mothers;
unemployed men.

How do traditional ideals around gender influence how we see these identities?

Rather than fixing masculinity or femininity as a property or structure within individuals, a contemporary critical feminist approach to gender tends to locate gender as a social construct and examines the meanings attached to gender within various (textual) presentations (speeches, magazine features, advertisements, interview transcripts). For example, some recent feminist/critical work has interrogated prevailing media representations of gender.

Gender, representation and discourse

Critical research on gender has examined the images and ideals reproduced in popular cultural forms, ranging from children's fiction to soap opera and art. A detailed content analysis is the normal method, which involves carefully reading the text and identifying predominant themes relating to the ways in which men and women are depicted. A standard finding, for example, is that much reading material for schoolchildren largely presents women in domestic or caring roles (Swann, 1992), and in many girls' comics patience, passivity and serving others are advertised as a means of 'getting a man' (see Walkerdine, 1987). Similar evidence of gender stereotyping has been gathered with respect to television output, with, for example, men deployed as experts offering advice or doing voiceovers in many advertisements (e.g. Gunter, 1986). And in a thorough analysis of women's magazines from 1949 to 1980, Ferguson (1983) listed a number of dominant themes including 'getting and keeping your man', 'keeping the family happy' and 'be more beautiful' – all ideals of femininity which persist despite social and economic changes (see Burr, 1998, for an overview of this literature).

Most critical psychologists agree, however, that people do not simply absorb dominant media messages passively and unthinkingly, as social learning theory would seem to suggest. Rather, the values and practices transmitted through popular media are considered in terms of their derivation from and contribution to the pool of cultural resources from which people fashion gendered identities. As Ballaster *et al.* (1991: 131) suggest in relation to women's media: 'The magazine determines the range of possible meanings and assumptions implicit in its own text, what kind of life is seen as a struggle, as what is easy, or can be taken for granted.' In other words, media consumers are thought to acknowledge, reproduce, re-work and even resist prevailing meanings in active, dynamic and sometimes contradictory ways. For example, Buckingham (1993) analysed the talk of young boys when discussing the television programmes they watched and concluded that these 'texts' operated as a powerful resource from which the boys constructed masculine identities. McRobbie (1991) suggests that teen romance stories are read in quite different ways by girls, depending on other reading habits and familiarity with the genre. Beyond media representations and their impact on gendered identities, critical social psychology is generally concerned with language – or discourse/s – around gender.

CRITICAL THINKING ON MEDIA REPRESENTATIONS

Compare representations of men and women presented in a 'woman's' magazine (e.g. *Cosmopolitan; Marie Claire*); a 'men's' magazine (e.g. *Arena; Loaded*). You could select the same 'units' from each magazine for consistency (e.g. every 30th page). Compare images of 'masculinity' and 'femininity' within and between maga-zines. Discuss reasons for any differences.

The analysis of language has provided an important focus for feminist and critical researchers interested in challenging gender ideals. Seminal work by Cameron (1992), for example, suggests that women are subordinated more often in talk through being addressed by their first name (rather than Mrs, Ms, Dr, etc.) or through terms of endearment ('love', 'dear', etc.). Equally significant work by Spender (1980) has critically examined 'man-made language', the most obvious example being the widespread use of generic words such as 'man' to refer to all people. The use of compliments by men directed at women's bodies can also be thought of as reinforcing female subservience: 'they serve as a reminder that a woman's appearance is available to be commented upon and that the person giving the compliment is in a position to pass judgement' (Swann, 1992: 31–2).

Remaining with language around sexuality, another common finding confirms a sexual double standard wherein promiscuous women are typically denounced as 'slags' and 'tarts' whereas men who sleep around attract more positive identities such as 'stud' (see Anderson, 1988; Hollway, 1989).

More specifically, however, much critical social psychology work concentrates on 'discourse/s' (see Chapters 2, 3). The (male) breadwinner can be regarded as a discourse, a traditionally powerful one which is signalled by a range of interconnecting 'statements' or assumptions, such as 'men at work' and 'women's place is in the home' and 'a man must provide for his family', etc. As Pleck (1987) notes, another role (or discourse) has emerged in recent times which construes fatherhood in terms of involvement, closeness and emotional support. So, at any given historical moment there will be more than one understanding of fatherhood (or any other 'object' for that matter) which a particular culture makes available. Further, following Foucault's (1972) notion that discourses exist in relations of power, it is usual that one discourse will be socially dominant at any one time. In the case of fatherhood, one could argue that the traditional 'bread-winner' discourse remains ascendant in spite of the evolution of alternative discourses.

Rather than simply identifying and describing the range of roles/ discourses present in society, there is an additional effort to study how discourses are re-presented (or 're-produced') in everyday talk and, significantly, how dominant discourses are resisted or re-worked (there is no assumption here that socially powerful ideals are accepted and practised uncritically). This form of critical research can be illustrated by considering recent empirical work within feminist social psychology which turns the spotlight on to men's talk and masculine identities.

Men and masculinities

Up until very recently, the topic of 'masculinity' had not featured prominently within psychology or social science generally. As feminist writers suggest, the history of the social sciences has been dominated by men and male-centred perspectives (the 'malestream') which adopted a 'male-as-norm' approach (see Wilkinson, 1986; 1996). In other words, social and psychological phenomena were understood from the position of (white, middle-class) men; after all, much psychological 'knowledge' has been generated from a subject base largely comprising male college students, as Gilligan (1982) pointed out in relation to morality. Masculinity was not thought about explicitly; it was assumed as natural, normal and beyond question – that is, until the intervention of feminism.

Critical feminist voices were powerfully raised in the late 1960s and 70s against 'the male gender' in the light of emerging evidence concerning male oppression of women. As statistics on sexual violence were produced, for example, masculinity came to be seen as damaging to women and children, thereby disrupting the myth of men as protectors of families. As role theories became fashionable, some men themselves began to regard traditional social expectations around masculinity as problematic and unhealthy (see Messner, 1997): hence the appearance of 'men's' groups' dedicated to resisting dominant ideals around emotional repression, work absorption, aggression, etc. and attempting to rethink masculinity along more positive lines. From within and without, what it means to be a man became an active subject for debate in the 1970s and has now produced a sizeable social scientific literature (see Connell, 1995; Wetherell and Griffin, 1991). More recently, critical and feminist social psychologists have subjected masculinity to critical, empirical scrutiny (see Edley and Wetherell, 1995).

For example, Willott and Griffin (1997) conducted a study on unemployed men in order to explore how their 'masculinity' was constructed in the absence of the traditional male resource of 'breadwinning'. The study is presented in the wider UK economic context which has witnessed a huge shift from heavy male-dominated work (e.g. coal mining, steelworking) to light industries (tourism, leisure) and created issues for many men around securing work and remaking masculine identities. The feminist aspect to this research was concerned with the possibility that unemployed men might reposition themselves actively within the household in terms of domestic chores and childcare responsibilities.

However, the analysis suggests that, rather than reinvent themselves as domestic workers or involved caregivers, the unemployed men often chose to adhere to the traditional discourse of the male breadwinner by resorting to 'fiddling', thereby finding money to support the family (and, of course, public consumption) – see Box 6.5.

Even with men who are positioned as relatively powerless (in terms of income, status, etc.) the pull of traditional discourses is so strong that it structures their talk – and practice. In this way these

---

**Box 6.5   Men, masculinity and breadwinning
(Willott and Griffin, 1997)**

Frank   I've done some casual, and it don't satisfy yer. But I'll tell
           you something it does do for yer, it gets you off your arse
           and 'cos you enjoy going to work it puts you . . .
Madge   And puts food on the table
Nick   It pays the bills don't it? .
Ray   Yeah.
Frank   You're not walking around the house and you're not
           getting around your missus and the child, you're going
           out and doing something. Whether you have to get up at
           five or six o'clock in the morning, you enjoy doing it.

'oppressed' men retain access to power and continue to affirm relations of inequality between themselves and their women (positioned domestically within this discourse).

As well as addressing how gender is constructed within multiple discourses, this discourse approach is also sensitive to contradictions within a given 'text' (such as an interview transcript, a newspaper report, a magazine article, or even a television programme). In other words, a speaker (or writer) may well employ two or more discourses during the course of conversation with diametrically opposed meanings and implications. In one study on political arguments (McNaughten, 1993) we encounter any given participant using both pro-privatization arguments and arguments in favour of increased public spending. In the field of gender, research on masculinity (e.g. Gough, 2001) has generated many instances where competing discourses are deployed, often in the same extract – hence the popularity of the term 'masculinities'. In Box 6.6, for example, two heterosexual male university students are discussing homosexuality, with one speaker adopting a 'gay-friendly' position whilst the other makes remarks which could easily be construed as homophobic.

Moreover, the deployment of anti-gay sentiment is not straightforward – the same speaker attempts to present himself as tolerant or liberal at the same time as presenting homophobic comments. One could argue that the two discourses used here – one reactionary, one liberal – are 'objectively' in conflict, although scrutiny of the text would invite the view that the liberal discourse works in the service of the homophobic discourse by functioning to mitigate and therefore

Box 6.6 Constructing masculinities in relation to (homo-)sexuality (Gough, 2001)

Joe	[...] and I know, like, a few gay lads that work at the club and when they see me they come up to me and give me a kiss on the cheek.
Trev	Oh no! Uhhh, I just couldn't, it's just not ...
Joe	I call you 'love' and 'flower' but you don't get offended do you?
Trev	Yeah, I mean ...
Joe	But what if I turned round and said I was gay? Would you instantly dislike me because of it?
Trev	No, I mean I've got, I have one gay friend and ... [I wasn't chuffed about it]. I'm not bothered – as long as they don't come on to me.
Joe	So what makes you think that any homosexual's gonna come on to you?
Trev	Well, I'm not bothered if they come on to me ... as long as they don't! [*laughter*] No ...
Jo	Is it just that it would repulse you to give a guy a kiss?
Trev	Oh yeah, big time, yeah.
Joe	But why?
Trev	It's just disgustin', I just can't stand it [...] I just don't think it's right.
Joe	What about a couple of girls snoggin'?
Trev	No, it's not ...
Joe	If they were attractive?
Trev	If they were attractive, if they were attractive it [*laughter*] ... No, it has its sexual tone yeah, but ...
Joe	What about if it was two attractive blokes?
Trev	There's no such thing, is there?
Joe	Two of the guys from Levi ads with six pack and all muscly and that ...
Trev	I just don't [understand it] I don't know, I can't help it, not that I'm that [bothered] anyway, I just can't stand it, it's just not [on] [...] bit close to the mark ...

enable its expression in a cultural climate which eschews overtly prejudiced talk. In other words, contemporary norms of equality and political correctness may be used to 'cover' any prejudiced content or present the speaker as liberal so as to deflect potential accusations of bias. The classic formulation would be 'I'm not homophobic but ... gay men shouldn't flaunt their sexuality', where a disclaimer is inserted before the controversial statement is offered. Such discursive strategies have been studied in the context of 'new racism' (see Billig, 1990; van Djik, 1984) and 'new sexism' (Gill, 1993; Gough, 1998) (see also Chapter 9).

The extracts also highlight the relational dimension to masculinities, whereby men define themselves in relation to other 'objects', in this case gay men. Further, the 'other' is presented as somehow inferior ('disgusting'; 'not right') so that (heterosexual) masculine self is implicitly favoured (as morally superior etc.). Forms of masculinity which frame other identities (women, gay men, etc.) as subordinate have been labelled 'hegemonic' (Connell, 1995). For example, recent work by Wetherell and Edley (1999) has identified a range of subject positions which men inhabit and which are defined in relation to other masculine identities (Box 6.7).

So, conceptualizing gender in terms of discourse rather than role moves beyond the one-dimensional deterministic ethos of psychological theories (where individuals are at the mercy of normative expectations) to consider how social ideals are 'negotiated' during social interaction. The common theme within recent feminist and critical approaches is 'the social construction of gender', that is, a concern with how men and women are variously re-presented at various 'sites', such as media, education, family, and how these images/ideas are re-produced by people in their everyday understandings. This turn to discourse thus situates particular identities in social, cultural and historical contexts and often signals an analysis of power, in recognition that roles and representations exist in relations of difference/dominance.

The foregoing discussion should not be taken to imply, however, that a discursive approach to gender is without blemish; there have been some significant objections from feminists on the grounds that individual women's (and men's) experience of particular subject positions within discourse has not been adequately theorized (see Chapter 4, the section headed 'The problem of subjective experience'). In other words, discourse theory allows little scope for exploring how

Box 6.7   Discourse and masculinities (Wetherell and Edley, 1999)

Three subject positions are highlighted which male interviewees use to construct themselves as masculine – the heroic, the ordinary and the rebellious – with all three considered problematic in terms of gender politics. The heroic refers to construals of self which rely on traditional ideals of masculinity around drinking, sport, being in control, etc. (and which can be seen as criticizing contemporary forms of masculinity centred around nurturance or part-time work). The ordinary concerns self-identifications as 'normal' or 'regular' in which distance is created between self and social conventions around masculinity (here recognized as negative and stereotypical). Although this second position could easily be read as unproblematic, Wetherell argues that it can also be as reinforcing masculine myths – around individualism, autonomy and rationality. Both the heroic and the ordinary, then, may be regarded as privileged subject positions available to men as resources for fashioning masculine identities (and for creating difference and excluding women). As for the rebellious position, in which men define themselves as unconventional in resisting gender ideals (e.g. enjoying knitting or cooking), the problem here is that the rebellion remains on an individual level – nonconformity is perceived as an individual character trait rather than a political activity. The men assuming these positions appear to congratulate themselves for their courage and independence in pursuing such unusual options thereby rendering gender relations unchanged.

one individual personalizes or negotiates within specific discourses; for example, a discourse which constructs 'women as natural carers' will provoke a range of emotional and political responses from different women, depending on personal biographies as well as social circumstances. One mother might resist this positioning on the basis of her own negative experiences of mothering and being mothered, whilst another might position herself within this discourse on account of her perceived suitability for and history of parenting. The meaning of 'mothering' will depend on subjective, emotional reactions and memories as well as broader societal and cultural understandings (see Hollway, 1989).

As well as personal 'reality' or experience, discourse analysis might also overlook societal or material realities encountered by groups such as women and ethnic minorities. Again, feminist social psychologists have been foremost in pondering the limits of discourse analysis for a feminist project committed to speak for women as a collective (see Chapters 3 and 10). Although the focus on discourse is endorsed for highlighting the social construction of femininities and opening up alternative discourses of gender, the relativist insistence on endless diversity and the exclusive focus on language makes it difficult to settle on one version of reality beyond or supported by discourse, such as the reality of women's oppression. For this reason several feminist writers adopt a 'critical realist' stance in that personal and political values are asserted to support a fixed view of gender relations whilst also acknowledging the motivated or constructed nature of the account (see Gill, 1995; Willig, 1998).

Nonetheless, discourse analysis has proved critically useful in shifting from the biological connotations around concepts of traits and sex-roles. As such, the idea that men and women unproblematically accept or follow prescribed roles is challenged and replaced by the notion that negotiating gender is now a complicated, dynamic business informed by particular perspectives and social meanings, as well as the positions of class, race, sexuality and so on. The concept of role seems far too shallow and simplistic to fully account for gender, as it implies straightforward internalization and unquestioned practice of a limited range of scripts. It does not allow for societal power to be incorporated into the equation and it is important to look at discourse theory (or more broadly, 'social constructionism') to provide a more satisfying account of gender.

Summary

There are many different feminist and social psychological perspectives on gender and, as a result, several ongoing debates on important issues such as that between essentialism and constructionism. The trend within recent feminist and critical social psychological work has been towards an analysis of gender within discourse, with an emphasis on gendered identities as socially constructed, fluid and conflictual. There have also been recent attempts to rework psychoanalysis to produce a theory of gender and identity which accommodates subjective experience as well as discourse.

Key references

Burr, V. (1998) *Gender and Social Psychology* (London: Routledge). A slim book which clearly and critically outlines different traditions in the study of gender within social psychology. Good coverage of feminist approaches.

Edley, N. and Wetherell, N. (1995) *Men in Perspective* (London: Sage). The later chapters are especially relevant as they cover 'cultural' and feminist perspectives on men and masculinities. Lots of examples presented to develop points.

Sexualities and Psychology

7

This chapter will highlight:

- Essentialist thinking on sexuality
- Social constructionist thinking on sexuality
- New representations of sexuality emerging from 'queer' theory
- Understandings of heterosexuality as a normative, coercive institution.

2001

Introduction

" Twenty years ago the psychological establishment still viewed homosexuality as a perversion, a mental illness that needed to be 'cured'. Since then psychologists appear to have mellowed. According to the *Introduction to Psychology*, one of the most popular undergraduate textbooks, they now concede that homosexuality is 'a variant rather than a perversion of sexual expression and not in itself an indication or cause of mental illness'. (Kitzinger, cited in Holder, 1993)

The above quotation is taken from an article describing the difficulties faced by psychologists arguing for the recognition of lesbianism as a valid area of psychological study by their professional body. Although related to the study of lesbianism, the quotation reflects ongoing debates within social psychology about what sexuality means and how it can be researched and theorized by psychologists. This chapter explores the debates within social psychology concerning sexuality and the implications for understandings of sexuality within the discipline of psychology. Traditional perspectives exploring notions of sexualities as biologically-based, the favouring of heterosexual identities and its impact, and the male norm dominating much of this work, are critically reviewed. Drawing on more recent research from within critical social psychology, this chapter will argue that the study of sexuality should be viewed within wider political, social, cultural, scientific and other discourses regarding the body and its uses.

The nature debate:
essentialist models of sexuality

Within social psychology, discussions about the origins of sexuality have traditionally been situated within the nature vs. nurture debate. Prior to the 1960s, understandings of sexuality as biologically determined existed relatively unchallenged. However, since the 1960s, alternative understandings of sexuality have emerged from feminist and 'queer' theorizing, introducing new dimensions to discussions on the origin and practices of sexuality. In this section we will review some of the essentialist writings on sexuality.

The sociobiological perspective

> Since sex is often referred to as one of our more animal instincts, perhaps we should 'naturally' turn to biology for an explanation of our sexuality. (McFadden and Sneddon, 1998: 41)

There is a long tradition of work that views various aspects of human sexual and social behaviour from within a wider biological context. The origins of this work lie in a much-respected body of research exploring the reproductive arrangements of non-human species (Gould and Gould, 1989). From the 1970s, there have been various attempts to understand human sexuality within a similar framework, but the success of such theoretical forays remains a contentious issue (Lees, 1993; Mahony, 1985; Miller and Fowlkes, 1980).

Within the sociobiological tradition (Hutt, 1972; Wilson, 1978), sex and sexuality are depicted as determined through the mechanism of hormonal activity and shaped by parental investment which is based on Darwinian ideas of natural selection. Individuals are assumed to be driven to maximize the number of offspring that they successfully produce but because of differences between males and females, the sexes approach this task differently. Describing 'reproductive strategies' in terms of differences in the size of the female ova and male sperm, sociobiologists argue that women have a greater investment in the embryo, and eventual child, than men. Thus females are best served by, firstly, being selective about the males with whom they mate, and secondly, ensuring the survival of any offspring produced. In contrast, sociobiologists argue that as males invest less reproductive material (sperm) than their female counterparts, their most successful strategy is to compete for, and reproduce with, as many females as possible. Depending on the environmental contexts in which species are situated, male polygamy or promiscuity is proposed as the most effective biological means of servicing the survival of male genetic material.

Furthermore, within this paradigm hormonal activity is treated as sex-specific and linked directly to the physiology and behaviour of the sexes. Hutt (1972) suggests that the sexes differ physiologically and behaviourally from birth due to the effects of different sex hormones. The male hormone plays a critical role in the sexual and social development of males, inducing behaviours such as aggression, ambition and drive. In contrast the female hormone is inextricably geared towards reproduction and the behaviours this incorporates.

Despite the popularity of this theoretical perspective for understanding sexual behaviour and gender differences across the animal kingdom, it has been dismissed by many as an inadequate explanation of the range and diversity of human sexuality. For example, Mahony (1985) suggests that the aggression that Hutt (1972) associated with boys was probably learned and subsequently reinforced within a society where aggression pervades perceptions of masculinity. These notions of aggression as an acceptable way for young men to assert their masculinity are reinforced in the work of Willis (1977) and Lees (1993). Other theorists have questioned the primary assumption within this perspective that the sole function of sex is the production of offspring and that males and females has different forces driving them to this end. As McFadden and Sneddon (1998: 43) note, 'It is but a short step from making this assumption to viewing non-reproductive sex as aberrant, and to prescribing different roles to males and females.'

The science of sexology

Since the late 1800s, research into and understandings of sexual identity and sexual practices have been informed by the discipline of sexology. Predominant among this tradition is the work of psychologists such as Freud (1933) and Ellis (1913; 1936). Freud viewed sexuality as a lifespan development, starting from infancy and progressing through a series of age- and sex-related phases. His theory intertwined the influence of the psychic (unconscious drives), biological and social factors on sexual development. Freud envisaged female and male infants as initially sharing common development until the phallic phase. However, according to Freud the primary factor in the acquisition of masculine and feminine sexualities is the differential resolution of the Oedipus complex experienced during the phallic phase. This complex is perceived as occurring when the child becomes aware of others (especially the father) and how they impinge upon her/his exclusive relationship with the mother (who is, according to Freud, the primary object of the child's love).

For the young boy, the awareness that the father shares a relationship with the mother leads to a bitter hatred for the father. Indeed the son fantasizes about killing the father and securing the love of the mother for himself. However, Freud points out that at the same time, the young boy is also aware of the power of the father and fears he will be punished by the father if he challenges him. For the young boy at this stage in his development, his sexual drive is satisfied through masturbation and he fears that the father will punish him by removing this treasured part of his anatomy. The anxiety experienced by the young boy in relation to the removal of his penis Freud refers to as castration anxiety. This anxiety is further fuelled by the young boy's recent awareness that his female counterparts are lacking a penis and according to Freud he experiences these young girls as 'mutilated creatures'. Castration anxiety motivates the young boy to repress his desire for the mother and to identify with the father. This identification requires the young boy to respect not only the father but that which he represents on a societal level – law and morality. Through the processes of identification, the young boy acquires not only a masculine identity but, with development of the superego, a place in the societal structure.

For the young girl, Freud presented the resolution of the Oedipus complex as more problematic. Indeed throughout his writings Freud consistently muses over the enigma that is female sexuality. This is reflected most clearly in the following quotation from his 1933 lecture on femininity: 'Throughout history people have knocked their heads against the riddle of femininity. Nor will you have escaped worrying over this problem – those of you who are men; to those of you who are women this will not apply – you are yourselves the problem' (1933: 224).

For the young girl, then, the resolution of the Oedipus complex is perceived as complicated and disappointingly incomplete. Like the young boy, the girl becomes aware of the presence of others (especially the father) in the relationship with her primary love object, the mother. Again, like the young boy, the girl becomes enraged by the mother's desire for the father and wishes to kill him. However at this stage the girl becomes aware of differences in her primary source of satisfaction, the clitoris, and that of her male counterpart. This results in what Freud (1933: 225) calls penis envy: 'girls hold their mother responsible for their lack of penis and do not forgive her for their being thus put at a disadvantage'. In despair she turns to the father in the hope of winning back that which all women desire, the penis. At this stage the girl's object of love changes from being that of the mother, to the father. However, the girl soon realizes that she cannot possess the father (and the penis) and, accepting her loss, reluctantly identifies with the mother. Completion of this phase, Freud suggests, occurs when the girl substitutes her desire for the anatomical penis and what it symbolizes (identity, power and a place in human culture) with that for a (male) baby: 'if woman can positively wish for a baby as a substitute source of power and identity, so much the better for the quality of her femininity' (Freud, 1923: 231).

In Freud's writing it is clear that the young girl encounters more hurdles and conflicts in her development towards adult sexuality, often with negative consequences. Freud argues that because girls do not experience castration anxiety, they lack the psychic energy necessary for the development of a strong supergo, or sense of morality. As a result, women are presented as passive human beings rather than active human subjects. The wound of inferiority resulting from the realization that she lacks a penis means the young girl limps into adulthood feeling incomplete: 'They will feel seriously wronged, often declare that they want to "have something like it too", and fall victim to "envy for the penis", which will leave ineradicable traces on their development and the formation of their character' (1923: 226), resulting in a character structured by jealously, insecurity and masochism. It is not surprising, then, that Freud views the task of building civilization as the domain of 'mankind' characterized by rationality, moral strength and emotional security. Nor is it surprising that many traditional psychoanalysts view femininity as spawning a variety of neuroses (see Figes, 1970; Minsky, 1996).

CRITICAL THINKING ON FREUD

What contribution do you think Freud has made to our understanding of psychosexual development? In what way does his work continue to shape our understanding of sexuality in the twenty-first century?

The main themes to emerge from Ellis's writings relate to the idea that sex is based on a biologically determined power relation and that, technically, no sexual act is ever abnormal as it is merely an extension of 'innocent and instinctive biological impulses' underlying all sexual activity. Ellis's ideas on male and female sexuality are couched in the language of survival and reproduction; sex is described as being like a biologically orchestrated dance, with the dance partners occupying distinct biologically based positions. In relation to female sexuality, Ellis perceives women, like men, as possessing biological instincts or impulses that motivate them to indulge in sex. In volume 1 (1936:69) of his work he expands on the nature of female sexual impulses by employing notions of modesty: 'The female's primary role in courtship is the playful but serious one of the hunted animal who lures her pursuer, not with the aim of escaping but of finally being caught.' He refers to women as psychologically characterized by an instinctive fear or reluctance to indulge in sex, which he links to the instincts of animals, who in oestrus are not physiologically ready for mating. He does acknowledge that the situation in humans is more complex, as women do not have designated biological times when they are available for sex. However, this modesty is key to the act of courtship, as Ellis (1936:1) explicitly links female reluctance and male sexual arousal: 'The woman who is lacking this kind of fear is lacking also, in sexual attractiveness to the normal and average male.' Therefore a 'natural' aspect of heterosexual acts is the pursuing and conquering of the reluctant female by the male; it is an 'inevitable by-product of the naturally aggressive attitude of the male in sexual relationships, and the naturally defensive attitude of the female' (1936:40).

The language of aggression and conquering introduces the second major theme of Ellis's work – that women's sexuality includes natural experiences of pain and violence. Ellis suggests that, for men, the inflicting of pain and use of force are necessary to conquer the women's natural inhibitions towards sex; moreover that these are the by-products of different instinctive impulses characterising masculinity and femininity: 'The masculine attitude in the face of feminine coyness may easily pass into a kind of sadism, but is nevertheless in its origin an innocent and instinctive impulse' (1936:42). Ellis, like Freud, suggests that women have masochistic tendencies and enjoy being taken by surprise and force. Indeed, in the writings of Ellis, force appears key to women's sexual pleasure; as Jackson (1994) points out, Ellis goes to extraordinary lengths to claim that women need pain in order to experience sexual pleasure. Pain and pleasure, Ellis continues, are indistinguishable in women; 'the normal manifestations of a woman's sexual pleasure are exceedingly like pain' (Ellis, 1936: 84). Furthermore Ellis asserts that the use of force is a reflection of a man's desire for a woman and indeed that women feel sexually wanted through the use of force by a male partner. The modesty of women – in its primordial form consisting of resistance, active or passive, to the assaults of men – aided selection by putting to the test man's most important quality, force. Thus it is that when choosing among rivals for her favours a woman attributes value to violence' (Ellis, 1936: 33).

Thus, within the writings of Ellis, heterosexual sex is presented as a mutually sado-masochistic act between man and woman. Male sexual impulses are presented as innocent, but violent impulses and are aroused by the complementary sexual coyness of the female. Finally, Ellis, like Freud, suggests that different social positions and practices for men and women are the natural outcome of sexual desires and practices. Ellis refers to motherhood as a woman's supreme function and something that required all her energies: 'The task of creating a man needs the whole of a woman's best energies' (Ellis, 1936: 7). Thus Ellis berated political groups such as the Women's Movements as drawing women away from their natural reproductive duties (Jackson, 1994).

Although producing different types of knowledge and utilizing differing methodologies, Freud and Ellis share a number of fundamental assumptions about human sexuality:

- Sexuality as biologically determined
- Female and male sexual identities and practices as complementary
- Heterosexuality as the natural expression of instincts
- Social identities, relations and practices as biologically connected to sexuality

However, both theories' contribution to understandings of sexuality remains a highly contested issue. For many psychologists, both theorists were trailblazers, constructing the foundations of modern sexuality and generating powerful insights into gender inequality (Mitchell, 1974). For others, including many critical and feminist social psychologists, the conceptualization of sexuality in the work of Ellis and Freud and their research philosophies are viewed as extremely problematic on many levels (Figes, 1970; Jackson, 1994; Jeffreys, 1986; McFadden and Sneddon, 1998; Weeks, 1981).

Many commentators have suggested that Freud and Ellis did not provide objective scientific accounts of sexuality as they claimed, but rather maintained and reproduced notions of male supremacy

(Faderman, 1991; Jackson, 1989; Penelope, 1992). Both theorists have been criticized for failing to challenge stereotypes of masculinity and femininity in relation to both sexuality and social roles. Weeks (1977) draws attention to tensions in Ellis's writings on women's sexuality. On the one hand Ellis advocates a distinct sexuality for women which they should be able to control, yet on the other argues that women's sexuality is expressed most naturally (and satisfactorily) in motherhood. In addition, many feminist theorists argue that the representations of female sexuality (linked to male orgasm and motherhood) emerging from the writings of Freud and Ellis are inextricably linked to increasing calls from the Women's Movement, in the late nineteenth century and early twentieth, for female sexual and social autonomy (Jackson, 1989; Jeffreys, 1986).

Also, central concepts in the writings of Freud and Ellis have been subjected to critical scrutiny. Commentators such as Cixous (1975) and Frosh (1987) suggest that Freud's insistence on femininity as a riddle indicates the male agenda underpinning his work and has also meant that female sexual identity and practices are not explored, nor the social consequences of femininity investigated. Similarly, Ellis's representation of sex as a natural pleasure–power couplet has been challenged as obscuring the negative sexual and social implications of biologically determined definitions of masculinity and femininity. Jackson (1984a) notes that Ellis's descriptions of female modesty and male aggression as natural merely legitimized and maintained male power (and control) over women. In an attempt to make visible the negative social consequences of a female sexuality based on inferiority and anatomical mutation, Horney (1924a, b) dismissed Freud's notion that girls experience penis envy during the phallic stage. Instead she suggested that young girls do not desire the anatomical penis but the social penis – the power and identity that the possession of the phallus seems to provide her male counterparts, in society.

Inversion and fixation: homosexuality

In the writings of Freud and Ellis, homosexuality was pathologized, defined as a developmental or genetic abnormality, an illness that endangered the stability of both the individual and society as a whole, and therefore was something that needed to be cured. For example, in the work of Ellis, lesbian women were defined as sexual inverts and perceived as being in some way biologically abnormal. Indeed, according to Ellis, although sexual inverts may maintain the clothes and appearance of 'normal' women, their innately masculine characteristics and practices, especially their lack of female modesty (and therefore sexual attractiveness), were telltale signs. Ellis (1936: 250), describes the lesbian as follows:

> When they still retain female garments, these usually show some traits of masculine simplicity, and there is nearly always a disdain for pretty feminine articles of the toilet. Even when this is not obvious, there are all sorts of instinctive gestures and habits which may suggest to female acquaintances the remark that such a person ought to have been a man. The masculine straightforwardness and sense of honour, and especially the attitude towards men, free from any suggestion of either shyness or audacity, will often suggest the underlying psychic abnormality to a keen observer.

A further dimension to Ellis's thesis on lesbianism was the detrimental impact of such women on society. Ellis linked lesbianism to various forms of social instability including feminism and the demise of heterosexual marriages, and in particular through his explicit reference to the 'pseudo-homosexual'. This phrase denoted instances when a naturally heterosexual woman was temporarily seduced into an immoral lesbian lifestyle by a real lesbian woman. For Freud, an overly possessive and seductive mother who rejects her son's attempts at independence precipitated the development of male homosexuality in boys. For girls, lesbianism resulted from their failure to resolve the Electra complex, to repress their more masculine, active sexual desires and accept the more passive sexual practices that constituted femininity.

Many 'queer' and feminist theorists have challenged essentialist accounts of gay men and lesbian women (presented by Freud and Ellis). Penelope (1992) and Faderman (1991) believe that Ellis's pseudo-homosexual was heavily influenced by the changing social and sexual contexts of the early twentieth century. Faderman (1991) notes that through the eighteenth and nineteenth century intimate relationships (sometimes involving physical or genital contact, sometimes not) between women were tolerated, often viewed as a way of training women for the skills they would require to sustain a successful marriage. However, the twentieth century witnessed an attack on 'romantic friendships' with such relationships increasingly talked about in the language of lesbianism (abnormality, inversion, etc.) and redefined as a danger to the moral fabric of society. In addition, Jeffreys (1984) highlights the disdain of sexual theorists such as Freud and Ellis for the burgeoning women's movement by drawing attention to the links between feminism and lesbianism within their writings.

'Just like us': liberal-humanistic explanations of homosexuality

Within psychology, representations of homosexuality as socially deviant and an illness were challenged in the 1960s and 1970s backlash against essentialist theories of sexuality and replaced by understandings of homosexuality situated within liberal-humanistic paradigms (Kitzinger, 1987). Within this context, the social stigma associated with gay identities was challenged through representations of gay and lesbian people as normal individuals who had had made a personal lifestyle choice that was as healthy and normal as that made by their heterosexual counterparts. In addition, representations of such individuals as a danger to moral and social instability were contested through the emphasis on their 'personal choice' and 'private lifestyle'. Such representations of gay and lesbian identities were embraced by many who had lived with pathologized understandings of their identities, and theorists who had challenged the persuasiveness of essentialist definitions of lesbianism and homosexuality. For many others, liberal-humanistic definitions were also viewed as problematic. For example, rather than liberating lesbians, Kitzinger (1987) believes that the reduction of lesbian identities to a matter of personal choice denies the opportunity for many women to define themselves in socio-political terms. In particular, couching lesbianism in the language of personal choice and equating it with heterosexuality renders invisible other important discourses around lesbianism, as, for example, a source of empowerment (Kitzinger and Wilkinson, 1997b), or pleasure (Dancey, 1994), or as resistance to heterosexuality (McFadden, 1995). Now read Box 7.1.

> **Box 7.1 Its more than a personal choice: alternative experiences of lesbianism (McFadden, 1995)**
>
> In the following extract, Molly talks about how she feels about being lesbian:
>
> 'I just find being a lesbian – and that's across-the-board, not just how I express myself sexually – very liberating. I think lesbians

have [*pause*] greater opportunities for self-expressions and just developing confidence that the parameters of heterosexuality don't either allow or encourage. And I think there's some strain in heterosexual relationships to do with the power imbalance. [*pause*] I'm trying to think of friends who are straight and who are excited and fulfilled by their relationships [*laugh*]. I just can't think of any, like I know some of these people really enjoy sex with men but I don't know on the wider level how satisfied they are in their relationships with men. I kinda feel that women and men communicate differently and [*laugh*] I don't know what that says but I think they have different understandings of words and expressions and to that end I think women in relationships are more likely to speak the same language. They have the same understandings of things like support or companionship or just needin' to let off steam or whatever; you know men, they're just not in the same head-set as women. So to that end I think that women are one step up when in relationships with other women [*pause*] I mean most women I know would say that it's in their relationships with other women that they have most expression and intellectual stimulation. It's not like hard work.'

CRITICAL THINKING ON SEXUAL IDENTITY

Explore the language in Box 7.1. Consider how Molly experiences being lesbian? What aspects of heterosexuality does she identify as problematic? Is lesbianism for Molly simply a personal choice as suggested in liberal-humanistic perspective introduced in the above section?

Discursive and social practices: the social production of sexualities

From the 1970s onwards, understandings of sexuality and gender, including those discussed in the preceding sections, have been increasingly challenged from a diverse number of sources including feminism, 'queer' theorizing, social theory, anthropology, and critical social psychology. Epistemological, methodological and political aspects of more traditional theorizing on sexuality and gender have been increasingly problematized and many of the understandings of femininity, masculinity, gay and heterosexual identities re-evaluated. This section will introduce these revised conceptualizations.

One of most important themes to emerge from the critique of theories discussed so far is the dismissal of sexuality as something that is innate or biologically determined. Rather, within critical social psychology, sexuality is viewed as socially constructed and negotiated. Foucault (1978) offered an alternative reading of sexuality, presenting it as an historical concept, constructed through a number of discourses including the legal, the religious, the medical and the scientific. The crux of Foucault's theoretical argument was the rejection of sexual identities and practices as resulting from an inner essence (anatomical, psychological or biological): 'sexuality must not be thought of as a kind of natural given which power tries to hold in check, or as an obscure domain which knowledge tries to uncover' (1978: 105).

In Foucault's thesis, sexuality provided a means of controlling the body through legislation on birth control and homosexuality, as well as a means of policing the population as a whole with campaigns against immorality, prostitution and venereal disease. He argued that from the eighteenth century onwards, sexuality increasingly provided the central focus around which social bodies, relationships, positions and practices were organized.

Rather than describing the history of sexuality as repressive Foucault (1978) depicts it as a history of discourses on sex that generated relationships of power and understandings of bodies and their associated pleasures. Charting the inception of our inclination to talk about sex in the penitential practices of the Middle Ages, Foucault develops his main thesis by exploring the defining and redefining of sexuality through later political, economic and technical incitements to converse on sex. Central among the institutions redefining sexual identities and practices was that of science, including medicine, psychiatry and psychology. To illustrate this, Foucault draws on the increasing clinical codification of normal (heterosexual, reproductive) and abnormal (homosexuality, masturbation, hysteria) sexuality in the twentieth century.

Prior to this period, prohibitions on sex had been predominantly of a judicial nature with both transgressions of marriage and deviant sexualities defined under a 'general lawlessness' (Foucault, 1978: 38). Foucault argues that the gradual establishment of heterosexual monogamy as the norm, and the scrutinizing of those whose sexualities did not fit this norm, not only facilitated the establishing of a natural order of desires but created an abnormal annexe of sexuality within which deviant sexualities could be disciplined (or, in the language of Freud and Ellis, cured). New forms of knowledge brought new structures of power through which sexuality could be defined, controlled and disciplined. Consequently the governance of sex became grounded in two systems, and offences became separated into those against the law of marriage and those against 'the regularity of a natural function' (1978: 38). Thus, as Foucault (1978) argued, sexuality came to provide multiple areas of power and control, as it became not only a means of regulating actual sexual behaviour but also a key area in social relations: 'The deployment of sexuality has its reason for being, not in reproducing itself, but in proliferating, innovating, annexing, creating and penetrating bodies in an increasingly detailed way, and in controlling populations in an increasingly comprehensive way' (1978: 107).

Box. 7.2   Interrogating Foucault

Foucault's writings on the history of sexuality have been widely acclaimed for the insights they provide into the social dimensions of sexuality and issues of power and control (Turner, 1984; Weedon, 1987; Weeks, 1985). Notwithstanding this favourable reception, Foucault's (1978) hesitancy to address issues of gender earned him criticism from some Feminist and Queer theorists. Walby (1990) notes that while Foucault takes into account competing discourses, historical specificity and power, he does not specifically address the issue of gender and power. Penelope (1992) takes this criticism further, accusing Foucault of not only failing to address inequalities relating to power and gender in the construction of sexuality, but of going 'to great lengths to construct a fortuitous history, one in which male domination is reduced to a happenstance intersection of "relationships of force" in which some discourses are privileged (male) while others (female) are silenced' (1992: 25). Furthermore she suggests that Foucault's omission of lesbian sexuality and his subsequent illustrations concentrating on male homosexuality, not only made lesbians invisible but distorted the impact of sexology on this and other aspects of female identity and practice. Similarly, Bleier (1984) argues that while Foucault addressed the issue of power, he did this in a non-direct way where he questions neither the source nor direction of its invention. To counteract this she suggests reading Foucault as a metaphor and applying his analysis to the position of women in the last century. In doing so, it becomes apparent that those who invented the discourses (medical, psychological, religious, legal, etc.) were more than likely men, while those who went to confess, to be cured or punished were women.

A second theme framing accounts of sexuality within critical social psychology is the relationship between sexuality, language and social practice. Sexuality is viewed as the product of social, cultural and historical discourses. Within this perspective, then, the dualistic representation of the individual and social underlying many traditional perspectives is dismissed and replaced by the 'individual' as inextricably connected with the social. Subsequently notions of sexuality as an innate (or biologically determined) private identity are deconstructed and rather sexualities are understood as fluid and multifaceted identities that are negotiated and structured through various social, cultural and historical discourses. The crux of a constructivist perspective, then, as Naus (1987: 39) argues, is that: 'Human sexuality has no essence or nature that transcends historical and cultural circumstances, but rather encompasses a diversity of sexualities that are made, constructed, as a result of personal, social and economic factors.'

Within the literature on femininity in America and the United Kingdom, the construction and control of women's sexual identities and practices through a number of distinct though interconnected discourses is a pervasive theme (Daniluk, 1991; Holly, 1989; Lees, 1993; Thomson and Scott, 1991). One of the most prominent discourses relating to femininity is that of reproduction and motherhood. Lees (1993) and Thomson and Scott (1991) note that within the context of school and home, sexuality for many young women is discussed only in relation to their future roles of wives and mothers. In addition, within this and other discourses on female sexuality, married heterosexuality is represented as the most natural type of sexuality. Such observations, although recent, are not new – as Oakley (1979: 13) commented: 'In Western cultures today, motherhood is the chief occupation for which females are reared. It is the major component of the female gender role as taught to a female child by her parents and others with whom she comes into contact.' In addition, Fine (1988) identified a number of common discourses pervading representations of female sexuality, and subsequently the information those women receive regarding sexuality. The first she notes is victimization, where women are portrayed as potential victims of an uncontrollable male sex drive. Through this discourse, women are informed not only of the dangers that men present to their virginity and reputations, but also of bodily dangers such as pregnancy and disease. Another common theme in the discourses on female sexuality is the portrayal of women as moral vanguards. This approach involves, as Jackson (1984a) points out, the complimentary portrayal of women as morally stronger and thus as responsible and sensible (unlike their male counterparts). Within this discourse, then, female subjectivity is given recognition in the language of self-control and sexual restraint.

Vance (1984) notes that regardless of the presentation of women's sexuality, the various discourses discussed share a common theme that starkly distinguishes female from male sexuality – that is, little recognition is given to women's desire to be sexually active. Indeed Fine (1988) notes that the naming of pleasure, entitlement or desire is noticeable only by their absence in contemporary discourses on female sexuality. In the writings of many theorists, the absence of a discourse on female desire is perceived as a reflection of the ways in which sexualities have been historically and socially constructed. To illustrate, Burke (1980) suggests that since women are not bequeathed either practices or a discourse specific to their sex, they are forced to solicit their practices from male-defined relations and structures, resulting, as Cixous (1975) points out, in the naming of female sexual desire and pleasure as the joys of surrender, sacrifice and service to others. This elusive discourse of female sexual pleasure is maintained at many social sites, including, as Holland *et al.* (1990) argue, through the consistent teaching of women about their bodies in the language of biology, and as the following extracts in Box 7.3 illustrate, through censorships imposed on desire by both men and women.

However this is not to suggest that within critical social psychology, individuals are perceived as passive recipients of social practices. On the contrary, individuals are understood as actively working towards various social positions and representations. For example, McFadden (1995) describes how the women in her study illustrated different forms of resistance to the dominant representations of female sexuality discussed by Fine (1988). These strategies included delaying marriage until they had 'had some fun', choosing to be celibate and seeking alternative sources of information to construct their notions of sexual pleasure and desire. Holland *et al.* (1991) and Smith (1988) have highlighted similar findings. In her work with lesbian women, Dancey

Box. 7.3 The construction of female pleasure and desire (McFadden, 1995)

R. Is it more difficult for a woman to say that she enjoys sex?

Z. Yes, I think its cause men kinda see it like as they own it [sex] like and that its their right to enjoy it. Like women should but they find it difficult I would myself [*pause*] judging from my own experience I wouldn't say it . . .

R. What would stop you?

Z. The men just kind of looking at me thinking I was a bit of a slut, they'd probably call you names, you know think you might get about a bit or something.
(Extract 1: Zoe, aged 18)

F. I mean like, even when they're [men] standin' on the street with a group of people and a girl they fancy walks past it's all 'Oh I wouldn't mind a piece of that'. But for girls it's different, like men are really funny, for example I was walking down the road with male friends and I saw this really nice guy and I said 'He's nice', and they were all really funny [*pause*] really annoyed and all 'What are you talking about'. They're really funny you see because girls aren't meant to do things like that.
(Extract 2: Frederica, aged 19)

(1994) noted similar resistance among the women interviewed to what they perceived as negative representations of lesbianism. These strategies included emphasizing the positive benefits associated with a lesbian lifestyle, including the removal of the perceived necessity to conform to role expectations and the solidarity and companionship they experienced living as lesbian women.

Box 7.4 Queer theory (Butler, 1990; 1993)

The pervasiveness of heterosexuality as a cultural norm and the multiple ways in which this is resisted and re-inscribed are dominant strands of feminist (Kitzinger and Wilkinson, 1997) and gay and lesbian studies (Plummer, 1992; Weeks, 1991). Within the last decade, diversification of these themes has occurred in the writings of queer theorists, (most notably Butler, 1993) on sexuality. The main aim of 'queer' theorizing is to destabilize normative understandings of what it is to be a heterosexual wo/man or homosexual wo/man through subversion – the embodiment/representation of the unexpected, for example the macho gay man, female dominatrix, the cross-dresser or the transvestite.

Drawing on post-modern notions of the 'self' as fragmented, queer theory explicitly challenges the perceived traditional link between sex (fe/male), gender (femininity as passive; masculinity as active) and sexuality (heterosexuality as the most natural mode of sexual expression). Such ideas, however, do not exist unchallenged. Many feminist writers question the reduction of sexuality to the staged personas or performances, believing that such representations contribute to the invisibility of oppressive social and political practices experienced by many so-called straight and gay people. The use of subversive tactics as a political strategy to address prejudice and oppression is also severely questioned. As Segal (1997: 216) notes, 'What seems shocking and disturbing today can become part of the mass media spectacle tomorrow.'

In addition, this theoretical perspective has been critiqued for its failure to account for the diversity of oppression mediated through factors such as race and class.

A third theme framing understandings of sexualities within critical social psychology is how to incorporate concepts of power and ideology into theoretical explanations. Understandings of sexuality as the product of culturally produced discourses rather than innate, introduce new types of questions for psychologists researching and theorizing issues relating to gender and sexuality. For many critical social psychologists these questions include reflecting on the functions of sexuality, exploring the processes defining sexuality (including psychology as an academic discipline) as well as issues of power, ideology and equality (Brown, 1997; Gough, 1998; Hollway, 1989; Kitzinger and Wilkinson, 1997b; McFadden and Sneddon, 1998). A dominant strand of this work relates to the suggestion that traditionally sexuality has been constructed as synonymous with heterosexual ideology and practices. A key text challenging the prevalence of heterosexuality as the most 'natural' type of sexuality is Adrienne Rich's (1980) 'Compulsory Heterosexuality and Lesbian Existence'.

Within this work, Rich (1980) challenges representations of hetero-sexuality (more specifically, definitions of masculinity as different though complementary identities and practices, marriage as the only legitimate expression of sexuality and penetrative sex the most natural sexual relationship) as the 'natural' type of sexuality for women (and by implication men) through two interrelated arguments: the first relating to the socially manufactured and coercive nature of hetero-sexuality, and secondly, through her dismissal of restrictive clinical definitions of lesbianism in favour of a broader understanding based on the notions of lesbian continuum and lesbian existence. With respect to the naturalness of heterosexuality, Rich presents the ideology of heterosexuality as an extensive socially manufactured matrix that is coercively imposed on many women through a variety of means, including romantic ideologies, the stigmatizing of alternative types of sexuality, and physical and verbal force. Women, she argues, are not born heterosexual but rather are coerced into it through a variety of social mechanisms (e.g. through scientific, legal and educational discourses) that bind them into a 'socially acceptable' sexuality and punish them if they step outside these boundaries:

> Whatever its origins, when we look hard and clearly at the extent and elaboration of measures designed to keep women within a male sexual purlieu, it becomes an inescapable question whether the issues feminists have to address are not simply about 'gender ine-quality' nor the domination of cultures by males nor merely 'taboos against homosexuality', but the enforcement of heterosexuality for women as a means of assuring male rights of physical, economic and emotional access. (Rich, 1980: 488)

As the above extract illustrates, Rich believes that the pervasiveness of heterosexual definitions of sexuality in Western cultures masks its political function (assuring men's access to women's physical, eco-nomic and emotional labour), coercing women into accepting subordi-nate sexual roles (wives, mothers) and limiting their opportunities for developing a critique of the so-called 'naturalness' of heterosexuality. In addition, Rich argues that such definitions of femininity create false and divisive boundaries between women, obscuring the sense of com-munity and practical support that many women experience. In order to give recognition to the women's shared experiences, Rich dismisses clinical definitions of lesbianism centred on genital contact and adopts the broader concept of the lesbian continuum. This incorporates not only women who desire sexual contact with other women but what Rich describes as women-identified experience, including 'the sharing of a rich inner life, the bonding against male tyranny, the giving and receiving of practical and political support' (1980: 635). In doing so Rich strives to give recognition to the rich and varied relationships that women have historically experienced.

CRITICAL THINKING ON HETEROSEXUALITY

Take time to think about how you experience your sexuality. What types of information did you receive about sexuality in your school, from friends and from your parents? Was there the assumption that you are/were heterosexual? (For example, was there recognition that you might be attracted to a same-sex partner? Were marriage and parenthood talked about as things that would 'naturally' happen when you were older?).

Rich's (1980) radical critique of the ideology of heterosexuality has influenced recent theorizing on sexuality. For example, Bleier describes the ideology of heterosexuality as so pervasive 'that it is as taken for granted as the air we breathe' (1984: 83), and argues that within a society where young women learn about the inevitability of inter- course as well as their subordination within 'heterorelations', notions of choice, consent and expression become nonsensical. Indeed such notions are consistently replicated in research. For example Holland *et al.* (1990) argue that the ideology of heterosexuality creates powerful models of sexual behaviour that shape young women's (and subse- quently young men's) understandings of what is normal and accep- table; in particular that young women educated within the hetero- sexual matrix that Rich (1980) described, learn not only about their relationships in terms of male–female relationships within which sexual intercourse is required, but come to equate this with penetration and male orgasm. Finally, Gavey (1993) suggests that broader definitions of heterosexuality not only constrain women by prescribing particular sexual identities and practices but also by depicting women who resist these or indulge in 'other sexual relations' as abnormal.

**Box 7.5   Living on the fringes: lesbianism as absence
(McFadden, 1995)**

From a study with 10 lesbian women living in Northern Ireland, a dominant discourse to emerge from the talk of these women was their experience of lesbianism as a site of exclusion and the absence of personal and social structures. As suggested by Rich (1980), social taboos against homosexuality were a common experience, with all of the women commenting on a lack of information about lesbianism within the contexts of school and home. In addition, these women highlighted other sites of socially imposed censorship that constructed their experiences as lesbian women. Many of the women experienced this social invisibility as having no future directions or developments mapped out. As the extract below suggests, with heterosexuality comes some signposting about what is possible (marriage, parenthood, material success, etc.) and this is reflected in the social structures and processes that support it. In contrast, with lesbianism comes a social vacuum where the concept of a socially manufactured 'lifestyle' is absent and individuals are left to find their own pathways.

R. Do you feel a type of liberation from the pressures of heterosexual living?

C. I think it's not really about escaping from the heterosexual agenda for me, as personally I'd already gone through the stuff – dated, married and divorced. The big problem at the minute is mapping out the future, because for heterosexual people they sort of think early twenties, late twenties and everything looks clear for them. They sort of get a job, get married, have some kids and then try to improve your job, get the kids grown up and get them to university. You know the problem for me is that I can't see the future clearly, I'm not exactly sure what I'm meant to be doing at a certain age. No one has actually told me forty-five and the kids are grown up, it's you and the wife again [*laugh*]. I don't really know what direction my life is going to take, I think you take on board certain career ideas, things like I'll get a job when I leave university, I'll buy a house and a car but apart from that I haven't thought much further. I can see myself sittin' at thirty odds with the house and the car and sayin' [*laugh*] what should I do with these things. (Clare, extract 9; 22)

In Molly's case, she likens the situation to a conspiracy of silence; individuals (e.g. family) may notice that she is not following the heterosexual pathway but no one wants to know why or to give recognition to the life she lives with her partner.

M   I think it's at times like, you know, when there's markers in straight life, gettin' engaged, gettin' married, pregnancy, I do feel very (. . .) excluded. I suppose because I can't put down my markers and say this is it, I've come back to Belfast to live with my girlfriend and we're going to do this and that. I mean there will come a time, I mean I think there already is a kinda silent acknowledgement that I won't be gettin' married and the big why has been left unquestioned. I do get really pissed off about all the assumptions that are made. (Molly, extract 10; 23)

CRITICAL THINKING ON HOMOSEXUALITY

Think back to the ways in which you thought about how homosexual women and men experience the world before you saw and read Box. 7.4. Has reading these extracts (and indeed this chapter) influenced how you think about homosexuality? If so, why?

Summary

This chapter has attempted to offer an overview of the debates around sexuality within psychology. Essentialist perspectives, grounded in the language of anatomy and biology, have been critically discussed using a range of research from within critical social psychology, feminism and queer theorizing. Understandings of sexuality as cultural and socially produced have been introduced through a constructionist perspective and the recognition of sexuality as a multifaceted and diverse social phenomenon emphasized. Representations of heterosexuality as 'natural' have been challenged through the consideration of its coercive implementation, and alternative sexualities have become visible through continued theorizing on issues relating to power and ideology. It seems that only one safe certainty can be written at this stage, that in this new millennium the debates and issues relating to sexuality remain complex and hotly contested within psychology and other social science disciplines.

Key References

Rich, A. (1980) 'Compulsory Heterosexuality and Lesbian Existence', *Signs: Journal of Women in Culture and Society*, 5 (4): 631–57. A seminal paper that challenges definitions of heterosexuality as natural and instead suggests that in Western societies, this representation has been carefully manufactured and imposed to the detriment of many women and homosexual individuals.

Segal, L. (1997) 'Sexualities', in K. Woodward (ed.), *Identity and Difference* (London: Sage). This provides interesting additional readings on sexuality. The section on lesbian resistance is particularly good for those who want to develop their understandings of 'queer' theory in practice.

Aggression in Social Contexts

8

This chapter will highlight:

- Problematic aspects of unitary definitions of aggression
- Traditional social psychological perspectives on aggression
- Critical understandings of aggression as social actions
- The invisibility of female aggression in traditional psychological theories

Introduction

Defining aggression: the discussion

The everyday use of the terms 'aggression' and 'violence' would suggest that there is some shared, agreed meaning to these terms. However, if we reflect on our own uses of the terms we become aware that they are used in different contexts for different purposes. Despite this commonsense knowledge, since the early 1900s many psychologists have attempted to produce precise, operational definitions of aggression, often centred on 'injurious intent' (that is, that the action is carried out with the intention of injuring the person to whom the activity is directed). For example, Dollard *et al.* (1939) defined aggression as 'any sequence of behaviour, the goal response of which is the injury of the person toward which it is directed' (1939: 11). Later definitions, such as that of Buss (1961), incorporated a wider understanding of 'injury' by including insults or verbal harassment, defining aggression as 'a response that delivers noxious stimuli to another organism' (1961: 1). Although the preceding definitions emphasize intent and action, the emotional states that many of us associate with aggression are not salient (Geen, 1990). This issue led Feshbach (1964) to differentiate between affective and instrumental aggression:

168

- *Affective*: Aggression accompanied by strong emotional states; in lay terms, anger, used to injure or harm the provocateur
- *Instrumental*: Aggression as a means to some desired end (e.g. obtain money, self-defence, military contexts, etc.)

Critical social psychology dismisses unitary definitions of aggression such as those discussed above. In contrast, aggression is understood as a diverse social phenomenon intimately linked to the historical, social and cultural contexts in which aggressive activities are situated. Within this perspective, the role of social psychology as an institution contributing to definitions of aggression is critically reflected upon. Understandings of aggression situated at either the level of the individual or the social environment are rejected and replaced instead with multiple narratives relating to the 'origins' and 'causes' of such actions (Stainton-Rogers *et al.*, 1995).

This chapter is informed by the ongoing discussion outlined above. In the first part of the chapter, traditional social psychological understandings of aggression are reviewed and questions relating to their theoretical origins and methodological approaches asked. Drawing on the limitations associated with traditional perspectives, the second part of the chapter explores understandings of aggression produced by critical social psychologists.

Traditional social psychological explanations

Within social psychology, levels of explanation tend to fall into two domains: firstly, explanations of aggression based on internal mechanisms (drives, genetic inheritance), and secondly, theories identifying external causes as underlying aggression (situational factors, contexts of learning). The following two sections will review such theories and critically reflect on their utility for those interested in understanding aggression.

Aggression as instinctual (Freud, 1933; Lorenz, 1966; Wilson, 1975)

Instinctive theories classify aggression as a universal human trait: we behave aggressively because we are somehow programmed to do so. Psychoanalytic explanations of aggression are among the most popular. Within this paradigm, aggression was seen as part of the libido, the pleasure-seeking drive that stimulated psychosexual development. However, Freud (1920; 1923) later refined his thinking on aggression and identified it as a separate instinct – 'thanatos', the powerful death instinct. The individual was seen as being driven by two competing biological mechanisms, the life instinct (Eros) and a death instinct (Thanatos). The death instinct, according to Freud, drove the individual to strive for personal obliteration and ran contrary to the life instinct. Although this self-destructive instinct could be controlled (usually via the ego) it could not be completely eliminated and therefore Freud visualized defence mechanisms as central to dealing with this self-destructive aggression. Thus aggression could be combined with the libido, manifesting as sadism and/or masochism; it could be displaced on to others resulting in aggression/violence, absorbed into the superego and consequently repressed or expressed through other activities, for example physical sports.

In psychoanalytic terms, then, aggression is seen as inevitable, an instinct that builds up and requires some type of outlet: 'It really seems as though it is necessary for us to destroy some other thing or person in order not to destroy ourselves, in order to guard against the impulse of self-destruction. A sad disclosure indeed for the moralist' (Freud, 1933:588). Consequently 'catharsis' is an important aspect of this approach – that is, the idea that if people can vent their hostility and aggression in relatively non-harmful ways (the classic means is hard physical sport) then this reduces their tendencies to engage in more harmful acts of aggression.

Box 8.1 Does catharsis work?

Dollard *et al.* (1939) suggested that if an individual can vent anger and hostility in relatively harmless ways, the tendency to engage in more harmful types of aggression will be reduced. However, the validity of this popular hypothesis has been brought into question by a relatively mixed bag of evidence. Research such as that by Zillman (1979) indicates that participation in relatively harmless activities (e.g. vigorous physical activity, shouting obscenities in an empty room) leads to reduction in the emotional arousal resulting from frustration or provocation. However, such relief, as Caprara *et al.* (1994) note, is temporary, as the emotional arousal returns when the individual remembers the incident that made her or him angry. Various studies using other 'socially acceptable' methods of expressing aggression paint a similar picture. Studies involving watching violent media scenes, verbal criticism of an aggressor to a third party, or the attacking of inanimate objects, indicate that there is no reduction in overt physical aggression (Ebbesen *et al.*, 1975; Geen, 1978). Indeed, perhaps more disturbing, several studies have indicated that participation in relatively harmless activities can lead to an increase as opposed to decrease in aggression (Turner and Goldsmith, 1976; Geen *et al.*, 1975).

CRITICAL THINKING ON HUMAN AGGRESSION

Do you agree with the pessimistic picture that Freud paints of human beings on a mission of destruction?

The ethological approach, like the psychoanalytical approach, sees aggression as spontaneous, as an instinct that builds up, needs to be discharged and then builds up again. In particular, Lorenz (1966) viewed aggression in humans as arising from a fight instinct that humans share with other species (the other three of the 'big four' being hunger, sexuality and flight). In contrast to the psychoanalytic approach, aggression within this perspective is set within the context of evolution; it is defined as an instinct that ensured that only the strongest individuals would pass their genes on to the next generation. Consequently, ethologists view aggression as a positive adaptive instinct necessary for survival.

The second major thread running through the work of Lorenz (1966) relates to the ways in which aggression is performed among animals and humans. Lorenz suggests that animal aggression follows a fixed pattern or set of evolved rituals among different species. He argues that ritualization preserves the adaptiveness of aggression by ensuring a winner and a loser without too much harm occurring to either. In particular, he notes the diverse appeasement strategies that many species indulge in to avoid aggression. But he suggests that among humans expressions of aggression have become distorted due to advances in weapons and technology. Much human combat no longer occurs face to face but at long distances and so appeasement rituals are more remote and non-physical among humans.

The basic principles underlying ethological accounts of human behaviour were revised with renewed vigour in the 1970s and 1980s among sociobiologists. This theoretical perspective aimed to provide an account of human social behaviour couched in the language of genetic advantage and biological fitness. Wilson (1975) argued that three evolutionary mechanisms – the personal survival of the individual, reproduction of the group to which the individual belongs, and altruism – direct all human behaviour. He adopted a wide definition of behaviour that included both overt, observable behaviours and emotional aspects of behaviour. Therefore, for Wilson, behaviours such as fighting and mating as well as the associated emotions (hate, fear, love, guilt, etc.) are shaped by genetic predispositions that have evolved among species to enhance personal survival, reproduction and altruism (Siann, 1985). Wilson works retrospectively, using information about the population, communication and social structures of animal species and early human societies as a basis for understanding how genetic transmissions influence the behaviour of man in contemporary society.

In his later work, Wilson (1978) develops his ideas further, suggesting that aggression, although an adaptive behaviour, is not present in all cultures but rather that certain conditions provide the breeding ground for aggressive activities. In doing so, he turns the logic of social scientific thinking on its head by arguing that certain social conditions awaken in people the genetic predisposition to aggress. Siann (1985) cites an illustration of this logic when he points to Wilson's explanation for the conflict among the Selmay of Malay in the 1950s. The history of this people was one of non-conflict until the 1950s, when as a result of a British military campaign against the Communist guerrillas, many of the population became what Wilson describes as 'hardened soldiers'. Wilson (1978) argues that it was not the change in the environmental conditions that resulted in conflict but rather that the conflict had awakened their hereditary predisposition to aggress.

CRITICAL THINKING ON ETHOLOGICAL ACCOUNTS

Wilson (1978) suggests that the conflict simply acted as the spark that ignited the Selmay people's predisposition to aggression. Can you think of other reasons why this conflict may have occurred?

Box 8.2 Anthony Storr

Both the psychoanalytic and ethological perspectives on aggression influence the work of Storr (1970). Storr, in agreement with Lorenz (1966), defines aggression as an innate impulse that needs to be discharged. This impulse is viewed as positive for both animal and human populations, in the former contributing to population control, sexual selection, protection of the young, and social order, whilst in human populations aggression is said to contribute to the development of human civilization and the maintenance of social order. Central to this theory is the idea that the aggressive instinct aids the development of identity and interpersonal interactions. Storr adopts a developmental approach to identity formation suggesting that it is in childhood resolutions of conflict between the aggressive instinct (need for independence) and its opposite, the sexual instinct (need for connectedness and dependency), that one's fledgling identity emerges. The opposition that parents express in relation to a child's urges for independence must be delicately balanced as, according to Storr, if parents do not provide sufficient opposition, 'the child's aggression tends to become turned inwards against the self so that he pulls his own hair, bites his own nails, or becomes depressed and self-reproachful' (1970: 69). This conflict between these opposing needs is perceived to continue into adulthood with identity born out of the ongoing struggle to balance the need for company and the maintaining of a separate identity. In Storr's work, then, striving for a separate identity is a healthy derivative of the aggressive instinct.

The work of Freud (1933), Lorenz (1966) and Wilson (1975: 78) on aggression is now largely rejected by many social psychologists for a number of reasons; in particular:

- *Myth of the beast within*: These perspectives have been critiqued for promoting as unproblematic the idea that humans, like other animals, are naturally aggressive (Klama, 1988). The acts of aggression are neutralized as inevitable responses and located as the ideological portrayal of the individual (as beast-like when the veneer of civilization is removed) produced by Western industrialized modernity.
- *Biological reductionism*: These perspectives on aggression have been widely criticized for failing to address the role of social contexts in precipitating and maintaining conflict. The problems with

such omissions are illustrated in Wilson's (1978) rather illogical explanation of conflict among the Selmay people (see above). As Stainton-Rogers *et al.* (1995: 152) argue, the problem with explanations of aggression in terms of drives or instincts is that they deny 'that things (like aggression) can be explained in a diversity of ways because of the ways they appear to, or are encouraged by, different people at different times and in different situations'.

• *Analogies between animals and humans*: The reliance of the ethological and sociobiological perspectives on studies of animal species that are then unproblematically applied to human species is considered a fundamental flaw by many contemporary psychologists (Baron, 1977). This criticism is two-pronged. Firstly many psychologists have emphasized the tenuous links between acts of animal aggression and survival, citing the multiple strategies including co-operation that many animals employ to enhance survival (Bateson, 1989; Trivers, 1985). Secondly, it is argued that such evidence leads to oversimplified understandings of human aggression that fail to recognize the complexity of human social and cultural organization and the diversity in human acts of aggression, including those facilitated by increasingly sophisticated technology (Heelas, 1986; Segal, 1987).

Experimental perspectives on aggression

Experimental research on the origins and maintenance of aggression has dominated social psychological knowledge of this phenomenon for much of the twentieth century. The intellectual origins of this work are within the epistemological framework of 'psychology as science' (Armistead, 1974). Consequently, theoretical understandings of what aggression is, how it can be studied and managed, are constructed around a common set of assumptions (Siann, 1985). Firstly, experimental approaches view aggression as an innate tendency; however, they diverge from the previously discussed theories in an important way by emphasizing environmental factors and their effect on the individual. Thus, the observation of actual behaviours forms the basis for causal explanations of behaviour. The social world of the individual is assumed to be a single objective reality and therefore the external sources of aggression can be isolated, manipulated and preferably measured. Finally, there is an adherence to the use of experimental methodology which, it is believed, provides those researching with a concrete collection of facts from which general laws about human social behaviour can be drawn. This section will provide an account of the various ways in which external factors have traditionally been assumed to influence the behaviour of the individual.

One of the earliest experimental approaches to the study of aggression was the work of Dollard *et al.* (1939) which attempted to integrate some of Freud's ideas on the repression of aggressive and sexual instincts with the notion of frustration. This approach was based on the commonsense view that if you prevent a person from achieving a goal that they thought was within grasp, they become frustrated, and this frustration results in aggressive behaviours. This particular formulation of the causal link between frustration and aggression was extremely persuasive and spawned a proliferation of studies that continued to consolidate the link. In 1941, Barker, Dembo and Lewin set up a playroom for children that contained a large number of attractive toys. One group of children was allowed to play with these toys immediately while the other group was 'frustrated', as they were only allowed to view the toys through a window. During the second stage of the experiment, both groups of children were permitted to play with the toys and their behaviour observed. Researchers observed the level of 'constructive play' by the children and it was found that those who had been frustrated in the earlier phase were more likely to engage in destructive play (e.g. hitting the toys, breaking the toys, etc.).

The concern that the causal link between aggression and frustration was too general and did not take account of the person's motives for aggression led to attempts to classify different types of aggression in the 1960s (Buss, 1961; Feshbach, 1964). Aggressive activities were classified into two types: hostile aggression, where the primary goal of the aggressor was to inflict suffering on the victim, and instrumental aggression, where aggression was a means of achieving some other goal (e.g. money, status, etc.).

Box 8.3   Buss (1961) and instrumental aggression

In this experiment, Buss (1961) set out to explore and refine the relationship between frustration and aggression. Subjects were told that they were taking part in a learning exercise where they would work with a partner (a confederate). The subjects were asked to give the confederate an electric shock each time a mistake was made (subjects could vary the intensity and duration of the shock). Subjects were divided into two groups: the 'frustrated' were told that their partner's speed of learning was a result of their own skills and knowledge, or that their grade on their introductory psychology course depended on the partner's speed of learning; the other group were not made aware of these conditions. In order to measure whether subjects used aggression to achieve other goals (i.e. increase learner's speed and therefore achieve a good grade), some subjects in the two groups were informed that higher levels of shock would result in faster learning. The results of this experiment indicated to Buss (1961) that frustration does not lead to aggression unless it is instrumental in achieving other goals, as only those in the frustrated conditions, who were told that higher shocks would increase learning, used such methods.

Leonard Berkowitz (1962) has revised the link between frustration and aggression in his cognitive associational model of aggression. Berkowitz (1974) redefines the link between frustration and aggression by focusing on the emotional responses that frustration elicits. These negative affects, as Berkowitz (1974) refers to them, are produced by unpleasant situations, experienced as, for example, pain or anger at being insulted, and thus initiate aggressive behaviours. In later work, he argued that these affects were further mediated through cognitions, in particular in relation to the interpretation of situational cues associated with aggression (weapons, viewing of media violence, etc.). In doing so, Berkowitz (1966) drew on the learning principles of classical conditioning whereby a previously neutral stimulus becomes capable of provoking or triggering an emotional response. This led Berkowitz (1966) to conclude that the presence of such cues would increase the likelihood of aggression being expressed. Evidence to support these assertions was collected using a rather dramatic series of experimental studies. Using the learning paradigm discussed earlier, Berkowitz introduced aggressive cues, including a .38 calibre revolver or a badminton racquet that he left beside the shock machine. He found an increased tendency to use electric shock among those groups of subjects who were exposed to aggressive cues compared with those who were not.

Experimental understandings of aggression have been widely critiqued. These criticisms are presented below:

• *Individualistic explanations*: Although the frustration–aggression hypothesis focuses on environmental cues, many critics have questioned the degree to which it addresses the social context of aggressive activities. Billig (1982) argues that such perspectives ignore the historical, social and cultural contexts of aggression and provide overgeneralized, simplistic and sanitized versions of aggression. Take for example the violence that has until recently defined understandings of Northern Ireland. It seems quite simplistic to assume that over the last thirty years people in Northern Ireland have reacted en masse to difficult social conditions (poverty, poor housing, etc.) and the presence of aggressive cues (e.g. guns, army jeeps). Such an understanding loses sight of the diverse social and political positions and rhetoric adopted by various groups and communities within Northern Ireland. It fails to address the complex issues of national identity and rights that are central to many of the arguments and violent activities that take place within Northern Ireland. In addition, the peaceful political routes and protests engaged in by many citizens in Northern Ireland are also eradicated from an understanding of Northern Ireland's violent history.

- *Aggression in the laboratory*: Psychology's claims to investigate social phenomena using objective methods and as such uncover universal truths relating to human behaviour have resulted in the experimental approach being heavily criticized (Frodi *et al.*, 1977; Siann, 1985; Stainton-Rogers *et al.*, 1995; also see Chapter 2 for a general critique). Critics argue that the exploration of aggression in the laboratory is artificial and reductionist and as such fails to address the full social complexity of such behaviours. Many theorists highlight the problematic assumptions surrounding the use of electric shocks, pointing out that how subjects interpret what they are doing in that laboratory can have a diverse number of meanings (e.g. if you are told that you are aiding learning by giving shocks rather than viewing this as an act of aggression, you may view yourself as being 'cruel to be kind'). Other theorists note that the subjects' understandings of what is expected of them in the laboratory situation may influence their activities and lead them to behave in ways contrary to those in the 'real world'.

- *Ideological influences*: The lack of recognition of ideological rhetoric shaping experimental definitions and investigation of aggression is consistently highlighted as problematic among critics of this approach. This is summed up by Sedgwick (1974: 36): 'Violence, for psychology, becomes translated into a discussion about aggression displayed by the individual subject; it is never seen as the property of institutions like the police or the Mafia; or historically contingent situation like the picket line.' Consequently, the historical recognition of psychology as an instrument of social power and control is invisible in experimental understandings of aggression.

Traditional social accounts of aggression

Social learning theory

Central to this perspective is the understanding that aggression is not an innate tendency but rather is a learned behaviour. People are perceived as indulging in aggressive activities for a purpose (similar to the definition of instrumental aggression discussed earlier); they have learned that aggression can enable them to achieve a desired outcome. The primary mechanisms through which such learning takes place are reinforcement and modelling. In 1973, Bandura conducted a series of studies to demonstrate the processes through which aggression is learned. Based within the laboratory, children watched films where they observed adults behaving aggressively towards a large inflatable toy – 'the bobo doll'. The adults indulged in a number of specific aggressive activities (sitting on the bobo doll, hitting it with an inflatable hammer, etc.) and were either rewarded or punished for their actions. Later, when the children were allowed to play with the bobo doll, it was found that those children who had observed those adults who were rewarded indulged in similar activities. Bandura (1973) argued that the experimental evidence illustrated how children learned aggression through imitating the adults observed. The second aspect of this paradigm relates to the understanding that behaviour is controlled by its consequences, and therefore if aggression is rewarding for the individual it will increase the likelihood of it occurring again. In 1983 Bandura developed this work further by focusing on cognitive dimensions of aggression, in particular the effect of 'self-regulatory' mechanisms on aggression. The origin of these mechanisms lie in the learning of social standards (e.g. that it is morally wrong to kill), norms related to how individuals behave. Bandura (1983) visualized these mechanisms as having an inhibitory effect on aggression because if the person transgressed these internal values, they would experience negative consequences (e.g. guilt, self-disapproval). Although the focus on the social antecedents of aggression were initially viewed in a positive light, social learning theory suffers from some fundamental flaws (Billig, 1976; Stainton-Rogers et al., 1995).

- *Level of explanation*: Although social learning theory appears to offer an escape from the notion that aggression is an innate tendency, the focus of this explanation remains situated at the level of the individual, in her or his learning capacities. Consequently the wider social, historical and political contexts of aggressive activities and the ways in which people construct understandings of activities remain relatively untheorized. In particular, power inequalities and the ideologies that currently legitimize particular types of aggression (e.g. male violence, violence perpetrated by authority figures such as the police, armed forces, etc.) remain absent from the theoretical picture.

- *Ideological influences*: Stainton-Rogers *et al.* (1995) argue that social learning theory, like many of the perspectives previously discussed, lacks reflexivity. Bandura and other theorists presented a grand theory of aggression in which they claimed to provide universal truths about what initiates and sustains aggressive activity. In addition, the nineteenth-century angst about aggression and its detrimental impact on society coloured understandings of aggression as something which needed to be socially controlled. As Billig (1976: 214) concluded, 'most psychologists in their interpretation of which aspects of aggression it is important to study have concentrated on those aspects that which do not lead them to ask searching questions either of the society in which they live, or their own ideological assumptions'.

Box 8.4   The media violence debate

One of the most popular offshoots of social learning approaches on aggression is the presumption that media violence causes 'real life' incidents of aggression. Most recently this link was passionately revisited in Britain following the killing of James Bulger and the speculation around whether his killers had watched the film *Child's Play III*. So what does the evidence say? You might be surprised to know that research relating to this proposed link is highly inconsistent and does not provide any evidence to support the popular belief that media violence causes aggression (Barker, 1997; Eysenck and Nias, 1980).

In his article 'The Newson Report: A Case Study in Common Sense', Barker (1997) cautions against accepting experimental research evidence on media violence and aggression, for a number of reasons. Firstly he notes contradictions in research studies, and problematic conceptualizations of 'media violence' and how this is measured and understood. In addition, he draws attention to the historical contexts of current anxieties around media violence and social stability and subsequently the ideological framework within which 'experts' produce knowledge.

CRITICAL THINKING ON MEDIA VIOLENCE

As an activity you might like to think about where you stand on the media violence debate. Is the concern with media violence a big social panic or do you think there is a link between media violence and everyday aggression?

Phenomenological perspectives

In 1978 Marsh *et al.* attempted to integrate sociological understandings of aggression with ethological perspectives in social psychology (e.g. Lorenz, 1966). One of the most interesting aspects of this work is the methodology, which attempted to understand aggression from the perspective of those participating in it. Marsh *et al.* (1978) argues that aggression has a biological basis, defining it as 'a property of human beings in virtue of which they are prone to act upon others in a typically thrusting and imperious way' (1978: 27). The main focus of this work is not an understanding of the origins of aggression *per se* but rather the motivations underlying such behaviours and an understanding of the rituals in society through which this is executed by the individual. Prescribing to a similar ethos as the ethologists, Marsh perceives aggression as a positive force providing people with the rules through which they can achieve a personal sense of worth and identity. In order to theorize these links, Marsh *et al.* (1978) explored the function of aggressive rituals among youth gangs and football hooligans (for details of these studies, see Marsh and Campbell, 1982; also see Chapter 2 on ethogenics).

Although at face value this work appears to address many of the flaws associated with the perspective discussed earlier, it seems to have been overly ambitious in its claims. Siann (1985) critiques this work on the basis of its evolutionary deterministic stance, as despite Marsh's

(1978) claims to be working within a critical theoretical space his bottom line is that aggression is an innate disposition and is manifested when the rituals governing behaviour break down. Other criticisms relate to the inability of this theory to address in its full complexity the social contexts in which particular types of violence occur (e.g. sexual violence and football hooliganism). For a fuller critique see Stainton-Rogers *et al.* (1995).

Critical themes in understandings of aggression and violence

A brief review

Much critical work on psychological understandings of aggression and violence are centred on addressing the limitations that characterize many of the traditional theories discussed in the preceding sections (and chapters of this book). Critical work rejects the doctrine of individualism that underpins much traditional psychological thinking, and rather is interested in the negotiations that people engage in when constructing and making sense of their social worlds. Implicit in this, then, is a critique of psychologists who isolate explanations at the site of the individual or social circumstances. Indeed such theorizing is recognized as being ideologically biased, intimately linked with the position of psychology as a powerful institution. More specifically, as Billig (1976) argues, psychology is implicated as the producer of knowledge and interventions that maintain the social and political status quo embedded in differing historical contexts. Consequently, explanations for aggression, such as in the case of social unrest (e.g. cyber and street protest during the World Trade Organisation meeting in November 1999, and more recently the unrest in Washington in April 2000), are situated in the activities of protestors as deviant groups as opposed to the activities of institutions (e.g. governments) that may have contributed to and ultimately deal with incidences of social violence.

Critical social psychologists reject notions of aggression as originating through biological drives, dysfunctional learning or the activities of deviant sub-cultures. Rather, representations and understandings of aggression are understood as social constructs or narratives of human behaviour that emerge within particular historical, social and cultural contexts. As Stainton-Rogers *et al.* (1995) suggest, critical analysis of traditional social psychological approaches allows us to gain insights into the different meanings that were attributed to aggression by different theorists. The rejection of the dualistic representation of the individual and the social, inherent in much traditional psychological theorizing on aggression, is central to critical theories. Rather, as Ritzer (1992) suggests, people create their notions of society through their social negotiations, and this 'society' in turn provides the context in which identities and activities are negotiated and sanctioned. This reconstruction of the individual and social couplet enables critical social psychologist to ask different questions relating to the origin and maintenance of aggression. These include an exploration of the ways in which aggression is 'talked about' (legitimized) within prevailing historical, social and cultural contexts, how access to discourses is socially negotiated, and finally, the function of these discourses. Consequently, the epistemological context of understanding aggression shifts to one where 'aggression can be seen not as an action or state but as a set of interwoven textual identities, actions and descriptions' (Stainton-Rogers *et al.*, 1995: 169).

CRITICAL THINKING ON THE CAUSES OF AGGRESSION

So far this chapter has introduced you to a continuum of explanations for aggression. At one end, aggression is perceived as at an individual level (biological drives, genetic predispositions), and at the other, socially legitimized. Drawing on your own experiences what do you think are the causes of aggression?

A further level to the argument that aggression is socially constructed is through the understanding that different representations of what constitutes aggression generate a language with which we can collectively talk about aggression in our everyday experiences. For example, we might talk about an individual as being 'a nasty piece of work', an opinion that focuses on perceived personal dispositions, or we draw on situational factors, commenting that a colleague is aggressive in a meeting. This language is not static but rather changes over time and context, and more importantly, as Burr (1995) points out, different constructions allow different kinds of human social action. For example, in Britain until the early 1950s, people who committed murder were perceived as 'innately bad' and capital punishment was viewed as a legitimate form of state punishment. In the twenty-first century, however, capital punishment is reconstructed by many as an inhumane means of intervention.

Critical research in practice

Male violence

Segal (1994) notes the continuing anxieties among the media and the public relating to violence from men – in particular, football violence and gang-related violence (Armstrong, 1998; Canaan, 1996). Griffin (1993) notes that, traditionally, violence among men (especially young working-class men) has been represented predominantly through three discourses – deviance (as a consequence of belonging to a sub-culture), dysfunction (as a consequence of some hormonal or biological malfunction) and deficiency (as a consequence of poor learning). Critical social psychologists seek the explanations for acts of male violence not within the individual or his environment but, rather, within the cultural framework through which men conduct and make sense of their experiences. Within this perspective the ideological construction of masculinity forms an importance focus for explanations of male violence (Connell, 1995; Mac an Ghaill, 1996). In her work with young white working-class men, Canaan (1996) describes how fighting functioned as a central mechanism through which the young men constructed their masculinity. While many of the participants' accounts of fighting were situated within the context of drinking, as the following extract illustrates, participants clearly defined fighting as a way of proving their 'hardness' (masculinity):

> Andrew had been forced to fight a young man who drew a picture of him and would not tear it up. He did not want to fight this young man, 'but everyone was saying hit him'. 'If I didn't hit him, it would look like I was soft ... I didn't want to hit him but I didn't have a choice so in the end I did.' (Canaan, 1996: 120)

As well as providing a site through which physical toughness could be illustrated, for many of the young men interviewed fighting providing a context for dealing with what they perceived as negative emotions and feelings (e.g. hurt and anger). As Canaan suggests, for many of the young men interviewed who lacked a language for dealing with emotional upset, fighting allowed emotions to be shifted to 'a physical level where they could be contained, tangibly balanced' (1966: 121)

This understanding of aggression as negotiated within local contexts and against the wider social and cultural circumstances within
which men are situated has also been illustrated in Armstrong's (1998)
book on football hooliganism among young men in Sheffield. Armstrong presents football hooliganism as a range of complex social
activities (periodically involving negotiations with rival fans) through
which social identity, power and status are negotiated. He points out
that football is extremely significant in the identity of Sheffield as the
home of organized football. The history of football in Sheffield is, as
Armstrong documents, intimately linked with the local male cultural
mores. Fishwick (1989: 86) also notes that football provided an important social function in times of social unrest with pit-managers in 1912
organizing teams and competitions for striking miners to keep the men
from trade union activity. In addition, throughout the early twentieth
century, football was encouraged by local employers (especially in the
steel industry) to increase the fitness and productivity of workers as
well as providing a means of combating industrial unrest.

Armstrong (1998) suggests that the behaviour of football followers
has always attracted the attention of the authorities who have historically been concerned about the wayward energies of 'mob' behaviours.
In his book he charts the increasing definition and regulation of the
'football hooligan' through various institutions including the police
and the legal system. He also discusses the more recent impact of the
media in terms of assigning meaning to the activities of football fans.
The media disapproval of the behaviour of some football fans includes
representations of football supporters as 'thugs', as evil, as ill and as
troublemakers. Armstrong, however, rejects such representations
of football hooliganism and the associated implications that aggression and violence are central to such activities. Rather, he perceives
the football arena as providing football fans with a recognized social
domain within which they expressed their masculinity via the ability
to fight and hold a reputation. In addition, he notes the diverse
activities or rules that govern the behaviour of football supporters.
Violence may be one means of negotiating identity but other, less
visible, dimensions include dress codes, drinking and ritualistic
chants. Rivalry between supporters of the two home teams in Sheffield (the 'Blades' and the 'Owls') and between home and visiting fans
is seen to generate a dialogue of 'winners' and 'losers' and the associated positive ('hard', fair players, etc.) and negative (cowardice,
using dirty tactics, etc.) representations of fans that accompanied such
public identities.

Sexual violence

In the twenty-first century sexual violence continues to be an area of concern for many feminists and critical social psychologists. Academic critiques of sexual violence have traditionally been situated within feminist writings (Brownmiller, 1976; Faludi, 1991; Stanko, 1985) and more recently the critique of hegemonic masculinity within men's studies (Kimmell, 1987). Theories on sexual violence have been structured around two main issues: firstly the prevalence of sexual violence and secondly the cause. One of the major problems in estimating the prevalence of sexual violence is the continued under-reporting of incidences to the police and the small number of cases that produce criminal convictions. Moane (1998) notes that in Ireland only 28 per cent of those attending the Dublin Rape Crisis report crimes of sexual violence to the police, and that of those reporting only 20 to 40 per cent (depending on the year of reporting) result in legal proceedings. This under-reporting of sexual violence is confirmed in international research findings (Rollins, 1996).

Within the academic literature differences in experiences of sexual violence are well documented. Whilst acknowledging that earlier feminist writings failed to recognize that men also experience sexual violence, many theorists agree that incidences of sexual violence are higher among women than their male counterparts (Lees, 1998; Stanko, 1985; Walby, 1990). Explanations for acts of sexual violence against women are diverse. Theories situated within the tradition of individualism have generated explanations that focus on individual pathology among perpetrators of sexual violence, producing profiles of the 'types of men who rape' (Brittan, 1987). Such men include those who have had a disturbed upbringing, or possess extreme ignorance and guilt about sex, anger against women, or a personal sense of failure and inadequacy especially relating to their masculinity (West et al., 1978). In other studies, the social conditions of the perpetrator are emphasized. For example, in *Patterns of Forcible Rape*, Amir (1971) suggests that rather than exhibiting forms of psychological abnormality, men who raped were distinguishable from other men primarily in terms of their socio-economic status (that is, those of lower-class/ lower-status groups). Both these approaches however have been criticized by many feminist writers as producing misleading understanding of men who rape and why they indulge in these activities.

In contrast, many feminist writers emphasize the socially sanctioned and diverse nature of sexual violence against women. Sexual violence is, as Moane (1998: 222) argues, 'not just something that occurs between a man and a woman in isolation from social and cultural forces. Indeed, it occurs with sufficient frequency to make it clear that its occurrence is linked to economic, political-judicial and socio-cultural factors.' Consequently, feminist writers are at pains to stress the pervasive and socially sanctioned nature of sexual violence against women. This is illustrated in Liz Kelly's (1988) notion of sexual violence as not simply rape but rather as something more insidious and everyday in its occurrence – a continuum of sexual violence. This continuum emphasizes the everyday abuse of women through sexist jokes, pornographic images, sexual harassment, marital rape, so-called domestic violence and murder.

Within this analysis then, sexual violence cannot be understood as situated within the pathology of individual men or problematic social conditions, but rather requires an awareness of how we as a society construct notions of femininity and masculinity. Consequently, issues of ideology and power become central to feminist understandings of male sexual violence. This is reflected in feminist writings that critique essentialist definitions of sexuality that dominated psychological theorizing until the 1960s: in particular, theorists such as Freud and Ellis whose work enshrines acts of sexual violence between women and men as natural, originating from 'innocent and instinctual sexual impulses'. In contrast, feminist thinking on sexual violence takes issue with such notions and rather stresses the ideological context of such ideas as a means of ensuring men have power and control over women's bodies and consequently as disempowering women in a variety of sexual and social situations. As Kelly argues, 'rape is but one of many of the ways men maintain power over women through sexual violence. It is men's "taken for granted" use of aggression – for example in sexual harassment in workplaces – which enables men's power to override other power relations like that between teacher and pupil' (cited in Segal, 1994: 244).

One of the main advantages of this type of analysis is that it allows us to define and expose incidences of sexual violence not as situated within the activities of individual men but as embedded within a socially constructed and legitimized culture of male violence. Consequently many feminist writers seek to challenge explanations of sexual violence that often exclude women and maintain a considerable degree of silence about the issue of sexual violence. This is reflected in Lees' (1997a) paper entitled 'Naggers, Libbers and Whores', in which she highlights the ways in which the judicial system in Britain (and indeed internationally) legitimizes and protects the perpetuators of violence against women. More specifically, she notes how violence is accepted as a normal response in circumstances where women are perceived as behaving in non-feminine ways. Similarly, Larkin and Popaleni (1994) document the ways in which sexual violence and harassment facilitated the social and sexual control of young women in their sample. These authors showed how the young women's activities were controlled by the young men they were in contact with in a variety of social and sexual contexts through acts of diminishment, intimidation and force. Larkin and Popaleni (1994: 219) argue that these male activities ensured control of young women in a diverse number of ways:

> Acts of diminishment objectify and degrade young women through behaviour that includes criticism, rating and the display of pornographic material. Acts of intimidation, such as threats and surveillance, warn young women of the violent consequences should they challenge their ascribed position in relation to young men. And acts of force punish those young women who resist their assigned subordinate positions.

CRITICAL THINKING ON SEXUAL VIOLENCE

Is It useful to consider sexual violence in terms of a continuum from rape to harassment as suggested by Larkin and Popaleni (1994)?

Female aggression: addressing the imbalance

Within critical social perspectives, the lack of knowledge on the use of aggression by women is highlighted. This is perhaps because, as Segal (1987) notes, aggression has traditionally been constructed within psychological literature as a male 'trait' and, as such, not associated with normative femininity. Historically, this is illustrated within psychological literature on sex differences that 'proves' that males (from a young age) are more aggressive than their female counterparts. Notions of aggression as a male trait have been challenged more recently in the work of Kirsta (1994) and Day (2000). Both authors identify a male bias in traditional research that aligns closely with the ideological construction of masculinity and femininity within the discipline of psychology. In her study involving working-class women in Yorkshire, Day (2000) explores the prevalence and function of aggression among the women interviewed. Similarities between this work and that of Canaan (1996) are evident, with the young women in the Day study using violence to establish reputations and positions within their immediate social contexts. As Day (2000) notes, acts of violence for these young women were central to establishing working-class feminine identities. As the following extract shows, violence was often used as a means of settling scores and maintaining 'face' in front of friends:

> *K.* 'I've only had one [fight] and that was at a feast. That was just all me mates winding me up. I'd had an argument with her a couple of weeks before that, an I tried chasing her around Miggy [Middleton, a local district] an I couldn't catch her. Then I saw her at t' feast, an me mates were nudging me "Look she's over there", so I waited for her getting off this ride, an then I had a fight with her. But like, she was on the floor, an then that wor it, you know, end of fight, an me mate kept saying, "Go on kick her ed in", an I was going "Ave a to? Oh alright then", so I'd go back an punch her again, an I'd walk away, an she was goin, "Go on it er again", so I'd go back an smack her again.'

Such discourses, however, did not exist in isolation but were often followed by the speaker positioning herself as restrained, a strategy that allowed the women to align themselves within more traditional discourses of femininity. For example K. then went on to describe how most of the time she uses other means such as shouting her way out trouble.

In addition, for these young women violence was also often located within the context of 'nights out' and, as the following extract illustrates, were used to foster positions of social respect and identity:

> *J.* 'This girl came up to me an basically poured a drink all down me dress, like she didn't go "Oops, sorry that was an accident", she just kind of laughed and poured it down me, an I went "you fuckin' bitch, you can pay for that dress", an I was all over the place, an I was really pissed, an I had hold of her hair an stuff, an Nigel was trying to grab me an pull me off, an I was going fuck off you, an I punched him in the face ... an I just ran at her, an I remember grabbin' her by the neck an pullin' her the full length of the dance floor, an I banged her, an punched her. I think I cut her eye open, an I stood back an went "Oh my God" [*laugh*], you know when you don't know your own strength? ... but she turned round and went deech [*makings hitting*

sounds] with the back of her hand, and I was like "Ow you fuckin bitch" [*laughing*]. An everyone was going, "Cat fight, cat fight" [*stamps her feet on the floor when she says this*]'.

As Day (2000) discusses, and as the above extract illustrates, within accounts of violence women represent and position themselves through a number of different (and often contradictory) discourses. Joanne, the participant above, draws on her aggressive activities as a means of securing her social position, to retaliate against what she perceives as an unprovoked attack by another. In addition she challenges traditional discourses around femininity by drawing on a discourse situating women as able to look after themselves (without male partners intervening). Joanne also talks about being scared after realizing that she hurt the other woman, thereby constructing limits as to how far violence should be taken.

Summary

This chapter offers an overview of definitions and understandings of aggression situated within traditional social psychology. Limitations to these theories are highlighted and discussed and alternative understandings of aggression from within critical social psychology are explored. Within this latter theoretical context, representations and understandings of aggression are understood as social narratives that emerge within particular historical, social and cultural contexts. As such, then, the meaning and functions of aggressive activities are prioritized, and explanations that focus beyond the level of individual analysis offered by many traditional social psychological theories are presented.

Key references

Segal, L. (1994) 'The Belly of the Beast (II): Explaining Male Violence', in Segal, *Slow Motion: Changing Masculinities, Changing Men* (London: Virago). This chapter, informed by feminist theories, places the concepts of power and ideology as central to understandings of male violence.

Siann, G. (1985) 'Laboratory and Experimental Approaches to Aggression and Violence', in Siann, *Accounting for Aggression* (London: Allen & Unwin). This chapter provides a good overview of the limitations of laboratory and experimental accounts of aggression and violence.

Prejudice in Practice

9

This chapter will highlight:

- Strengths and limitations of traditional social psychological explanations of prejudice
- Critical readings on prejudice that emphasize the importance of social, cultural and political concepts
- New forms of 'politically correct' prejudice
- Links between critical theory and practice for psychologists

Introduction

Prejudice against others because of their gender, colour, religion, etc. has engaged the discipline of social psychology for much of the twentieth century and beyond. This chapter reviews explanations of prejudice proposed by traditional social psychology and introduces recent theoretical accounts of prejudice emerging from critical social psychology that argue for the need to understand prejudiced activities in terms of language, culture and ideology.

Traditional social psychological theories of prejudice

Prejudice as errors in thinking: social cognition approaches

Lippman (1922), in his text *Public Opinion*, provided a theoretical explanation of prejudice centred on distortions in the cognitive processes of the individual. Within this theory, the analogy of a computer is invoked to describe how the individual makes sense of the multitude of social information he or she encounters. Recognizing the complexity of this information, as well as the limited cognitive capacities of the human mind, the individual is perceived as simplifying this task by generating 'general categories' relating to self and others (on the basis of colour, race, age, sexuality, etc.). By doing so, Lippman and others (e.g. Hamilton and Trolier, 1986) suggest that the overloading of our limited cognitive processes is prevented, and thus categorization is presented as generally an advantageous cognitive process. Social cognition theorists, however, point out that at times this system of filing can short-circuit, and certain 'faulty categorizations' can be introduced, with people forming stereotypes about members of groups.

A stereotype is defined by Wetherell (1996: 189) as 'a selective over-generalization which prejudges any individual member of a group'. Common stereotypes include representations of Irish people as 'stupid' or 'bog trotters' or Asian people as 'money-grabbing owners of corner shops'. Within the social cognition perspective, it is suggested that stereotypic schemata/scripts can bias the encoding of new knowledge about individual or group members, as people will pay more attention to activities that confirm their pre-formed beliefs (Hamilton and Trolier, 1986). Much of the research within this tradition has focused on the content of stereotypes, the role of socialization in the development of stereotypes and, perhaps more controversially, how stereotypes can be changed. Hamilton and Trolier (1986) suggest that as well as information that reinforces stereotypes being salient, when perceived members of certain groups behave in ways other than those expected such information is likely to impress and be remembered by those observing.

Box 9.1   A classic social cognition experiment

Synder and Uranowitz (1978) conducted a study based on homo-phobic stereotypes. They argued that people are more likely to remember information about another person which is consistent with their stereotype of a social group or category. In their study, subjects were asked to read a case history about a woman called Betty. The case study described Betty's childhood, her education, career, social life, etc. Subjects returned a week later to carry out a recognition memory test on various details of Betty's life. Prior to the test, however, half the subjects were told that Betty was now living in a happy and successful lesbian relationship and the other half told that she was in a happy and successful heterosexual relationship. The above researchers found that the new information on Betty had a significant impact on the results of the memory recognition test. Subjects centred their memories and recall of information around the respective categories of 'lesbian woman' and 'heterosexual woman' – thus suggesting that people use category information to interpret information and recall memories.

The final strand of this approach consists of research suggesting how psychologists might work with people to challenge stereotypes. These remediation strategies include the 'book-keeping effect', with people gradually changing their accounts of certain groups based on new, inconsistent information (Rothbart, 1981). In general, then, within the social cognition tradition, prejudiced activities are viewed as the unfortunate by-products of limitations on our rational mental organization (Billig, 1985), and remediation strategies include having sufficient contact with those we have stereotyped to counter pre-judicial views.

CRITICAL THINKING ON STEREOTYPES

Read the following extract from Jeanette Winterson's (1985) *Oranges Are Not the Only Fruit*. Are you familiar with the representations of homosexual people presented by the mother character? In small groups discuss whether you think social cognition theory provides an adequate explanation for the prejudice illustrated in this account.

My mother wanted me to move out, and she had the backing of the pastor and most of the congregation, or so she said. I made her feel ill, made the house ill, brought evil into the church. There was no escaping this time I was in trouble. . . . It seems to hinge around the fact that I loved the wrong sort of people. Right sort of people in every respect except this one; romantic love for a woman was a sin. 'Aping men,' my mother had said with disgust. Now if I was aping men she had every reason to be disgusted. As far as I was concerned men were something you had round the place, not particularly interesting, but quite harmless. I had never shown the slightest feeling for them, and apart from my never wearing a skirt, saw nothing else in common between us. Then I remembered the famous incident of the man who'd come to church with his boyfriend. At least, they were holding hands. 'Should have been a woman that one', my mother had remarked (pp. 125–6).

Despite the currency of social cognition accounts of prejudice, this approach has been increasingly criticized by those within the discipline of critical social psychology along the following lines:

- *Individualistic orientation*: Wetherell and Potter (1992) question the image of the individual in social cognition theories. The individual is represented as a solitary figure, encoding information, sometimes erroneously, about others on the basis of perceived similarities and differences. The production of prejudiced cognitions does not have a logic to explain why only certain individuals perform prejudiced activities nor why, historically, certain groups have been the victims of racist thinking. Rather, the suggestion is that as all human minds function in similar ways it is possible that any one of us could develop stereotypes of anyone else in our social domain. As such, prejudiced thoughts and feelings are represented as universal traits, part of the conditions of being human.
- *De-contextualized accounts*: The representation of the social or society in social cognition theorizing has also been criticized as simplistic and reductionist. An objective physical reality is assumed to exist that people perceive or misperceive in linear ways, regardless of their individual, social, cultural and historical origins. So, for example, this theory would suggest that the religious and social conflict that has dogged Northern Ireland for decades is the result of misperceptions of 'Protestant' or 'Catholic' individuals or groups and is unaffected by cultural reinterpretations of historical events, political ideologies or material inequalities between communities. As Wetherell and Potter (1992: 41) suggest, the underlying assumption within the social cognition tradition is that 'a collection of individuals produce the same judgements, not because they talk and communicate with each other, but because each person faces the same set of stimuli with the same inbuilt cognitive limitations'.
- *Remediation strategies*: One of the most contentious aspects of social cognition theory relates to the 'contact hypothesis' – the idea that if

individuals or groups can have sufficient contact with others about whom they hold stereotypic views, in time sufficient inconsistent information will be experienced to erode erroneous beliefs. The implication here is that if only the gay man, black person, etc. would behave in *better ways* and offer images of their groups which contradicted stereotyped views, then the prejudiced views of individuals may be in some way altered. What many find unacceptable about such an explanation is that it places responsibility on those experiencing homophobia, sexism, racism, etc. to prove they are 'different' and naturalizes the prejudiced views held as simply problems with information processing. As Julian Henriques (1984: 74) concludes, 'the black person becomes the cause of racism whereas the white person's prejudice is seen as a natural effect of their information processing mechanisms. (This works as a subtle double exoneration of white racism, no doubt all the more effective because it is not conscious.)'

Prejudice as personality traits: psychodynamic approaches

The work of Adorno *et al.* (1950) produced a theory of prejudice that attempted to explain the social and emotional aspects. Such work, more recently developed by Frosh (1997), recognizes that prejudiced activities are not simply cognitive, but for many are accompanied by intense emotions and influenced by socio-political circumstances. In trying to understand where such emotions originate and the diverse ways in which such feelings are manifested, this tradition draws on Freudian psychoanalysis. In addition, Adorno *et al.* (1950), aware of individual differences in prejudiced activity, set out to explain why, at certain historical times, political ideologies appeal to different people to varying degrees. In particular, Adorno and colleagues were interested in the psychological processes shared by those who were attracted by anti-democratic, conservative ideologies such as fascism. A complex theory was proposed that considered the impact of conscious and unconscious activities, as well as parenting practices and social circumstances, on the development of personality. This theory suggests that there is a certain type of personality – the authoritarian personality – that is attracted to anti-democratic, conservative ideologies. The origins of this personality were not perceived by the above authors as being attributable to chance but rather to lie in particularly harsh childhood experiences. Parenting practices associated with the development of the authoritarian personality are also situated more widely within patriarchal, capitalist societies.

Through empirical research, Adorno and colleagues suggested that authoritarian personality types shared a number of recurring features, including,

- being conformist
- conventional (not only in terms of political beliefs but also in relation to family life, sexual relations, etc.)
- locked into stereotypical thinking
- organized and obedient
- respect perceived strength
- dislike perceived weakness, intolerance of ambiguity
- defer to authority.

In the language of psychoanalysis, a type of dualistic world is experienced by such individuals where one part of their world is over-idealized and the other structured by excessive negativity. Within this theoretical perspective, strict but often inconsistent parental discipline produces children who learn readily to obey authority but who fear expressing their own needs/feelings. As a result of such interactions, some children may become masochistic, believing themselves to be 'bad' and striving to meet parental norms and expectations, and who, at the same time, learn the importance of obedience. In psychoanalytic terms, children experiencing such parenting internalize the standards of parents, especially the father, developing a strong, punitive superego or conscience.

In lay terms, then, these children are constantly judging themselves according to harsh social standards. Furthermore, the initial instilling of beliefs about the importance of obedience and respect for authority persist in adulthood. Other authority figures (teachers, group leaders, political figures) substitute for the parents and an exaggerated respect is shown to those who are perceived to be as strong and disciplined as the parents. However, harsh parenting and excessive deference to authority also produces excessive resentment that cannot be vented at parents or other authority figures. In order to ease the psychic tensions experienced, Adorno *et al.* (1950) suggest that such individuals unconsciously employ defence mechanisms – projecting their resentment on to those perceived as weaker or inferior within the overarching political climate. Frosh (1997: 216) suggests that projection 'creates a world full of hated objects, thus confirming the racist's (or fascist's, in terms of *Authoritarian Personality*) vision of being ensnared in a dangerous situation in which the other has to be wiped out for the self to survive'.

This theory has been acclaimed by many authors, including Wetherell and Potter (1992), for its attempt to incorporate the ways that ideologies, such as fascism, in certain socio-economic situations, can psychologically engage certain individuals. In contrast to the social cognition perspective discussed earlier, this theory produces a complex theoretical explanation of prejudice that combines individual internal mechanisms and the social context. Within this theory prejudiced activities are linked to identity and individuals are conceived as fragmented and shaped by conflicting desires, desires to be both submissive and powerful. This representation of the individual stands in stark contrast to the unified individual presented in social cognition accounts of prejudiced activity:

> The chain of cause and effect is complex – from the mores and habits of certain social circumstances, to parent–child interactions, to the formation of personality, to the expression of political ideology, which then once more sets the scene for the reproduction of these personality forms in another generation. (Wetherell and Potter, 1992: 50)

However, others such as Pettigrew (1958) and Billig (1978) have indicated that this perspective provides a limited explanation of prejudiced activity. Firstly, it is suggested that this theoretical perspective links racism too narrowly with child-rearing practices and so cannot cope with the multiple contexts and diverse content of prejudiced activities. For example, the work of Minard (1952) with black and white miners stressed the variability in racist activities among this group, with racism occurring above ground but not below in the mines. Thus the context in which interactions occur is highlighted as significant for understanding prejudiced activity. Secondly, the authoritarian personality approach is criticized as oversimplifying the complex links between the internal world constructed by the individual and the external social world (Wetherell, 1996). Pettigrew's (1958) work illustrated how the prevalence of authoritarian personalities remained constant across Western societies and across southern and northern regions of the United States, yet instances of racism varied widely in different societies and between these regions in the United States. Such instances suggest a more complex interplay between the individual and her or his social worlds than Adorno *et al.* (1950) can account for. In addition the methodological approach adopted by Adorno and colleagues has been critiqued (see Wetherell and Potter, 1992, for further discussion).

Prejudice and group membership

This third theoretical approach to prejudiced activity suggests that the earlier works on cognitive processes and personality structure are too rigid to explain prejudiced activities and instead focus on the effects of group membership on the psychology of individuals. Central to this perspective is the Realistic Group Conflict Theory (Sherif and Sherif, 1969) and Social Identity Theory (Tajfel and Turner, 1979).

Sherif and Sherif (1969) rejected what they considered to be the overly simplistic analogies between human and animal social aggression that had been noted by earlier theorists (Lorenz, 1966), arguing that animal aggression lacked the organization and diversity of human social aggression, prejudice and group conflicts (see Chapter 8). Sherif and Sherif presented the processes underlying animal social aggression, witnessed in defensive behaviours relating to territory and resources, as mediated through straightforward chemical and visual discrimination, the 'sniffing out' of unfamiliar opponents. In contrast, they argued that prejudiced activities among humans were more complex, mediated through the cultural meanings of perceived territory (or homeland) and the rights that accompanied this. Theirs is a strongly environmental account of prejudiced activity where the immediate social situation (membership of a group and the group's relations with others) causes the psychological states involved in aggression. Central to the 'realistic group conflict theory' is that the positioning of groups, for example in relation to scarce resources or particular goals, causes the various psychological states that characterize intergroup relations. To quote Wetherell (1996: 204), 'People's perceptions of those who belong to their own group and to the other group, their emotions, identifications or lack of identification will fall in line with the state of relations between the groups.' Sherif and Sherif (1969) illustrated their theoretical ideas with a series of experiments conducted in a boys' summer camp (see Box 9.2).

Based on the evidence collected from the summer-camp experiments, Sherif and Sherif (1969) claimed to demonstrate a clear link between the objective relations between groups and the psychology of individuals. In phase three of the experiments, where the groups competed in the tournament, in-group identification and loyalty were consolidated

Box 9.2 The summer-camp experiments

Sherif and Sherif (1969) set up a summer camp over a two-week period. The boys who participated were unaware that they were part of the experimental research and all were selected for their 'normal' characteristics. The researchers set up four social situations. Firstly, the boys were allowed to mix freely, and spontaneous friendship groups emerged. The second phase occurred a few days later and involved the establishing of two groups. Although the groups appeared to the boys to be chosen arbitrarily, the researchers established them to cut across established groups and allegiances. The two groups worked separately on activities and quickly new friendships emerged, to the extent that the boys developed their own codes of behaviours and names such as the Bulldogs and Red Devils.

During the third phase of the study, the groups were brought together and a tournament announced. Each group could compete to earn points for their own group. Initially the points for each group were kept artificially equal. At this stage norms of good personship were discarded and open hostility emerged between the groups and in-group loyalty became evident. The final stage involved the groups working towards mutual superordinate goals (e.g. solving problems with the camp water supply). Over time, indulging in co-operative activities reduced intergroup hostility, which was further reduced by the introduction of a third group of boys from a nearby camp (common enemy). This period introduced a climate in the summer camp that resembled that in the first phase.

and hostility towards members of the perceived out-group intensified. Behavioural and emotional indicators of prejudice were evident in the name-calling and stereotyping that occurred. Later experimental research (Tajfel and Turner, 1979) supported the findings of Sherif and Sherif (1969).

CRITICAL THINKING ON METHODOLOGY

Read the experiments described in Box 9.2. What do you consider are the limitations of experiments for exploring prejudiced activities?

Although Sherif and Sherif (1969) acknowledged that real-life incidences of intergroup conflict were more complex than those illustrated
through the summer-camp experiments, various limitations of the
'realistic group conflict theory' have been discussed:

- *Intergroup conflict as a natural response to conflicts of interest*:
  Wetherell (1996) suggests that such a conclusion carries serious
  moral and political implications for understanding prejudiced
  activities. If prejudice is a natural response to group conflict then
  how can it possibly be problematized; rather, it is simply a predictable outcome based on a conflict of interests. So, for example, is it
  sufficient to say that racism in the UK is as a result of competition
  over jobs, and that by creating more jobs, racism could be eliminated? In many ways such an explanation obscures the diversity and
  pervasiveness of prejudiced activities and ignores historical representations of particular groups in societies and the ways such
  discourses are used to legitimize prejudiced activities. Also, if prejudiced activities are viewed as a natural response to group conflict,
  how do we define someone involved in such activity in terms of
  personal accountability?
- *Prejudice as a universal trait*: The suggestion that membership of a
  group will affect people in stable, predictable ways has been heavily
  criticized. Such an approach neglects important issues such as
  the history of the development of perceived groups, social positioning and how this affects access to resources, culture and ideology.
  It fails to explain variation in prejudiced activities and to explore
  why specific groups in society are discriminated against.
- *The invisible third group*: The work of Billig (1976) draws attention to methodological considerations, in particular the role of
  the experimenter(s). Billig challenges the taken-for-granted scientific understanding of the experimenter as a neutral observer and
  instead draws attention to her or his social position and power in
  experimental contexts. In the summer camp experiments, Sherif
  and associates effectively formed a third 'authority' group, instrumental in creating the social structure within which the activities
  of the boys were framed. They instigated the establishment of two
  distinct groups, defined competitive and superordinate tasks, and,
  perhaps more important, intervened when competition between the
  boys took place at 'unexpected' stages of the experimental process.
  The lack of analysis of the influence of the experimenter(s) and
  competition between the boys even when they were not directly in

competitive situations calls into question the theoretical validity of Sherif's work for understanding 'real-life' instances of intergroup hostility and conflict (for a fuller discussion see Billig, 1976).

Tajfel's experimental work in the 1970s (e.g. Tajfel, 1978) concentrated further on the identification that occurs within group situations and the consequences of the psychological changes this identification involves. Tajfel believed that group contexts introduced specific psychological changes in the ways individuals identify both themselves and others. In contrast to the work of Sherif and Sherif (1969), Tajfel argued that the processes of group identification would result in intergroup conflict in the absence of competition for resources or the attainment of some goal. Tajfel conceptualized behaviour in terms of a continuum. At one end he visualized 'interpersonal behaviour', that is the behaviours and characteristics that are manifested when we act as individuals. When perceiving oneself as a unique individual, Tajfel suggested that we relate to others as individuals, viewing and evaluating them in terms of their unique characteristics or personality. At the other end of the continuum is intergroup behaviour, the characteristics and behaviour we indulge in when we perceive ourselves as a group member (e.g. student, teacher, even our family). Again, Tajfel viewed this as having consequences for our relations with others, in particular the tendency to overgeneralize the characteristics attributed to other groups, leading to perceptions and evaluations of others as homogeneous masses. Tajfel acknowledges that these behaviours in their purest form rarely exist and that factors such as cultural context will also influence how we understand situations and react to them.

Tajfel (1981) explored the processes of identification with an interesting series of experiments known as the minimal group experiments. In contrast to Sherif and Sherif's (1969) work, where competition between two groups was deliberately fostered, Tajfel's subjects were randomly assigned to two groups under the pretence of a preference for the paintings of artists such as Klee and Kandinsky. The students participating were not aware of the group others were assigned to, and for the rest of the experiment subjects performed individually in cubicles. Students were presented with matrices and asked to divide points worth money between the two groups. The matrices contained code numbers for individuals and the subjects were asked to assign points to individuals in each group, never to themselves. Despite the fact that the groups shared no history or contact and were not in a situation of direct competition (in contrast to the summer camp experiments), the results indicated signs of in-group favouritism and discrimination against those perceived as out-group members.

Tajfel and Turner (1985) suggested that the results of the minimal group experiments could be explained in terms of the changes to personal identity that result from group membership. They suggest that when individuals perceive themselves as members of groups (working-class, Catholic, Asian, etc.), they categorize their social world according to their group's characteristics and beliefs. These changes, they propose, occur through a three-stage psychological process theorized in the social identity theory. This theory links the negative processes such as stereotyping and the inequitable allocation of resources illustrated in the earlier experimental work, with the individual's desire for a positive self-image. Firstly, Tajfel and Turner suggest a change in cognitive processing within group contexts whereby categories based on the salient features of groups emerge which structure the individual's view of her or his social world. It is argued that similarities within groups are accentuated and differences with other groups emphasized. This, Tajfel and Turner argue, promotes a change in self-definition. Identification with a group erodes individuality as the person begins to define herself or himself in line with the char acteristics, beliefs and traits of the group. Turner (1982) described this process as depersonalization, with the social identity of the group providing an important basis for self-esteem. The final process of social comparison is, according to these theorists, vital for a positive social identity and self-esteem and provides the final key to understanding collective actions. As Wetherell (1996: 213) points out, 'self-esteem, according to this logic will be tied to the position of one's groups vis-à-vis other groups. To think well of ourselves, it is necessary to think well of our groups.'

Consequently, if people compare their group with others and do not feel highly valued they will feel dissatisfied. If the relationship between themselves and the other group(s) is seen as legitimate, individuals will accept this and attempt to move to the more favourable group(s). If however, the intergroup relationship is perceived as illegitimate, group members will take collective action or individual action to improve their social identity and enhance self-esteem. So, for example, collective action could take the form of the violence in Northern Ireland that has recently diminished, with various terrorist groups (e.g. IRA, UVF, etc.) fighting for the rights of their so-called communities (Catholics, Protestants). Or on an individual basis, if one identifies oneself as 'working class', self-worth and self-esteem may be achieved by focusing on characteristics such as being down-to-earth, honest, hard-working, etc., and the perceived characteristics of the 'middle class' (such as pretentious, snobbish, artificial, etc.) that maximize difference may be emphasized. According to social identity theory it is these psychological processes that not only lead to intergroup conflict but also maintain it.

In many ways this latter account of social identification, categorization and comparison could be considered a more social account of the causes of prejudiced activities than the other perspectives discussed earlier in this chapter. The social context is emphasized as central to understanding group conflict and resulting discriminatory practices. From a critical social psychology perspective, however, a number of fundamental anomalies underlie social identity theory, two of which are discussed below:

- *The 'individual' and the 'social'*: This theory attempts to explore the interface at which aspects of the individual (cognitions, motivations, identities) and the organization of the social (groups/categories) combine and result in prejudiced activities. However, Wetherell and Potter (1992) argue that for the theory to hold, certain representations of the individual and the social need to pre-exist. Individuals within this theory are conceptualized as self-contained units sharing sets of internal processes (cognitions, motives) that function in some universal way (categorization, comparison, differentiation) regardless of individuals' social, cultural and historical contexts. Consequently, prejudiced thoughts, emotions and activities are seen as residing within the individual with no theoretical exploration of their social origins or the diverse socially constructed ways in which these are legitimized and manifested. The social in this theoretical perspective is represented as a collection of discrete groupings (class, religion, gender, minority, majority, etc.), and a social reality is assumed which the individual visibly perceives and processes in particular ways. The processing of such social stimuli in turns produces observable, predictable forms of social action such as racism, sexism, homophobia, etc. However, as Billig (1978) points out, the diverse cultural, social, political and legal representations of identities mediated through institutional representations/language and everyday talk are an absent level of analysis in such accounts. Instead the ever-present dynamic socio-historical reminders of 'who we are' and how we are situated in relation to others are theorized as a universal and static backdrop to activities, existing as 'traditions' (religion, race, sex) that are conceptualized as having some type of naturally existing status.

The problem with such assumptions has been highlighted through work on the minimal group experiment in a variety of cultures. In her work with Pacific Island Maori and white European New Zealand children, Wetherell (1982) illustrated differences in the strategies chosen by the children that reflected the social and cultural meanings of group relations. Unlike the European white New Zealand children, who chose strategies similar to those subjects in the original minimal group experiments, the Pacific Island children consistently chose to maximize the joint profit of both groups even on occasions where their group would receive considerably less than the out-group. As Wetherell (1996: 217) concluded, 'this behaviour makes sense in terms of the cultural and social frameworks of Polynesian societies and the emphasis these societies place on generosity to others as a marker of high status'. This example would provide evidence to argue against the notions of universal cognitive processing offered by Tajfel and Turner (1985) and also calls into question the concept of an objective, observable social reality. Rather, what appears to be important is the ways in which people in groups interpret and make sense of intergroup relations in line with the social and cultural frameworks shaping their worlds.

- *Prejudice as a cognitive by-product*: Despite its emphasis on the social context, social identity theory, like the social cognition perspective, has been criticized for its representation of prejudiced activity as an inevitable product of perceptual processing. Presenting the individual as a processor of information, structured in this instance within the context of social groups and categorizes, in order to maximize self-esteem, implies that racism, sexism etc. are unfortunate by-products of universal perceptual systems. As Wetherell and Potter (1992: 47) suggest: 'because these types of group phenomena are expressions of a universal psychological dynamic, racism is more likely to persist than not, and, if racism did disappear, it would simply be replaced by some other grounds for group differentiation'.

Box. 9.3   Social identity theory (SIT), conflict and Northern Ireland

In the 1980s, Northern Ireland, with its two large independent groups and their associated power differentials seemed to offer a natural laboratory for SIT. Much work relating to the influence of social identity on intergroup conflict and discrimination was conducted (Cairns and Mercer, 1984; Kremer *et al.*, 1986). Although producing many interesting findings, Gough *et al.* (1992) suggest that this work was confined by the limitations of SIT. The previous authors highlight difficulties with the assumption that groups can be objectively defined, in this case on the basis of religion, as such definitions are contested depending on the criteria adopted. For example, in terms of a simple head-count and using socio-economic criteria, Catholics are often classified as the minority group. Within Ireland as a whole, Protestants are the minority, and in the United Kingdom both Catholics and Protestants in Northern Ireland would be perceived as minority groups. Thus the permanence of terms such as majority and minority underlying much research on prejudice is called into question. In addition, variations in group affiliations depending on the context (Waddell and Cairns, 1986) and regional differences in prejudice and discrimination (Kremer *et al.*, 1986) that could not be fully explained within the context of SIT, were highlighted, leading Gough *et al.* (1992: 638) to conclude:

> it is dangerous to assume that situations can be readily and objectively defined. In reality, people will actively interpret situations according to their own needs and existing cognitions. SIT theorists have focused on more global processes of social categorization and social comparison without detailing how these processes impact at an individual level.

Identities, discourse and ideology: critical readings of prejudice

Social constructionism offers an understanding of prejudice that begins with a rejection of the dualistic concept of 'the individual and the social' embodied in the perspectives discussed previously. The individual as the possessor of internal psychological states (cognitions or motivations) linked to particular social actions is destabilized by representations of selfhood as multiple and fragmented (see Chapter 4). The identities in which individuals engage are perceived as neither unitary nor stable but rather are inextricably linked with socio-cultural contexts. In more contemporary work on prejudiced activities

(Gough, 1998; Hall, 1990; Wetherell, 1996), identity is perceived not as a static, consistent concept but rather is fluid, constructed and reconstructed through the interactions that occur. Talk, as Wetherell (1996) stresses, does not occur in a vacuum but is formed within a culture and directed at an assumed audience that fundamentally influences what is said and how it is presented. The accounts that are presented reflect how we interpret our historical, social and cultural positions as well as how we position others. For example, in the following extract from Cashmore (1987), the speaker draws on the colonial and military history of Britain to situate himself and others in relation to contemporary immigration policies (Box 9.4). The speaker talks about the Empire implying the power and domination Britain once enjoyed. He also implicitly falls back on early colonial ideas relating to natives as uncivilized and the role of countries such as Britain in taming this unruliness (... 'Right, now go back to your country and implement those things we've taught you'). In addition he incorporates more contemporary arguments relating to welfare and employment to justify his representations of ethnic minorities.

Box 9.4 'We gave them hell' (Cashmore, 1987)

'We gave them hell in the Empire; but just because they had no freedom then it doesn't mean they can have freedom in a different way now. They've become members of the Commonwealth, and all we should have done is have people who wanted to get education, educated them and then said "Right, now go back to your country and implement those things we've taught you". ... We always said "Anybody who's a member of our colonies is free to come into this country". Undoubtedly there's a lot who come in just to draw dole. ... They come here and within a month they're living off the state, whether they're black, yellow or any other colour. I think that's wrong' (p. 220).

Much critical work on prejudice emphasizes the social construction of such activities by highlighting the changing content of prejudice talk and actions. Billig (1988) in his work on racism refers to new, more subtle types of racist activities, where in cultures such as the UK blatant racism is on the decline, but where now people often present racist sentiments but deny their own prejudice at the same time (see Box 9.5).

Box 9.5   'I'm not prejudiced, but . . .'

Billig (1988) illustrates 'new racisms' by drawing attention to the diverse ways in which people present, for example, racist content while actively attempting to avoid being labelled as 'racist' in what Tony Blair calls 'multi-cultural Britain'. This according to the previous author is achieved through a denial of one's prejudice and a justification for treating others differently, not on the basis of colour but by using broader arguments relating to employment, housing, equality, law and order, etc. Similar prejudice targeted at women was highlighted in Gough's (1998) study on the reproduction of gender inequality by a group of university-educated men. In this study, Gough (1998: 44) highlights 'the deployment of "new sexist" discourse . . . a form of talk where liberal values are called upon to present the speaker in a positive light and enable the intimation of sentiments which can be viewed as sexist such that censure is discouraged'.

   This is illustrated in the following extract where prejudiced talk is framed by an expressed tolerance. For example, Kevin describes many feminist activities as being 'fair enough' but simultaneously criticizes these with his remark that 'at the same time they [feminists] take it too far'. Again, similar constructions are reproduced in Kevin's talk on equal employment opportunities. He begins by express-ing liberal values on women in the workplace – 'I mean women obvi-ously should be allowed to have jobs and stuff' – and then furthers his justifications for why women's access to jobs should be limited by representing women as biologically inferior to men: 'but there are some jobs they gotta accept they can't do, like you get bloody women pilots and stuff, they just can't make the fitness don't you think?' Later in the extract Kevin justifies his views on women's suitability for certain employment by recounting the tale of women's experi-ences in the American military, again on the basis of biological inferiority:

Brendan: What do you not like about feminist women?
Kevin: Ahh, they're just, I don't know, it's hard to put it into words, but I use to, like, inflame things, so many things I disagree with, like about 'em, quite a lot of it fair enough but at the same time they take it too far, I mean women obviously should be allowed to have jobs and stuff but there's some jobs they gotta accept they can't do, like

you get bloody women pilots and stuff, they just can't make the fitness don't you think?

Luke: You can't

Kevin: One or two campaigns like a few years ago in America in the, uh, corps or whatever and she lasted two weeks when she got in [*laughs*] so she had to go through all these court battles and like every [lesbian] in the country is up in arms about it and she's let the whole female race down because she couldn't take it, and there are situations where women shouldn't be in, I mean they're good in business and stuff like that, no problem, but it's just sometimes they take it too far, all this equal rights stuff. (Gough, 1998: 39)

Similarly, the social is understood not as a tangible, observable reality that can be distorted as a result of perceptual errors, but rather that the social worlds of individuals are themselves shifting and multiple constructions. Critical theorists (Billig, 1995; Wetherell and Potter, 1992) emphasize the centrality of language in the construction of identities and actions. Within critical theorizing, then, prejudiced activities are not viewed within the realms of personality or as the result of perceived social categorizations but rather as more pervasive, embedded in language and ideological practices. Wetherell and Potter (1992: 59) summarize this position when they state, 'The psychological and social field – subjectivity, individuality, social groups and social categories – is constructed through discourse. We shall thus suggest that action, the individuals and the social, the subject matter of social psychology, cannot be easily separated from discursive practice.'

Consequently prejudiced activities are explored as shifting social dialogues that reflect shared socio-cultural meanings and through which we negotiate our identities and relations with others. Consequently the historical, economic, political and social locations of the speaker become key to understanding how he or she positions himself or herself in relation to others. These are not objective positions but rather are interpretations, part of an unfolding cultural narrative the speaker presents (Thompson, 1984). For example, in their analysis of Maori–Pakeha relations in New Zealand, Wetherell and Potter (1992) note that in describing the position of the Maori people, the middle-class Pakeha sample not only talk about current relations but also try to make sense of their history and the colonialism that occurred in the mid-nineteenth century. Similarly, McCreanor (1996), in his review of anti-homosexual discourse in New Zealand, illustrates how the diverse range of historical and contemporary representations of homosexuals presented acquire meaning within a society that constructs hetero-sexuality as normal/natural and devalues homosexuality (see Box 9.6). Participants drawing on historical anti-Semitic images of Jews intensify the fear of contamination and the further destabilising of moral and social order 'poisoning the well'.

Box 9.6 'Why strengthen the city walls when the enemy has poisoned the well?' An assay of anti-homosexual discourse in New Zealand

This paper by McCreanor is based on the reading of public sub-missions to the New Zealand Select Committee on Homosexual Law Reform in 1985. These submissions were sent in response to pro-posed changes in the legislation regulating homosexuality in New Zealand.

[1] Homosexuality as abnormal, unnatural, unhealthy etc.
'Sodomy is UNNATURAL COPULATION-LIKE ACT that is exactly how I view homosexuality'
'Homosexual practices, which the Bill justifies, are anti-social and destructive to normal family conditions. Homosexuality is unnat-ural sexual activity and decadent ... Homosexual practices are unhealthy and deadly'

McCreanor (1996) notes that the terms used to describe homosexu-ality implicitly draw on the privileged discourse of heterosexuality as the proper/normal sexuality, and concludes, 'For example to say that homosexuality is unhealthy references heterosexual practice as healthy. My point is not at this stage to point out the weakness of such a position but to draw attention to the ways in which such statements rely upon an ideological heterosexism' (p. 85).

[2] Homosexuality as danger to society
'Homosexuality is lust. Lust is the most powerful form of selfish-ness in the world today. Homosexuality is a lust that is insatiable and if allowed to grow will become the all-consuming aim of the homosexual person, whether male or female. Homosexual lust is a destructive force that will bring mental disorder and pres-sure to the individual by way of jealously, anger, frustration and an ill conscience. Homosexual lust is a destructive force that

will bring physical breakdown to the individual by reason of venereal disease, gonorrhoea, syphilis, AIDS and other unidentified anal diseases' (p. 87).

McCreanor (1996) comments that in this instance homosexuality is represented solely in terms of sexual activity with no reference to other social and personal behaviours (love, commitment etc.). Any similarities between homosexuality and heterosexuality are obscured and homosexuality is implicitly devalued as a rather dangerous type of lust. Such a representation, McCreanor (1996) points out, allows for the expression of various 'logical' extensions by the speaker to justify his position. In the latter stages of the extract, the speaker draws generalizations, outlining the dangers that homosexuality implies for society as a whole. The entire social fabric (with its cultural imperative of heterosexuality) is endangered by sexual activity that results in physical disease, mental instability and more general social disorder.

Gough (2001) illustrated similar representations of homosexuality in a more recent study. Many of the male participants drew on discourses of heterosexuality as the normal/natural sexuality to depict homosexuality as perverse and as a danger to the normative heterosexual society. For example in the following extract the speaker, Martin, compares gay marchers to monsters and constructs gay men as potential rapists, and justifies this on the basis of perceived 'normal' behaviours and styles of dressing. Heterosexuality is equated with privacy and restraint, the implication being that homosexuality is bound up with unacceptable public displays and, as stated more explicitly later in the extract, should be controlled.

Martin: If it's (homosexuality) if it's treated like conventional heterosexuality, you've got your partner and you keep it to yourself, it's not flaunted. I've always tolerated it but what annoys me is when you see these gay marches, they're all dressed up in these perverted leathers, whatever it is, bondage gear – if they wanna do that in their own home then that's alright, but I think they're gettin' themselves a bad name when they all turn up dressed as transvestites and they've got tights on like the Rocky Horror Show and they're all walkin' down the street; you look at them and you think what are they? and they look like monsters. If they're dressed fairly conventionally, just say 'look I'm a homosexual, accept me', I'd have no problem with that whatsoever – you're not tryin' to rape me, you're not tryin' to force it on me, I accept it, but it's that perversion that they seem to put over, not all of 'em, I mean it's a public minority, but it's that that I don't accept. If it was a heterosexual march and everybody was like in bondage gear and handcuffs, it's not on this ... you can't have this walkin' down the street. It goes off, you know it happens, you accept that ... but for them to force that on people, now whether they're dressin' to that extent to make a point, this is what you gotta accept. (Gough 2001: 12)

As Gough (2001: 13) concludes, 'these themes of abnormality and danger are embedded in and enabled by reference to certain (heterosexual) ideals.

CRITICAL THINKING ON HOMOPHOBIA

Extracts in this chapter have illustrated some of the ways in which gay men and lesbian women can be problematically represented. Can you add any other representations to this list? List the similarities and differences between representations of gay men and women.

This is not to suggest that prejudiced activities within critical work are believed to simply exist in talk; we are all too aware of the violence and social discrimination that can occur to those perceived as different. Indeed, central to a critical analysis of prejudiced activities is a consideration of the ways in which discourses can obscure or attempt to rationalize power relations. For example, many feminist theorists, including Jackson (1984b), point to nineteenth-century representations of women as better suited to the domestic domain and men to the public domain of production as 'natural', arguing that such a system of social relations ensured that all men had free access to women's domestic labour and that women's activities continued to remain outside the realm of value. (See Box 9.7.)

Box 9.7   Illustrations of critical practice

Feminist theorists have been very much at the forefront in connecting critical theory and practice. Nicolson (1992) draws attention to the

ways in which the female body has been problematized as biologically volatile within traditional academic psychology theories.
She makes explicit the disempowering positions that such representations place women in within the wider contexts of health care
and medicine. The absence of women's voices in decision-making
and control in childbirth, as well as the narrow biomedical definitions of depression which may women encounter when experiencing
postnatal depression, are fundamentally challenged and understandings of practice re-worked within Nicolson's (1992) work.

In *Deconstructing Psychopathology*, Parker *et al.* (1995) challenge
what are perceived as clinically inappropriate and limiting definitions of mental illness. Blanket definitions of mental health experiences are exposed as ethnocentric, i.e. based on values associated
with white, middle-class men, resulting in potential serious mis-
diagnosis (Boyle, 1996). In addition, Parker *et al* (1995) suggest that
diagnostic labels and the consequent lack of attention to the lived
experiences of people with 'mental illness', function to protect the
existing status quo surrounding established expertise and practice
in the disciplines of clinical psychology and psychiatry. Consequently many critical practitioners have rejected the scientific paradigm that drives much research on mental health and rather focus
on exploring how individuals experience their mental illness, and
prioritize this information as the starting point for clinical practice.

Mental Health Matters: A Reader (Heller *et al.*, 1996) provides
interesting examples of critical practice.

In order to explore power relations, many social constructionists
have employed the notoriously slippery concept of ideology, defined by
Burr (1995) as 'knowledge in the service of power' – that is, the use of
discourses in the interests of relatively powerful groups in society, and
subsequent oppression of others often through representations of their
status as 'natural' or 'fair' (Gill, 1995). It is important to note that it
is not the ideas themselves that are oppressive but the ways in which
the ideas are used and the outcomes they produce. Consequently, the
construction of discourses on 'class', 'race' and 'sex' become central to
understanding prejudiced activities.

Guillaumin (1995) in her book *Racism, Sexism, Power and Ideology*
situates the ideology of 'race' 'sex', etc., within the broader framework

of naturalism. By this she means the assigning of specific social positions and status to groups on the basis of assumed characteristics internal to groups themselves (e.g. colour, sexual anatomy). She develops her thesis by stressing the socially constructed nature of these categories, linking their emergence to rapid economic and political changes that occurred across Europe in the late eighteenth century and early nineteenth century. The destabilizing of the nobility, and the emergence of the bourgeoisie and proletariat set into motion chains of developments that not only resulted in new political and economic structures (including colonization) but also social identities (nation), philosophy (individualism) and social relations (appropriation). Guillaumin argues that the assigning of certain *natural* characteristics (e.g. biological reproduction, smaller brain size, etc.) was produced in the context of the broadly defined labour needs of the ruling class (the bourgeoisie). In particular, the rise of the discipline of science in the nineteenth century is highlighted as consolidating the connection between biology and social relations by producing the *biological facts* that supported the processes of racialization and sexualization. As Guillaumin (1995: 7) reminds us:

> The processes through which these categories are constructed and through which social agents are allocated certain positions are rendered invisible; more importantly the appropriation of their labour is occluded. ... Naturalism thus makes history invisible and hides the fact that the association between the social category and the signifier is born in the context of specific social relations.

Foucault's (1978) work on the power–knowledge couplet is an important dimension in understanding how prejudiced activities are produced and maintained by and within institutions. He stresses the network of power bases that historically have defined human existence through the production of knowledge (medicine, law, philosophy, science etc.), producing definable categories of people and structuring social relations (1978: 88). With respect to women, Guillaumin (1995) and other feminist scholars stress how historically knowledge about women's *nature* has been produced by men in positions of power (e.g. sexologists such as Ellis, 1913, and Freud, 1923) to structure social relations (e.g. marriage), to justify their exclusion from public arenas and their confinement to certain activities such as child production and the servicing of men's needs. Blakemore *et al.* (1997) illustrated the persistence of such representations of women in the institutions in the 1990s in their study 'Exploring the Campus Climate for Women Faculty'. This study illustrates how such ideas continue to shape women's existence and reproduce power relations on a daily basis. The women participating in this study recounted stories of professional devaluation and differences in promotion and tenure opportunities existing between them and male colleagues. Similar differences were enacted by students who addressed male staff using professional titles (Professor, Dr, etc.) while frequently referring to female staff as Miss or Mrs. In addition these women lecturers spoke of students expecting more nurturing from them than from male colleagues:

'They [students] expect women to be softer – sometimes it really pisses me off that they don't expect men to cut them a break.'

'Now I have a male graduate student who expects me to do his grunt work. He expects me to make his [chemical] solutions and wash his dishes. When I leave my glassware in the sink to clean up later, he piles his in on top of mine and expects me to clean his, too.' (Blackmore *et al.*, 1997: 59)

Furthermore, sexual harassment, exclusion from social networks and demeaning remarks based on gender were also reported by the female participants:

'In a department meeting one women faculty member got quite outspoken and a male colleague meowed.'

'This semester according to some information I was given by a student who was in my class and another class that met in the same room immediately after mine, the professor in the next class picked up the large piece of sidewalk chalk that I use for my lectures, raised it up and remarked: "Obviously a case of penis envy". I found that demeaning.' (ibid: 67)

CRITICAL THINKING ON PREJUDICE

What do the men in the above scenarios achieve from using such practices? What strategies can you think of to address such instances of discrimination?

Summary

In this chapter, theories of prejudice from the 1920s to the more contemporary accounts of critical social psychology in the 1990s have been critically reviewed. The second section dealt with traditional social cognition accounts that frame prejudice in terms of limitations on cognitive processes (that is, the ways in which people categorize and group stimuli together). Understandings of prejudice based on character structure, and the authoritarian personality, were then examined, with proponents of this approach suggesting that personality is central to understanding whether or not people indulge in prejudiced activities. Finally, the 'realistic group conflict' theory and 'social identity' theory were discussed in this section. These theorists argue that group situations fundamentally influence individual psychology and lie at the heart of explanations of prejudiced activities.

The third section of the chapter argued that people's identities and social positioning are fundamentally influenced by the social and ideological contexts in which they are situated. The social positions that different individuals or collectives of people occupy are not perceived as natural, observable phenomenon but rather are constructed and re-constructed through the social interaction in which they are engaged. Critical social psychologists suggest that the possibilities for identity negotiation are not finite but rather are limited by social and ideological constraints. Consequently prejudiced activities are constructed within the struggles over representation and identity that individuals or collectives of people go through and are fundamentally linked to conflicts of interests and power inequalities.

Key references

Gough, B. (1998) 'Men and the Discursive Reproduction of Sexism: Repertoires of Difference and Equality', *Feminism & Psychology*, 8(1): 1–49. An interesting and accessible journal article that provides insights into the ways in which liberal and so-called politically correct discourses can be re-worked to produce a range of complex and subtle prejudiced activities.

Wetherell, M. (1996) 'Group Conflict and the Social Psychology of Racism', in Wetherell, *Identities, Groups and Social Issues* (Milton Keynes: Open University Press). This easy-to-read chapter provides an extensive overview of psychological perspectives on prejudice and offers interesting individual and group activities.

Reflections on Critical Social Psychology 10

This chapter will highlight:

- Key themes in critical social psychology
- Important differences and debates between critical social psychologists
- Tensions between social constructionism and critical social psychology
- Further resources for developing 'critical' psychological thinking

Introduction

One message flagged in this book is that contemporary social psychology is a fragmented discipline, beset with difference and often disagreement. Indeed, it might be preferable to speak of social psycholo*gies*. Clearly, significant differences exist between 'mainstream' cognitive-experimental and 'critical' forms of social psychology, as we have stressed throughout this book. But there are other branches of social psychology not covered in much detail here, such as humanistic/experiential social psychology (Stevens, 1996) and psychoanalytic social psychology (Frosh, 1999). This situation is complicated further when we consider differences *within* given brands of social psychology. For example, Stainton-Rogers *et al.* (1995) outline a number of relatively separate types of (critical) social psychology, and in Box 10.1 we reproduce four brands relevant to critical social psychology.

So, we must be very careful not to regard labels such as 'mainstream' or 'critical' social psychology as reflecting neat, distinct bundles of coherent perspectives, for such thinking would be to mask serious internal debates and conflicts. Although such labels are difficult to avoid and can be useful for teaching purposes, it is important not to imagine critical social psychology as a unified set of concepts and

Box 10.1   Critical social psychologies (Stainton-Rogers *et al.*, 1995)

'Social psychology as social science'

It generally identifies social psychology as inter-disciplinary and accords considerable importance to its sociological roots. Here 'social psychology' is identified with relationships between individuals and social structures (from two-person 'dyads' to organizations and institutions). Individuals are held to be both influenced by and influential upon social structures. Where 'theories' feature, they are likely to be either 'grand theories' (such as structural-functionalism) or interactional models such as 'symbolic interactionism'.

'Social psychology as a social constructionist endeavour'

It declares itself early (e.g. in titles like The Social Construction of Death) in a challenge to all pre-emptive attempts to singularize (or even talk of) reality. However, social constructionism has become a buzz term, and you may find you have bought a pragmatist or social scientist underneath the snazzy bodywork! Do not be fooled. Social constructionism offers a powerful challenge to the enterprises listed above (e.g. social psychology as science/humanist endeavour etc.). But be warned – social constructionism is not on offer if it is presented as just one approach among many, or called constructivism. This is somebody trying to have their cake and eat it, since constructionism is incompatible with all the above approaches.

'Social psychology as a postmodern endeavour'

It will shout 'pomo'-speak from the start. You will soon find that its proponents would rather risk incomprehension than being misunderstood. If you don't rapidly find terms like 'deconstruction' being used or any mention of French theorists (like Foucault, Derrida and Deleuze) it must be something else.

'Social psychology as rebellion and resistance'

Sometimes this will be marked for you by the rapid recourse to words like 'feminist', 'marxist' or 'power'. But even where this does not happen, its polemical tone and rhetorical devices will soon show themselves. It dislikes and distrusts virtually all received social psychology. Some anti-social psychologists think that humanists and postmodernists have either 'sold out' or don't understand that they are being 'used' and that social constructionists are relativists.

practices. However, we will reiterate here what we feel to be key features of a critical social psychology perspective before moving on to discuss areas where consensus has proved elusive. Some concerns about critical social psychology voiced recently by advocates will then be summarized but we will finish by emphasizing arguments in favour of critical social psychology approaches.

Revisiting critical social psychology

Critical social psychology advocates critical theory and practice; indeed, the two are interlinked. The term critical implies a sceptical, questioning attitude towards present-ed 'knowledge' and the actions promoted thereof and represents the defining feature of social movements such as Marxism and Feminism. A popular 'target' for critical social psychology is the discipline of (social) psychology itself, but more broadly the (psychological) culture from which it derives and which it helps maintain. Parker (1994) uses the term 'psy-complex' to denote a powerful contemporary cultural inclination towards deploying individualistic concepts to understand human social experience. Similarly, critical social psychology repudiates accounts or 'discourses' which seek to explain social action in terms of psychological or individualistic categories such as 'personality', 'attitude', 'schema', etc. The argument is that such explanations are often used to oppress individuals and groups and/or to blame them for their predicament. For example, the 'class is dead' thesis could easily be used to portray a society of opportunities for all and to place responsibility for 'failure' (e.g. unemployment) on lazy or unmotivated individuals. This discourse would operate to obscure continuing class-based inequalities in education, health and employment. Previous chapters have presented criticisms of individualistic discourse applied to various topics such as prejudice and aggression; critical social psychology is firmly positioned against such a culture of 'self-contained individualism' (Sampson, 1977).

Instead, critical social psychology favours accounts of phenomena which stress the centrality of social relationships and practices. It is argued that socially embedded accounts make for more persuasive and complex insights into the topic in question – did you find this was the case in the previous chapters? For example, gender tends to be regarded as socially constructed within a given culture at a specific historical point and constantly negotiated in interpersonal relationships. In other words, 'femininity' and 'masculinity' are not biological or psychological essences pertaining to women and men respectively but culturally available discourses which open up and close off certain subject positions. As well as the focus on language and social construction, the issue of power receives great attention from critical social psychology such that a study of gender would examine how discourses of masculinity and femininity are used in practice – traditionally the 'masculine' is valued (reason, strength) and the 'feminine' slighted (emotional, weak), although discourses are emerging which attempt to reverse such thinking ('men as victims', 'career women') (see Chapter 6). As well as emphasizing the social embededness of experience and the operation of power, critical social psychology usually involves a commitment to resistance and social change. There is an affinity with groups identified as marginalized or oppressed and an expressed desire to work towards the betterment of their situation. Such explicitly political and pragmatic work is often labelled 'action research'.

Perhaps the most common activity performed by most critical social psychologists is the analysis of discourse. Discourses analysis is not necessarily a critical practice and other methods have been used for critical purposes, but critically informed discourse analyses inform the majority of research projects within critical social psychology. Emerging from the 'turn to language' within contemporary social theory (social constructionism, post-structuralism) and given a critical twist by Foucault and followers (see Parker, 1992), discourse analysis has proved a valuable and versatile tool for deconstructing a range of texts and offering critical readings. There are some valuable texts on discourse analysis available (e.g. Burman and Parker, 1993; Potter and Wetherell, 1987) and various book chapters on discourse analysis can be found in books on qualitative research methods (e.g. Banister *et al.*, 1994; Hayes, 1997). The chapters in this book also refer to useful papers where discourse analysis has been employed. Students are encouraged to tap into these and other sources in order to grasp how discourse analysis may facilitate the attainment of critical goals.

Deconstructing critical social psychology

We have devoted much space in this book to creating an image of critical social psychology as a positive force in opposition to more 'problematic' forms of social psychology and wider culture. This tactic has been useful, even necessary, to render basic 'critical' concepts and themes accessible for a student audience unfamiliar with such vocabulary. However, to construe critical social psychology as a happy family of academics who agree on shared policies against common enemies would be to give a mistaken impression, for there is widespread discussion, frequent disagreement and occasional acrimony to be found within critical social psychology texts. In fact, some writers who we have cited in this book may not be happy with the term critical social psychology, preferring alternative labels such as 'discursive psychology' (Edwards and Potter, 1992), 'social constructionist' (Gergen, 1999), 'postmodernist' (Kvale, 1992) or simply 'critical psychology' (Fox and Prilleltensky, 1997). The term critical social psychology works for us in the context of this book because it is counter-posed with mainstream cognitive-experimental social psychology and emphasizes the 'social' dimension to experience.

Varieties of discourse analysis

But the existence of multiple labels can cause confusion, especially considering that the same label may be interpreted differently by different authors! This diversity of categories, however, does denote different emphases and points of disagreement between 'critical' (social) psychologists and it is important to explore these. Consider the two forms of discourse analysis outlined in Chapter 3. One approach operates at a high level of abstraction by identifying broad discursive frameworks and the subject positions which these make available to different groups. This approach is associated with the work of Parker and colleagues (e.g. Burman and Parker, 1993) and is influenced by the work of the French philosopher Michel Foucault on the historical surveillance of 'problematic' subjects such as criminals and the mentally ill. An explicitly political project, this approach has been criticized by other discourse analysts for suggesting that people's lives are completely or largely structured by prevailing discourse/s. For example, a 'medical' discourse would define people as patients subordinate to the knowledge and practices of the medical institution, with little room for effective resistance. As well, it is not clear how discourses are identified or defined and it often seems as if a given discourse is portrayed as a powerful structure or object existing independently of social interaction (see Potter et al., 1990).

Such criticisms are valid enough, although in some versions of this Foucauldian approach to discourse notions of resistance and social action are paramount.

The contrasting emphasis of the other form of discourse analysis is on the active or 'performative' quality of everyday talk (see Potter and Wetherell, 1987). The focus tends to be on concrete social interaction as it occurs 'naturally' and the image of the person favoured is that of the social actor and user – rather than subject – of discourse. The term 'interpretative repertoire' is preferred to highlight the specific metaphors and vocabularies used by people during conversation to achieve particular goals. This more interpersonal or conversational level of analysis looks closely at the rhetoric used and the functions which language is made to serve, such as justification of one's actions, presenting self or another in a positive light, avoiding criticism, etc. For example, a game of football might be presented as 'beautiful' or 'poetic' by a speaker in order to fend of criticisms of macho aggression and preserve a positive identity for the speaker as a football fan. This form of discourse analysis has also been criticized, this time on the grounds of lacking a more cultural or political dimension (see Parker, 1990), although there are examples of such work which do tackle the ideological quality of talk. The debates between the two camps rumble on but increasingly there are calls for more integrated approaches and in practice both perspectives are often combined (e.g. Willott and Griffin, 1997).

Social relations as both 'real' and 'constructed'

A point worth stressing at once is that critical social psychology does not automatically imply a social constructionist analysis. It is true that many 'critical' theoretical and empirical publications do make use of social constructionist concepts such as the historical and cultural specificity of knowledge, but social constructionist influenced work could just as easily operate in non-critical or even oppressive ways. For example, arguments for equality and non-discrimination could be used by groups traditionally regarded as privileged (e.g. white middle-class males). Conversely, essentialist arguments can be used for critical ends whereby the 'unique' status of a group (women, blacks, the middle-classes, etc.) is emphasized in order to pursue positive outcomes for that group such as independence, freedom from oppression, a distinctive identity, etc. Some feminist authors, for example, have argued that men and women are fundamentally different (e.g. Daly, 1978; Gilligan, 1982) and this idea is firmly embedded in popular culture (e.g. Gray, 1993). The same points can be made with respect to discourse analysis, where an examination of language need not proceed to a political analysis (although some might argue that all talk and text is political in some way – note Parker's analysis of toothpaste instructions, chapter 3). Similarly, discourse analysis may be used to reinforce or defend positive representations of powerful groups and/or to undermine claims of subordination proffered by minority or powerless groups.

Clearly, the existence of multiple discourses making different and often conflicting claims about 'how things are' makes it difficult to argue for the validity of one version of events over the other. This presents problems for feminist and critical psychologists interested in identifying instances of oppression and inequality, since any account (e.g. the subordination of women) can always be countered by other accounts (e.g. 'it's men who are really oppressed'). This is the key point of tension between some social constructionists and critical psychologists – the issue of relativism. Within a postmodern climate, criteria used to judge the 'truth' or value of an account cannot be provided by science, religion, humanism, marxism or any of the 'grand narratives' of modernism, since these perspectives themselves have been deconstructed as mere stories rather than reflections of reality or truth. In other words, just as one person's masterpiece is another's banality, so one construction of reality is simply an interpretation presented from a particular vantage point within a given social context. The problem for feminism is underlined by Jackson (1992), for example, who wonders about the lack of basis for deciding between the rape victim's account of forced sexual intercourse and the rapist's construction of mutually agreeable fun.

So, in accepting poststructuralist ideas, however, it is difficult to say with certainty that certain social groups possess power whilst others lack power. Any one object, say 'men', can be seen as powerful and/or powerless depending on the social context and other sets of relations prevailing, such as social class, sexual orientation, race, etc. By this analysis, some (middle-class) gay men may occupy more powerful social positions compared with (working-class) heterosexual men, though on other occasions macho heterosexuality may work to oppress male homosexuality. The point is that social identities and relationships are complicated by multiple and sometimes conflicting discourses which prevents straightforward allocation of power/lessness to particular groups.

The critical/feminist emphasis on politics, however, urges discourse analysts to move beyond deconstruction in order to articulate positive, political positions. For example, Willig (1998) suggests that discourse analysts are destined to remain observers and commentators if they abstain from adopting particular viewpoints – simply to point up the constructed nature of dominant discourses is less politically effective than actually offering alternative discourses and practices. The task is to adopt a clear position to facilitate political action whilst simultaneously acknowledging the interested or constructed nature of the version presented and the possibility of other interpretations. This 'politics of articulation' recognises that the community which is being represented (e.g. women) must not be taken as homogeneous ('opening') whilst arguing for the need to stop talking/writing at some point in order to act ('closing') (see Wetherell, 1995). Similarly, Squire (1995) highlights the way in which feminist discourse analysts may oscillate between a 'pragmatic' use of discourse analysis which privileges specific versions of reality and 'extravagant' deployments which explore the complexities and contradictions pertaining to accounts.

So, discourse analysts who espouse a commitment to left-wing causes tend to straddle both structuralist and poststructuralist perspectives (e.g. Gavey, 1997; Parker, 1992). Using a structuralist framework typical of classic marxism and socialist feminism, for example, upper middle class and male sections of society enjoy access to power whilst working class and female groups exist in positions of relative powerlessness. In holding on to structuralism, discourse is related to social institutions and practices – gender ideals depicting women as mothers and men as breadwinners can be seen to reinforce patriarchal heterosexuality. The nature of this relation between discourse and social structures is subject to debate, however, with some arguing for the primacy of 'reality' in shaping experience and discourse (e.g. Collier, 1998) and others asserting the power of discourse to define 'reality' and our understanding of it (e.g. Brown *et al.*, 1998).

In the end, the argument goes, we have to convince the reader of the merit and persuasiveness of our own interpretation by providing supporting evidence and discounting competing explanations. Reflexivity is important here, that is, providing information which helps contextualize the reading, although a reflexive account is itself constructed, so that one can easily slide into agonising contemplation of one's rhetoric rather than promoting the account itself! (Burman and Parker, 1993). So, relativism is not necessarily a barrier to politically motivated enquiry since one's reading of the text can be promoted

---

Box 10.2   'Politically informed relativism' (Gill, 1995)

Relativists' refusal to deal with questions of value has led to political paralysis. There is no principled way in which they can intervene, choose one version over another, argue for anything. Against this, feminists who have engaged with postmodernism and poststructuralism have taken a rather different position. There is a growing awareness that questions of value are inescapable and must be addressed. In the absence of ontological guarantees, then, values, commitments, politics must be at the heart of analyses.

  We need a relativism which is unashamedly political, in which we, as feminists, can make social transformation an explicit concern of our work. This is something that feminists have always done, but which at present is ruled out by the relative commitments of some discourse analysts.

  Discourse analysts should adopt a notion of reflexivity which stresses the need for the analysts to acknowledge their own commit ments and to reflect critically upon them. By seeking to explain and justify the basis for their readings or analyses, discourse analysts become accountable for their interpretations and the social and political consequences of these interpretations. (Gill, 1995: 177–82)

---

whilst the status of the reading as one of several possible interpretations is acknowledged (see Box 10.2). For further reading on the realism–relativism issue and related debates see Gavey (1997); Wetherell (1996); Edwards *et al.* (1995); Parker (1992).

Recovering subjective experience

Although post-structuralism has produced a climate of scepticism regarding structures and essences, the strong view of human experience as entirely framed by language is rejected by a number of writers (see Chapter 4, section 'The problem of subjective experience'). Accepting the arguments for the deconstruction of the core self (or 'unitary, rational subject'), there is nevertheless some dissatisfaction with an image of personhood devoid of emotion and embodiment. Discourse analysis may well help identify those subject positions inhabited by a person and the implications thereof, but there is little said about how it feels for people to occupy those subject positions and relationships with others. As Burr (1995) notes, a woman might accept that current discourses of femininity and motherhood place limits on women's choices but nonetheless may feel a strong desire to have a child. Discourse approaches might connect this desire to powerful social conventions but this account does not seem to adequately capture the emotional experience. Consequently, some writers have looked to other traditions to help complement the insights proffered by social constructionism, notably psychoanalysis.

At first sight there is little common ground between discourse analysis and psychoanalysis since the latter is typically concerned with intra-psychic or mental events whilst the former concentrates on social relations. Recent articles by prominent 'critical' writers, however, have revisited psychoanalytic ideas and commented on similarities between discourse analysis and psychoanalysis. For example, both perspectives advocate a split subjectivity, emphasize the centrality of language and interpretation and are concerned with the relationship between individual and society (see Billig, 1997b; Parker, 1998). The psychoanalytic work of Jaques Lacan in particular has proved influential for feminist and social constructionist theorists working in the areas of gender and sexuality (e.g. Frosh, 1999; Hollway, 1989; Walkerdine, 1991). Lacan highlighted the role of language and culture in producing a subjectivity at once social and emotional. Briefly, the child enters the male-centred Symbolic or cultural order and is dis/placed within positions of gender and sexuality, but to take up these social roles pre-Oedipal infantile desires must be repressed (e.g. a boy must renounce his desire for the mother – and femininity generally). Identity is therefore bound up with loss and (unconscious) desire for a return to earlier fulfilment persists and punctuates the self.

Box 10.3   Subjectivity as defensive and discursive (Hollway, 1984)

According to Hollway (1984; 1989), people are not simply produced by discourse but rather actively identify with (or reject) particular subject positions among those on offer. The 'investment' shown in positions will not necessarily be conscious or rational but may actually involve the operation of defence mechanisms. In applying this analysis to heterosexual relationships, Hollway makes use of Klein's defences of 'splitting', where the 'object' (i.e. person) is divided into good and bad, and 'projection', in which feelings or desires denied by the subject are attributed to another person. These defences are construed as 'relational', as having implications for how the other in a relationship is seen. In the case of projection, for example, a man might locate his own (repressed) feelings of vulnerability on to the woman, thereby constructing her as weak or emotional and himself as strong and rational. Clearly such a manoeuvre is supported within discourses of gender difference which define masculinity and femininity differently, but cannot be reduced to the effects of these discourses since the individual will already have built up a unique, biographical and largely unconscious set of meanings pertaining to gender difference from childhood. Thus, discourse/s used by individuals will be partially informed by the anxieties and wishes evoked during interpersonal interactions, producing subject positions for self and others which variably reinforce and disrupt those provided by prevailing discourse.

So, Lacan's account emphasizes the connections between language and desire and opens up possibilities for social constructionist writers to incorporate an emotional or experiential dimension to human social interaction. What remains to be worked out, however, is how to combine aspects of discourse analysis and psychoanalysis in practice. For example, can psychoanalytic concepts be used in conjunction with discourse perspectives in order to analyse talk and text? One possibility here relates to defence mechanisms. Instead of regarding defence mechanisms as intra-individualistic practices, as Freud suggested, a more social view would see these as interpersonal, as negotiated in conversation with others (Hollway, 1984). Projection, for example, can be said to operate where feelings and ideas felt to be problematic or taboo are relocated to others, even the targets of the problematic statements. Consider discursive work on prejudice (see Chapter 9) which has studied how people often deny or ward off potential accusations of prejudice and re-place prejudice with the minority groups themselves (i.e. 'blaming the victims'). Such discursive activity could be read as a form of social or conversational projection, working to protect views perceived to be taboo. A lot more work is required in this area, but it is worth knowing that aspects of critical social psychology, discourse analysis and social constructionism are being fruitfully questioned by sympathetic writers and that efforts are being made to forge theories and practices which provide ever more eloquent and convincing accounts of human experience.

Summary

In attempting to introduce students to the arena of critical social psychology, it is perhaps inevitable that this book has overlooked or smoothed over some of the complexities and contradictions which are present. By contrasting critical social psychology with 'traditional' or 'mainstream' social psychology we have probably created the impression of a concerted and homogeneous alternative force. This image has perhaps been reinforced by our adherence to the format of conventional social psychology textbooks which cover a range of topics such as social influence, prejudice and gender. As well, this structure might serve to suggest clear boundaries between topics when we would actually wish to emphasize the opposite, i.e. that research questions and explanations regarding 'prejudice' might be very similar to those surrounding 'sexualities' (with both perhaps concentrating on discourses which define 'the other'). Similarly, by offering a dedicated chapter on methodology we do not wish to separate out theory from method – we have sought to continually underscore how 'knowledge' is constructed within particular social contexts and therefore always is partial and transitory.

In this last chapter, we hope to have illustrated diversity within critical social psychology by pointing up some issues and debates which inform current thinking, some of which have prompted intense disagreements. The commitment to challenging conventional psychological wisdom is clearly enacted in different ways by different theorists and researchers. Although the preoccupation with discourse is a defining feature of most critical work as we have shown in the book, an exclusive focus on language is increasingly rejected as attempts are made to theorise political and personal 'realities' by drawing on approaches such as structuralism and psychodynamics. Such contributions facilitate healthy and lively discussion and serve to illustrate the depth and breadth of critical social psychology. As the interest in critical social psychology grows further, certain challenges and opportunities are presented. In particular, there is a danger that critical social psychology may become sanitized and institutionalized as just another brand of psychology amongst a variety of alternatives. But by continuing to resist the discipline of psychology and by reflexively questioning the form/s and purpose/es of critical social psychology, we can help ensure a dynamic, stimulating and significant project.

Postscript

We hope that this book has proved a stimulating and rewarding introduction to critical social psychology and related fields. In attempting
to make complex concepts and debates accessible, we have probably
not done justice to the broad and fragmented arena of critical social
psychology, but in pursuing the recommended readings alongside this
preliminary text you will undoubtedly have attained a firm grasp of
the material. Critical social psychology does not lend itself naturally
to clear and unproblematic teaching or writing and our own experience of teaching critical social psychology and writing this text would
reinforce this view. Perhaps in the future you will take on other
'critical' courses during your studies and will have the opportunity to
conduct a research project informed by critical literature and using
methods such as discourse analysis. Chapter 3 on methods is an obvious starting place, but you would do well to consult other texts on
(qualitative) research methods in general and discourse analysis in
particular (e.g. Burman and Parker, 1993; Hayes, 1997).

It is also a good idea to consult a range of journal articles where
critical work is published. Journals such as *Discourse & Society* and
Feminism & Psychology are fine places to start, but it is worth brows-
ing other sociological and inter-disciplinary periodicals (e.g. *Sociological Review*; *Theory & Psychology*). As well, new dedicated critical
titles are starting to appear, such as the *Annual Review of Critical
Psychology*, the *International Journal of Critical Psychology* and *Radical Psychology*. The latter is also published on the internet and is part
of a larger website devoted to the presentation and discussion of critical issues in psychology and society (http://www.uis.edu/~radpsy/).

There are other critical social psychology websites which serve
similar functions, notably at the Centre for Critical Psychology in
Sydney (http://www.nepean.uws.edu.au/histories/ccp/) and links to
other related sites are easy to locate. One of the advantages of these
sites is the advice and encouragement offered to students and researchers interested in pursuing critical goals at work and in society
generally.

Glossary

Agency   Emphasizes individuals as active in negotiating their social worlds and directly challenges traditional notions of the individual as a passive recipient of social dictates and regulations.

Aggression   This a broad term that situates aggression not in the actions of the individual but rather as a set of social, cultural and historically located activities.

Androgyny   An androgynous individual is said to possess high levels of both 'masculine' and 'feminine' characteristics, but Bem's (1974) concept has been criticized for failing to account for the social construction of gender.

Collectivism   Cultural ideals prioritizing the group over the individual as expressed in norms such as duty and self-discipline common in 'Eastern' societies (contrast with Western individualism).

Compulsory heterosexuality   A term used to challenge prevalent representations of heterosexuality as 'natural' and to encourage notions of heterosexuality as socially constructed and managed.

Conformity   Within critical social psychology, conformity is redefined as a socially produced and managed activity. This is in contrast to traditional social psychological perspectives which define conformity at the level of the individual.

Continuum of sexual violence   In contrast to the traditional definitions of sexual violence as rape, the continuum emphasizes the everyday abuse of women (and some men) through sexist jokes, harassment, marital rape, domestic violence and murder.

Death of the self   A phrase which conveys widespread critique or 'deconstruction' of the psychological subject (the self as a discrete, rational and consistent entity) in favour of a dynamic, dispersed and socialized version of selfhood.

Deconstructionism   A joining together of destruction and construction which marks a critical stripping away of assumptions underlying a 'text' (e.g. a theory).

Determinism   A criticism levelled at various theories in social psychology which present the individual as shaped (or 'determined') by forces outside their control.

Discourse analysis A general term applied liberally to various forms of textual analysis, but the term 'discourse' is often traced to Foucault and associated with the identification of 'top-down' historical/cultural representations (e.g. discourses of medicine, science, individualism, etc.).

Empiricism A commitment to gathering data in a systematic manner in order to produce 'valid' knowledge.

Essentialism A view proclaiming the existence of an 'essential' core within individuals (and things) which can be identified; it has been used to argue that men and women are 'naturally' different.

Female aggression This term is used to challenge traditional representations of women as passive and non-violent and rather to highlight that, like men, women use violence for a number of reasons including to construct identities and maintain social positions.

Feminisms A recent term which highlights differences and debates within feminism in the light of the increasing range of experiences and positions articulated by women.

Football hooliganism Critical perspectives situate football hooliganism within its wider cultural and social contexts, as a range of complex social activities (dress codes, drinking, team rivalry) through which social identity, power and status is negotiated.

Homophobia Homophobia refers to practices that oppress gay, lesbian and bi-sexual people and derives from discourses that represent heterosexuality as the only natural, normal and acceptable sexuality.

Individualism A focus on the individual or parts of individuals (e.g. memory systems, genes, etc.), the main unit of analysis found in mainstream social psychological theories.

Institutional prejudice This refers to the many ways in which governments, churches, businesses, the media and other institutions discriminate against people on the basis of gender, sexuality, age, race, ethnicity etc. A central aspect of such practices is the desire to protect the status quo and maintain the positions of those in power.

Interpretative repertoire Used by Potter and Wetherell (1987) in their landmark text to signify a relatively discrete set of metaphors and images drawn upon in talk to construct a particular object (e.g. 'the self as an actor on the stage of life') and associated with their 'bottom-up' form of discourse analysis where individual creativity is apparent.

Masculinities Emphasizes the range of 'masculine' subject positions available to men in contemporary society; challenges the idea of masculinity as something fixed or essential.

'New' racism A term coined by Billig (1988), it refers to new more subtle types of racist activity where, in their talk, people often present racist sentiments while denying their prejudice at the same time.

Oedipal complex A Freudian term used to describe the feelings of hatred young children experience for their mother around the age of 3 or 4.

Positivism A belief in (natural) science as a positive social force capable of generating sound knowledge and moving society forward.

Post-modernism Often used alongside or as a substitute term for post-structuralism and signals a break with 'modernist' ideals such as truth, meaning and progress in favour of celebrating diverse (and equally valid) perspectives.

Post-structuralism A scepticism towards claims about underlying 'reality' such as those found in structuralist theories and a view of meaning as multi-faceted, partial and debatable.

Prejudice This term refers to oppressive social activities against an individual or individuals. In contrast to traditional psychological definitions of prejudice, critical definitions explicitly recognize the socially legitimized and power dimensions associated with prejudiced activities.

'Queer' theory A recent theoretical paradigm that aims to destabilize social norms and practices which present heterosexuality as natural and correct.

Realism A commitment to some notion of the 'real', whether this is said to exist independently of discourse or bound up with discourse; 'critical realists' accept constructionist arguments but argue that some constructions refer to reality (e.g. ethnic minorities as oppressed).

Reductionism An objection to mainstream psychological methods which tend to empty or reduce concepts of their meaning in order to render them measurable.

Reflexivity A practice popular with qualitative and many critical researchers whereby the constructed nature of one's analysis is made visible through highlighting personal and theoretical ideas which have informed the research process and outcomes.

Relativism A position following from post-structuralism and constructionism which rejects established notions of truth and reality and which, some argue, may lead to an inability to convincingly advocate or apply a particular political stance.

Saturated self A view of the self as penetrated by the many images, messages and fragments projected by contemporary media (e-mail, mobile phones, advertising, satellite television, etc.) and therefore chaotic and unpredictable, associated with Gergen (1991).

Sex roles Social psychological concept which explains gender (difference) in terms of socialization rather than biology but which neglects power relations and discourse.

Sexism Discourses and practices used to construct wo/men as inferior.

Sexology The scientific study of human sexual functioning and behaviour. Sexuality as an innate characteristic of human development forms a central assumption of this paradigm.

Sexual invert A term coined by Ellis to define homosexual individuals as biologically abnormal.

Slag A complex, derogatory term (predominately applied to women) and used to control sexual/social identities and activities.

Social constructionism A broad perspective which locates meaning within social/ linguistic processes, emphasises a critique of 'common sense' and highlights the plurality of constructions or interpretations.

Social control This term explicitly recognizes the functions of conformity/obedience as a means of controlling the social practices of populations.

Structuralism Explains human behaviour in terms of 'structures', which can be 'external', such as 'capitalism', 'patriarchy' or language, or internal, such as the unconscious, cognitive or biological systems.

Subject positions Those 'slots' made available by discourses which people may take up, re-work or reject, depending on resources and circumstances.

Subjectivity A term which avoids the individualism and realism implied in terms such as 'personality' and which emphasizes the self as an almost continuous process of construction.

Subversion Highlights one of the ways in which individuals resist oppressive social practices – that is, by re-working taken-for-granted social representations to produce more positive social meanings.

Working-class femininities Emphasizes the complex interaction of social class and gender in identity negotiation.

References

Adlam, D., Henriques, J., Rose, N., Salfield, A., Venn, C. and Walkerdine, V. (1977) 'Psychology, ideology and the human subject', *Ideology & Consciousness*, 1: 5–56.

Adorno, T.W., Frenkel-Brunswick, E., Levinson, D.J. and Sanford, N. (1950) *The Authoritarian Personality*, New York: Harper Row.

Allport, G.W. (1968) 'The historical background of modern social psychology', in G. Lindzey and E. Aronson (eds), *The Handbook of Social Psychology* (2nd edition, vol. 1), Reading, Mass: Addison-Wesley.

Althusser, L. (1984) *Essays on Ideology*, London: Verso.

Amir, M. (1971) *Patterns of Forcible Rape*, Chicago: University of Chicago Press.

Anderson, R. (1988) *The Power and the Word: Language, Power and Change*, London: Paladin.

Archer, J. and Lloyd, B.B. (1985) *Sex and Gender*, Cambridge: Cambridge University Press.

Argyris, C. (1975) 'Dangers in applying results from experimental social psychology', *American Psychologist*, 30: 469–85.

Armistead, N. (1974) *Reconstructing Social Psychology*, Harmondsworth: Penguin.

Armstrong, G. (1998) *Football Hooligans: Knowing the Score*, New York: Berg.

Aronson, E. (1988) *The Social Animal* (5th edition), New York: Freeman.

Asch, S. (1952) *Social Psychology*, Englewood Cliffs: Prentice-Hall.

Austin, J. (1962) *How to Do Things with Words*, London: Oxford University Press.

Ballaster, R., Beetham, M. Frazer, E. and Hebron, S. (1991) *Women's Worlds: Ideology, Femininity and the Woman's Magazine*, Basingstoke: Macmillan.

Bandura, A. (1973) *Aggression: A Social Learning Analysis*, New Jersey: Prentice-Hall.

Bandura, A. (1977) *Social Learning Theory*, Englewood Cliffs: Prentice-Hall.

Bandura, A. (1983) 'Psychological mechanisms in aggression', in R. Geen and L. Donnerstein (eds), *Aggression: Theoretical and Empirical Reviews*, vol. 1, New York: Academic Press.

Banister, P., Burman, E., Parker, I., Taylor, M. and Tindall, C. (1994) *Qualitative Methods in Psychology: A Research Guide*, Buckingham: Open University Press.

Barker, M. and Petley, J. (1997) *Ill-Effects: The Media/Violence Debate*, London: Routledge.

Barker, R., Dembo, T. and Lewin, K. (1941) 'Imitation of film-mediated aggressive models', *Journal of Abnormal and Social Psychology*, 66: 3–11.

Baron, A. (1977) *Human Aggression*, New York: Plenum.

Baron, R.A. and Byrne, D. (1999) *Social Psychology: Understanding Human Interaction*, Boston: Allyn & Bacon.

Bateson, P. (1989) 'Is aggression instinctive?', in J. Groebel and R.A. Hinde (eds), *Aggression and War: Their Biological and Social Bases,* New York: Cambridge University Press.

Baumeister, R.F. (1988) 'Should we stop studying sex differences altogether?', *American Psychologist*, 42: 1092–5.

Bem, S.L. (1974) 'The measurement of psychological androgyny', *Journal of Consulting and Clinical Psychology*, 42: 155–62.

Bem, S.L. (1981) 'Gender schema theory: a cognitive assessment of sex-typing', *Psychological Review*, 88: 354–64.

Bem, S. (1985) 'Androgyny and gender schema theory: a conceptual and empirical integration', in T.N. Sonderegger (ed.), *Nebraska Symposium on Motivation 1984: Psychology and Gender*, Lincoln, NE.: University of Nebraska Press.

Bem, S. (1987) 'Gender schema theory and the romantic tradition', in P. Shaver and C. Hendrick (eds), *Sex and Gender*, Newbury Park: Sage.

Bem, S.L., Martyna, W. and Watson, C. (1976) 'Sex-typing and androgyny: further explorations of the expressive domain, *Journal of Personality & Social Psychology*, 33: 48–54.

Benbow, C.P. and Stanley, J.C. (1980) 'Sex differences in mathematical ability: fact or artifact?', *Science*, 210: 1262–4

Berger, P.L. and Luckman, T. (1967) *The Social Construction of Reality*, Harmondsworth: Penguin.

Berkowitz, L. (1962) *Aggression: A Social Psychological Analysis*, New York: McGraw-Hill.

Berkowitz, L. (1974) 'Some determinants of impulsive aggression: role of mediated associations with reinforcement for aggression', *Psychological Review*, 81(2): 165–76.

Berkowitz, L. and Geen, R. (1966) 'Film violence and the cue properties of available targets', *Journal of Personality and Social Psychology*, 3: 525–30.

Bhavnani, K. K. and Phoenix, A. (1994) 'Special Issue: Shifting Identities Shifting Racisms', *Feminism & Psychology*, 4 (1).

Billig, M. (1976) *Social Psychology and Intergroup Relations*, London: Academic Press.

Billig, M. (1978) *Fascists: A Social Psychological View of the National Front*, London: Harcourt Brace Jovanovich.

Billig, M. (1982) *Ideology and Social Psychology*, Oxford: Blackwell.

Billig, M. (1985) 'Prejudice, categorization and particularization: from a perceptual to a rhetorical approach', *European Journal of Social Psychology*, 15: 79–103.

Billig, M. (1988) 'The notion of prejudice: some rhetorical and ideological aspects', *Text*, 8: 91–110.

Billig, M. (1990) 'Rhetoric of social psychology', in I. Parker and J. Shotter (eds), *Deconstructing Social Psychology*, London: Routledge.

Billig, M. (1992) *Talking of the Royal Family*, London: Routledge.

Billig, M. (1995) *Banal Nationalism*, London: Sage.

Billig, M. (1997a) 'Rhetorical and discursive analysis: how families talk about the royal family', in N. Hayes (ed.), *Doing Qualitative Analysis in Psychology*, London: Psychology Press.

Billig, M. (1997b) 'The dialogic unconscious: psychoanalysis, discursive psychology and the nature of repression', *British Journal of Social Psychology*, 36(2): 139–60.

Billig, M., Condor, S., Edwards, D., Gane, M., Middleton, D. and Radley, A. (1988) *Ideological Dilemmas: A Social Psychology of Everyday Thinking*, London: Sage.

Blakemore, J., Young, J., Dilorio, J. and Fairchild, D. (1997) 'Exploring the campus climate for women faculty', in N. Benokraitus (ed.), *Subtle Sexism: Current Practices and Prospects for Change*, London: Sage.

Bleier, R. (1984) *Science and Gender: A Critique of Biology and Its Theories on Women*, London: Pergamon.

Bond, M.H. and Cheung, T.S. (1983) 'The spontaneous self-concept of college students in Hong Kong, Japan and the United States', *Journal of Cross-Cultural Psychology*, 14: 153–71.

Boyle, M. (1996) ' "Schizophrenia" re-evaluated', in T. Heller, J. Reynolds, R. Gomm, R. Muston and S. Pattison (eds), *Mental Health Matters: A Reader*, Houndmills: Macmillan Press Ltd.

Brehm, S. and Kassin, S. (1993) *Social Psychology*, Houghton Mifflin.

Brewster-Smith, M. (1983) 'The shaping of American social psychology: a personal perspective from the periphery', *Personality and Social Psychology*, 9: 165–80.

Brittan, A. (1987) *Masculinity and Power*, London: Blackwell.

Brown, H. (1996) 'Themes in experimental research on groups from 1930s to the 1990s', in M. Wetherell (ed.), *Identities, Groups and Social Issues*, London: The Open University.

Brown, L. (1997) 'New voices, new visions: towards a lesbian/gay paradigm for psychology,' in M. Gergen and S. Davis (eds), *Towards a New Psychology of Gender: A Reader*. London: Routledge.

Brown, P. (1974) *Radical Psychology*, London: Tavistock.

Brown, S.R. (1980) *Political Subjectivity: Applications of Q Methodology in Political Science*, New Haven: Yale University Press.

Brown, S.D. and Pujol, J. with Curt, B. (1998) 'As one in a web? Discourse, materiality and the place of ethics', in I. Parker (ed.), *Social Constructionism, Discourse and Realism*, London: Sage.

Brownmiller, S. (1976). *Against Our Will: Men, Women and Rape*, Harmonds-worth: Penguin.

Buckingham, D. (1993) 'Boys' talk: television and the policing of masculinity', in D. Buckingham (ed.), *Reading Audiences: Young People and the Media*, Manchester: Manchester University Press.

Burke, C. (1980) cited in Hudson, B. (1984) 'Femininity and adolescence', in A. McRobbie and M. Nava (eds), *Gender and Generation*, London: Macmillian.

Burman, E. (1990) *Feminists and Psychological Practice*, London: Sage.

Burman, E. (1991) 'What discourse is not', *Philosophical Psychology*, 4(3): 325–42.

Burman, E. (1998) *Deconstructing Feminist Psychology*, London: Sage.

Burman, E. and Parker, I. (1993) *Discourse Analytic Research. Repertoires and Readings of Text in Action*, London: Routledge.

Burman, E., Alldred, P., Bewley, C., Goldberg, B., Heenan, C., Marks, D., Marshall, J., Taylor, K., Ullah, R. and Warner, S. (1995) *Challenging Women: Psychology's Exclusions, Feminist Possibilities*, Buckingham: Open University Press.

Burr, V. (1995) *An Introduction to Social Constructionism*, London: Routledge.

Burr, V. (1998) *Gender and Social Psychology*, London: Routledge.

Buss, A. (1961) *The Psychology of Aggression*, New York: Wiley.

Butler, J. (1990) *Gender Trouble: Feminism and the Subversion of Identity*, London: Routledge.

Butler, J. (1993) *Bodies That Matter: On the Discursive Limits of Sex*, New York: Routledge.

Cairns, E. and Mercer, G. (1984) 'Social identity in Northern Ireland', *Human Relations*, 37(12): 1095–102.

Cameron, D. (1992) *Feminism and Linguistic Theory* (second edition), Basing-stoke: Macmillan.

Canaan, J. (1996) ' "One thing leads to another": drinking, fighting and working-class masculinities', in M. Mac An Ghaill (ed.), *Understanding Masculinities: Social Relations and Cultural Arenas*, Milton Keynes: Open University Press.

Caprara, G., Barbaranelli, C., Pastorelli and Perugini, M. (1994) 'Individual differences in the study of human aggression', *Aggressive Behaviour*, 1: 61–74.

Cartwright, D. (1979) 'Contemporary social psychology in historical perspective', *Social Psychology Quarterly*, 42: 82–93.

Cashmore, E. (1987) cited in Wetherell, M. (ed.) (1996) *Identities, Groups and Social Issues*, London: Sage.

Castillejo, I. de (1973) *Knowing Woman: A Feminine Psychology*, London: Hodder & Stoughton.

Chodorow, N. (1978) *The Reproduction of Mothering*, Berkeley: University of California Press.

Choi, P.Y.L. (1994) 'Women's raging hormones', in P.Y.L. Choi and P. Nicolson (eds), *Female Sexuality: Psychology, Biology and Social Context*, New York: Harvester Wheatsheaf.

Cixous, H. (1975) cited in Minsky, R. (1996) *Psychoanalysis and Gender*, London: Routledge.

Collier, A. (1998) 'Language, practice and realism', in I. Parker (ed.), *Social Constructionism, Discourse and Realism*, London: Sage.

Condor, S. (1988) ' "Race Stereotypes" and racist discourse', *Text,* 8: 69–91.

Connell, R.W. (1987) *Gender and Power*, Cambridge: Polity.

Connell, R.W. (1995) *Masculinities*, Cambridge: Polity.

Coyle, A. and Kitzinger, C. (2001) *Lesbian and Gay Psychology*, Leicester: BPS Books.

Curt, B. C. (1994) *Textuality and Tectonics: Troubling Social and Psychological Science*, Buckingham: Open University Press.

Dahrendorf, R. (1973) *Homo Sociologicus*, London: Routledge & Kegan Paul.

Daly, M. (1978) *Gyn/Ecology: The Metaethics of Radical Feminism*, London: The Woman's Press.

Dancey, C. (1994) 'Lesbian Identities', in P. Choi, P. Nicolson, B. Alder, C. Dancey, L. Gannon, E. McNeill and J. Ussher (eds), *Female Sexuality*, New York: Harvester Wheatsheaf.

Daniluk, J. (1991) 'Female sexuality: an enigma', *Canadian Journal of Counselling,* 25(4): 433–46.

Davies, B. and Harre, R. (1990) 'Positioning: the discursive production of selves', *Journal for the Theory of Social Behaviour*, 20(1): 43–63.

Day, K. (2000) Women and alcohol: Discourses around femininity and pleasure in contemporary Britain', unpublished doctoral thesis, Sheffield: Hallam University.

Deutsch, M. and Gerrard, H.B. (1955) 'A study of normative and informational social influence upon individual judgement', *Journal of Abnormal and Social Psychology,* 51: 629–36.

Dollard, J., Doob, L., Miller, N., Mowrer, O. and Sears, R. (1939). *Frustration and Aggression*, New Haven: Yale University Press.

Ebbesen, E. G., Duncan, B. and Konecni, V.J (1975). 'Effects of content of verbal aggression on future verbal aggression: a field experiment', *Journal of Experimental Social Psychology*, 11: 192–204.

Edley, N. and Wetherell, N. (1995) *Men in Perspective. Practice, Power and Identity*, Hemel Hempstead: Prentice Hall/Harvester Wheatsheaf..

Edwards, D. and Potter, J. (1992) *Discursive Psychology*, London: Sage.

Edwards, D. and Potter, J. (1993) 'Language and causation: a discursive action model of description and attribution', *Psychological Review*, 100: 23–41.

Edwards, D., Ashmore, M. and Potter, J. (1995) 'Death and furniture: the rhetoric, politics and theory of bottom line arguments against relativism', *History of the Human Sciences*, 8(2): 25–44.

Ellis, H. (1913) *Studies in the Psychology of Sex*, F.A. Davis.

Ellis. H (1936) *Studies in the Psychology of Sex*, New York: Random House.

Eysenck, H.J. (1952) *The Scientific Study of Personality*, London: Routledge.

Eysenck, H. and Nias, D. (1980). *Sex, Violence and the Media*, London: Paladin.

Faderman, L. (1991). *Odd Girls and Twilight Lovers*, London: Penguin.

Fagot, B. (1974) 'Sex differences in toddlers' behaviour and parental reaction', *Developmental Psychology*, 4: 554–8.

Faludi, S. (1992) *Backlash: The Undeclared War Against Women*, London: Chatto & Windus.

Ferguson, A. (1982) 'Patriarchy, sexual identity and the sexual revolution', in N. Keohane, Z. Rosaldo and B. Gelpi (eds), *Feminist Theory: A Critique of Ideology*, Chicago: University of Chicago Press.

Ferguson, M. (1983) *Forever Feminine: Women's Magazines and the Cult of Femininity*, London: Heinemann.

Feshbach, S. (1964) 'The function of aggression and the regulation of aggressive drive', *Psychological Review*, 71: 57–72.

Figes, E. (1970) *Patriarchal Attitudes*, New York: Stein & Day.

Fine, M. (1988) 'Sexuality, schooling and adolescent females: the missing discourse of desire', *Harvard Educational Review*, 58: 29–53.

Fishwick, N. (1986) *From Clegg to Clegg House: The Official Century of the Sheffield and Hallamshire County Football Association 1886–1986*, Sheffield: The Sheffield and Hallamshire County Football Association.

Fishwick, N. (1989) *English Football and Society*, Manchester: Manchester University Press.

Ford, A. (1985) *Men*, London: Weidenfeld & Nicolson.

Foucault, M. (1972) *The Archeology of Knowledge*, London: Tavistock.

Foucault, M. (1976) *The History of Sexuality*, Vol. 1, London: Allen.

Foucault, M. (1977) *Discipline and Punish: The Birth of the Prison*, Harmondsworth: Peregrine.

Foucault, M. (1978) *The History of Sexuality: An Introduction*, London: Penguin Press.

Foucault, M. (1980) *Power/Knowledge*, Sussex: Harvester Press.

Foucault, M. (1988) *The Care of the Self. Vol.3: The History of Sexuality*, London: Penguin Press.

Fox, D. and Prilleltensky, I. (1997) *Critical Psychology: An Introduction*, London: Sage.

Freeman, M. (1993) *Re-writing the Self*, London: Routledge.

Freud, S. (1908) 'Character and anal eroticism', in J. Strachey (ed.), *Standard Edition of the Complete Psychological Works of Sigmund Freud Vol. 9*, London: Hogarth Press.

Freud, S. (1920) *Beyond the Pleasure Principle*, in J. Strachey (ed.) *Standard Edition of the Complete Psychological Works of Sigmund Freud Vol. 18*, London: Hogarth Press.

Freud, S. (1923) *The Ego and the Id*, in J. Strachey (ed.) *Standard Edition of the Complete Psychological Works of Sigmund Freud Vol. 19*, London: Hogarth Press.

Freud, S. (1931) 'Female Sexuality', in J. Strachey (ed.), *Standard Edition of the Complete Psychological Works of Sigmund Freud, Vol. 21*, London: Hogarth Press.

Freud, S. (1933) *New Introductory Lectures on Psychoanalysis*, London: Hogarth Press.

Friday, N. (1980) *Men in Love: Men's Sexual Fantasies*, New York: Arrow Books.

Frodi, A., Macaulay, J. and Thome, P. (1977) 'Are women always less aggressive than men? A review of the experimental literature', *Psychological Bulletin*, 84(4): 634–61.

Frosh, S. (1987) *Psychology and Psychoanalysis*, London: Sage.

Frosh, S. (1993) 'The seeds of male sexuality', in J. Ussher and C. Baker (eds), *Psychological Perspectives on Sexual Problems*, London: Routledge.

Frosh, S. (1997) *For and Against Psychoanalysis*, London: Routledge.

Frosh, S. (1999) *The Politics of Psychoanalysis* (2nd edition). London: Macmillan.

Gallagher, A.M. (1988) 'Identity and ideology in Northern Ireland: a psychological perspective', *Irish Review*, 4(7): 7–14.

Garfinkel, H. (1967) *Studies in Ethnomethodology*, Englewood Cliffs: Prentice Hall.

Garvey, C. (1977) *Play*, Cambridge, MA: Harvard University Press.

Gavey, N. (1993). 'Technologies and effects of heterosexual coercion', in S. Wilkinson and C. Kitzinger (eds), *Heterosexuality: A Feminism & Psychology Reader*, London: Sage.

Gavey, N. (1997) 'Feminist poststructuralism and discourse analysis', in M. Gergen and S. Davis (eds), *Toward A New Psychology of Gender: A Reader*, London: Routledge.

Geen, R. (1978) 'The effects of attack and uncontrollable noise on aggression', *Journal of Research in Personality*, 12: 15–29.

Geen, R. (1990) *Human Aggression*, Milton Keynes: The Open University Press.

Geen, R., Stonner, D. and Shope, G. (1975) 'The facilitation of aggression by aggression: evidence against the catharsis hypothesis', *Journal of Personality and Social Psychology,* 31: 721–6.

Geertz, C. (1974) 'From the native's point of view: on the nature of anthropological understanding', in K. Basso and H. Selby (eds), *Meaning in Anthropology*, Albuquerque, NM: University of New Mexico Press.

Gergen, K.J. (1973) 'Social psychology as history', *Journal of Personality and Social Psychology*, 26: 309–20.

Gergen, K. (1989) 'Warranting voice and the elaboration of the self', in J. Shotter and K.J. Gergen (eds), *Texts of Identity*, London: Sage.

Gergen, K. (1991) *The Saturated Self: Dilemmas of Identity in Contemporary Life*, New York: Basic Books.

Gergen, K. (1999) *An Invitation to Social Construction*, London: Sage.

Giddens, A. (1991) *Modernity and Self-Identity*, Cambridge: Polity.

Gill, R. (1993) 'Justifying injustice: broadcaster's accounts of inequality', in E. Burman and I. Parker (eds), *Discourse Analytic Research: Repertoires and Readings of Texts in Action*, London: Routledge.

Gill, R. (1995) 'Relativism, reflexivity and politics: interrogating discourse analysis from a feminist perspective', in S. Wilkinson and C. Kitzinger (eds), *Feminism and Discourse*, London: Sage.

Gilligan, C. (1982) *In a Different Voice*, Cambridge, Mass.: Harvard University Press.

Goffman, E. (1959) *The Presentation of Self in Everyday Life*, New York: Doubleday.

Goldberg, S. (1977) *The Inevitability of Patriarchy*, London: Temple-Smith.

Gough, B. (1998) 'Men and the discursive reproduction of sexism: repertoires of difference and equality', *Feminism & Psychology*, 8(1): 25–49.

Gough, B. (2001) 'Heterosexual masculinity and homophobia', in A. Coyle and C. Kitzinger (eds), *Lesbian and Gay Psychology*, Leicester: BPS Books.

Gough, B. and Edwards, G. (1998) 'The beer talking: four lads, a carry out and the reproduction of masculinities', *The Sociological Review*, 46(3): 409–435.

Gough, B. and Peace, P. (2000) 'Reconstructing gender in the 1990s: men as victims', *Gender & Education*, 12(3): 385–99.

Gough, B., Robinson, S., Kremer, J. and Mitchell, R. (1992) 'The social psychology of intergroup conflict: an appraisal of Northern Ireland research', *Canadian Psychology*, 33(3): 645–51.

Gould, J. and Gould, C. (1989) *Sexual Selection*, New York: Scientific American Library.

Gray, J. (1993) *Men are from Mars, Women are from Venus : A Practical Guide for Improving Communication and Getting What You Want in Your Relationships*, London: Thorsons.

Gray, J.A. (1981) 'A biological basis for the sex differences in achievement in science?', in A. Kelly (ed.) *The Missing Half: Girls and Science Education*, Manchester: Manchester University Press.

Griffin, C. (1991) 'Experiencing power: dimensions of gender, 'race' and class', *BPS Psychology of Women Newsletter*, (8): 43–58.

Griffin, C. (1993) *Representations of Youth: The Study of Youth and Adolescence in Britain and America*, Cambridge: Polity Press.

Griffin, C. (1995) *Feminism, Social Psychology and Qualitative Research*, The Psychologist, BPS, March.

Gross, G. (1974) 'Unnatural selection', in N. Armistead (ed.), *Reconstructing Social Psychology*, Harmondsworth: Penguin.

Guillaumin, C. (1995) *Racism, Sexism, Power and Ideology*, London: Routledge.

Gunter, B. (1986) *Television and Sex Role-Stereotyping*, London: John Libbey.

Hall, S. (1990) 'Cultural identity and diasporia', in J. Rutherford (ed.), *Identity: Community, Culture and Difference*, London, Lawrence & Wishart.

Halpern, D.F. (1992) *Sex Differences in Cognitive Abilities* (2nd edition), Hillsdale, NJ: Erlbaum.

Hamilton, D. and Trolier, T. (1986) 'Stereotypes and stereotyping: an overview of the cognitive approach', in J. Dovidio and S. Gaertner (eds), *Prejudice, Discrimination and Racism*, Orlando: Academic Press.

Hammersley, M. (1989) *The Dilemma of Qualitative Method: Herbert Blumer and the Chicago Tradition*, London: Routledge.

Hampson, E. (1990) 'Variation in sex related cognitive abilities across the menstrual cycle', *Brain & Cognition*, 14: 26–43.

Hare-Mustin, R.T. (1991) 'Sex, lies and headaches: the problem is power', in T.J. Godrich (ed.), *Women and Power: Perspectives for Therapy*, New York: Norton.

Hare-Mustin, R.T. and Marecek, J. (1997) 'Abnormal and clinical psychology: the politics of madness', in D. Fox and I. Prilleltensky (eds), *Critical Psychology: An Introduction*, London: Sage.

Harré, R. (1979) *Social Being: A Theory for Social Psychology*, Oxford: Basil Blackwell.

Harré, R. (1989) 'Language games and the texts of identity', in J. Shotter and K.J. Gergen (eds), *Texts of Identity*, London: Sage.

Harré, R. and Secord, P.F. (1972) *The Explanation of Social Behaviour*, Oxford: Basil Blackwell.

Hayes, N. (1997) *Doing Qualitative Analysis in Pschology*, London: Psychology Press.

Heelas, P. (1986) 'Emotion talk across cultures', in R. Harré (ed.), *The Social Construction of Emotion*, Oxford: Blackwell.

Heller, T., Reynolds, J., Gomm, R., Muston, R. and Pattison, S. (1996) *Mental Health Matters: A Reader*, Houndmills: Macmillan Press Ltd.

Henriques, J., Hollway, W., Urwin, C., Venn, C., and Walkerdine, V. (1984) *Changing the Subject: Psychology, Social Regulation and Subjectivity*, London: Methuen.

Hepburn, A. (2000) 'On the alleged incompatibility between feminism and relativism', *Feminism & Psychology*, 10(1).

Herzlich, C. (1973) *Health and Illness: A Social Psychological Analysis*, London: Academic Press.

Hogg, M.A. and Abrams, D. (1988) *Social Identifications: A Social Psychology of Intergroup Behaviour and Group Processes*, London: Routledge.

Holland, J.,Ramazanoglu, C. and Scott, S. (1990) *Sex, Risk, Danger: AIDS Education Policy and Young Women's Sexuality,* London: The Tufnell Press.

Holland, J., Ramazanoglu, C., Scott, S., Sharpe, S. and Thomson, R. (1991) *Pressure, Resistance and Empowerment: Young Women and the Negotiation of Safer Sex*, London: The Tufnell Press

Hollway, W. (1983) 'Heterosexual sex, power and desire for the other', in S. Cartledge and J. Ryan (eds), *Sex and Love: New Thoughts on Old Contradictions*, London: Women's Press.

Hollway, W. (1984) 'Gender difference and the production of subjectivity', in J. Henriques, W. Hollway, C. Urwin, C. Venn and V. Walkerdine (eds), *Changing the Subject: Psychology, Social Regulation and Subjectivity*, London: Methuen.

Hollway, W. (1989) *Subjectivity and Method in Psychology: Gender, Meaning and Science*, London: Sage.

Holly, L. (1989) *Girls and Sexuality*, Milton Keynes: Open University Press.

Horney, K. (1924a) 'On the genesis of the castration complex in women', in J. Miller (ed.), *Psychoanalysis and Women*, New York: Brunner/Mazel.

Horney, K. (1924b) 'On the genesis of the castration complex in woman', *International Journal of Psychoanalysis*, 5: 50–60.

Housden, M. (1997) *Resistance & Conformity in the Third Reich*, London: Routledge.

Huesmann, L.R. and Eron, L.D. (eds) (1986) *Television and the Aggressive Child: A Cross-Cultural Comparison*, Mahwah, NJ: Lawrence Erlbaum.

Hutt, C. (1972) *Males and Females*, Harmondsworth: Penguin.

Ibáñez, T. (1990) 'Henri, Serge and the next generation', *BPS Social Psychology Newsletter*, no. 24: 5–14.

Ibáñez, T. and Íñiguez, L. (1997) *Critical Social Psychology*, London: Sage.

Imperato-McGinley, J., Peterson, R.E., Gautier, T and Sturla, E. (1979) 'Androgens and the evolution of male-gender identity among male pseudohermaphrodites with 5 alpha reductase deficiency, *New England Journal of Medicine*, 300: 1233–7.

Ingleby, D. (1972) 'Ideology and the human sciences: some comments on the role of reification in psychology and psychiatry', in T. Pateman (ed.), *Counter Course: A Handbook for Course Criticism*, Harmondsworth: Penguin.

Ingleby, D. (1985) 'Professionals as socializers: the "psy complex"', *Research in Law, Deviance and Social Control*, 7: 79–109.

Jackson, L., Gardner, P. and Sullivan, L. (1992) 'Explaining gender differences in self-pay expectations: social comparison standards and perceptions of fair play', *Journal of Applied Psychology*, 77: 651–63.

Jackson, M. (1984a) 'Sexology and the social construction of male sexuality (Havelock Ellis)', in L. Coveney (ed.), *The Sexuality Papers*, London: Hutchinson.

Jackson, M. (1984b) 'Sexology and the universalisation of male sexuality (from Ellis to Kinsey and Masters and Johnson)', in L. Coveney (ed.), *The Sexuality Papers*, London: Hutchinson.

Jackson, M. (1989) 'Sexuality and struggle: feminism, sexology and the social construction of sexuality', in C. Jones and P. Mahony (eds), *Learning Our Lines: Sexuality and Social Control in Education*, London: The Women's Press.

Jackson, M. (1994) *The Real Facts of Life: Feminism and the Politics of Female Sexuality 1850–1940*, London: Taylor & Francis.

Jackson, S. (1992) 'The amazing deconstructing woman', *Trouble and Strife*, 25: 25–31.

Jahoda, M., Lazarsfield, P.F. and Zeisel, H. (1972) *Marienthal: The Sociography of an Unemployed Community*, London: Tavistock (first published 1933).

Jaspers, J. (1986) 'Forum and focus: a personal view of European social psychology', *European Journal of Social Psychology*, 16: 343–9.

Jefferson, T. (1994) 'Theorising masculine subjectivity', in T. Newburn and E.A. Stanko (eds), *Just Boys Doing Business?*, London: Routledge.

Jeffreys, S. (1984) 'Free from the uninvited touch of man: women's campaigns around sexuality 1880–1914', in L. Coveney (ed.), *The Sexuality Papers*, London: Hutchinson.

Jeffreys, S. (1986) *The Spinster and her Enemies: Feminism and Sexuality 1880–1930*, London: Pandora.

Johnson, R.A. (1976) *She: Understanding Feminine Psychology*, New York: Harper & Row.

Johnson, T.A. (1987) 'Premenstrual syndrome as a western culture-specific disorder', *Culture, Medicine and Psychiatry*, 11: 337–56.

Jourard, S.M. (1972) 'Psychology for control and for liberation of humans', paper presented to the BPS Annual Conference, Nottingham.

Kaminer, D. and Dixon, J. (1997) 'The reproduction of masculinity: a discourse analysis of men's drinking talk', *South African Journal of Psychology*, 25(3): 168–74.

Kelly, L. (1988a) *Surviving Sexual Violence*, London: Polity Press.

Kelly, L. (1988b) 'How women define their experiences of violence', in K. Yllo and M. Bograd (eds), *Feminist Perspectives on Wife Abuse*, Newbury Park, CA: Sage.

Kimball, M. (1994) 'The worlds we live in: gender similarities and differences', *Canadian Psychology*, 35: 388–404.

Kimura, D. (1987) 'Are men's and women's brains really different?', *Canadian Psychology*, 28: 133–47.

Kirsta, A. (1994) *Deadlier than the Male: Aggression in Women*, Glasgow: HarperCollins.

Kitzinger, C. (1986) 'Introducing and developing Q as a feminist methodology: a study of accounts of lesbianism', in S. Wilkinson (ed.), *Feminist Social Psychology: Developing Theory and Practice*, Milton Keynes: Open University Press.

Kitzinger, C. (1987) *The Social Construction of Lesbianism*, London: Sage.

Kitzinger, C. (1994) 'Problematizing pleasure: radical feminist deconstructions of sexuality and power', in H.L. Radtke and H.J. Stam (eds), *Gender and Power*, London: Sage.

Kitzinger, C. (1997) 'Lesbian and gay psychology: a critical analysis', in D. Fox and I. Prilleltensky (eds), *Critical Psychology: An Introduction*, London: Sage.

Kitzinger, C. and Frith, H. (1999) 'Just say no? The use of conversation analysis in developing a feminist perspective on sexual refusal', *Discourse & Society*, 10(3): 293–316.

Kitzinger, C. and Wilkinson, S. (1997a) 'Validating women's experience? Dilemmas in feminist research', *Feminism & Psychology*, 7(4): 566–77.

Kitzinger, C. and Wilkinson, S. (1997b) 'Virgins and queers: rehabilitating heterosexuality', in M. Gergen and S. Davis (eds), *Towards a New Psychology of Gender: A Reader* (403–20), London: Routledge.

Kitzinger, C., Wilkinson, S. and Perkins, R. (1992) Special Issue on heterosexuality, *Feminism & Psychology*, 2(3).

Klama, J. (1988) *The Myth of the Beast Within*, New York: Wiley & Sons.

Kleiner, B. (1998) 'The modern racist ideology and its reproduction in "pseudo-argument" ', *Discourse & Society*, 9(2): 187–215

Kline, P. (1988) *Psychology Exposed*, London: Routledge.

Kohlberg, L (1969) 'Stage and sequence: the cognitive-developmental approach to socialization', in D.A. Goslin (ed.) *Handbook of Socialization Theory and Research*, Chicago: Rand McNally.

Kremer, J., Barry, R. and McNally, A. (1986) 'The misdirected letter and the quasi-questionnaire: unobtrusive measures of prejudice in Northern Ireland', *Journal of Applied Social Psychology*, 16(4): 303–9.

Kretschmer, E. (1925) *Physique and Character*, New York: Harcourt.

Kuhn, T. (1970) *The Structure of Scientific Revolutions* (2nd edition), Chicago: University of Chicago Press.

Kvale, S. (ed.) (1992) *Psychology and Postmodernism*, London: Sage.

La Framboise, T., Helye, A. and Ozer, E. (1990) 'Changing and diverse roles of women in American Indian cultures', *Sex Roles*, 22: 455–86.

Laing, R.D. (1960) *The Divided Self*, London: Tavistock.

Laing, R.D. (1967) *The Politics of Experience and The Bird of Paradise*, Harmondsworth: Penguin.

Lakoff, G. (1987) *Women, Fire and Dangerous Things: What Categories Reveal About the Mind*, Chicago: University of Chicago Press.

Larkin, J. and Popaleni, K. (1994) 'Heterosexual courtship violence and sexual harassment: the private and public control of young women', *Feminism & Psychology*, 4(2): 213–27.

Larsen, K. (1974) 'Conformity in the Asch experiment', *Journal of Social Psychology*, 94: 303–4.

Latane, B. and Darley, J.M. (1970) *The Unresponsive Bystander: Why Doesn't He Help?*, Englewood Cliffs, NJ: Prentice Hall.

Lather, P. (1988) 'Feminist perspectives on empowering research methodologies', *Women's Studies International Forum*, 11: 569–81.

Lather, P. (1992) 'Postmodernism and the human sciences', in S. Kvale (ed.), *Psychology & Postmodernism*, London: Sage.

Leahey, T.H. (1992) *A History of Psychology: Main Currents in Psychological Thought* (3rd edition), Englewood Cliffs: Prentice Hall.

Le Bon, G. (1895) cited in R. Stainton-Rogers, W. Stainton-Rogers and P. Stenner (1995) *Social Psychology: A Critical Agenda*, London: Polity Press.

Lees, S. (1993) *Sugar and Spice: Sexuality and Adolescent Girls*, London: Penguin.

Lees, S. (1998) *Ruling Passions: Sexual Violence, Reputation and the Law*, Milton Keynes: Open University Press.

Lippman, W. (1922) *Public Opinion*, New York: Harcourt Brace.

Lorenz, K. (1966) *On Aggression*, London: Methuen.

Lubek, I. (1997) 'Reflexively recycling social psychology: a critical autobiographical account of an evolving critical social psychological analysis of social psychology', in T. Ibáñez and L. Íñiguez (eds), *Critical Social Psychology*, London: Sage.

Mac an Ghaill, M. (ed.) (1996) *Understanding Masculinities: Social Relations and Cultural Arenas*, Milton Keynes: Open University Press.

Maccoby, E. and Jacklin, C.N. (1974) *The Psychology of Sex Differences*, London: Oxford University Press.

Mahony, P. (1985) cited in Hester, M. (1992) *Lewd Women and Wicked Witches: A Study of the Dynamics of Male Domination*, London: Routledge.

Markus, H. and Kitayama, S. (1991) 'Culture and the self: implications for cognition, emotion and motivation', *Psychological Review*, 98: 224–54.

Marsh, P. and Campbell, A. (1982) *Aggression and Violence*, Oxford: Blackwell.

Marsh, P., Rosser, E. and Harre, R. (1978) *The Rules of Disorder*, London: Routledge & Kegan Paul.

Masters, M.S. and Sanders, B. (1993) 'Is the gender difference in mental rotation disappearing?', *Behaviour Genetics*, 23: 337–41.

McCreanor, T. (1996) 'Why strengthen the city wall when the enemy has poisioned the well? An assay of anti-homosexual discourse in New Zealand', *Journal of Homosexuality*, 3: 75–105.

McFadden, M. (1995) 'Female Sexuality in the Second Decade of AIDS', unpublished doctoral thesis, The Queen's University, Belfast.

McFadden, M. and Sneddon, I. (1998) 'Sexuality', in K. Trew and J. Kremer (eds), *Gender and Psychology*, London: Arnold.

McGhee, P. (1996) 'Defining social psychology', in R. Sapsford (ed.), *Issues for Social Psychology*, Milton Keynes, The Open University.

McNaughten, P. (1993) 'Discourses of nature: argumentation and power', in E. Burman and I. Parker (eds), *Discourse Analytic Research*, London: Routledge.

McRobbie, A. (1991) *Feminism and Youth Culture: From Jackie to Just Seventeen*, London: Macmillan.

Mead, G.H. (1934) *Mind, Self & Society*, Chicago: University of Chicago Press.

Messner, M. (1997) *Politics of Masculinities: Men in Movements*, Thousand Oaks, CA: Sage.

Milgram, S. (1974) *Obedience to Authority: An Experimental View*, New York: Harper & Row.

Miller, G. (1969) 'Psychology as a means of promoting human welfare', *American Psychologist*, 24: 1063–75.

Miller, P. and Fowlkes, M. (1980) 'Social and behavioural constructions of female sexuality', *Signs: Journal of Women in Culture and Society*, 5(4): 256–73.

Millett, K. (1970) *Sexual Politics*, London: Virago.

Minard, R.D. (1952) 'Race relationships in the Pocahontas coal fields', *Journal of Social Issues*, 25: 29–44.

Minsky, R. (1996) *Psychoanalysis and Gender*, London: Routledge.

Mischel, W. (1966) 'A social learning view of sex differences in behaviour', in E.E. Maccoby (ed.), *The Development of Sex Differences*, Stanford, CA: Stanford University Press.

Mitchell, J. (1974) *Psychoanalysis and Feminism*, London: Allen Lane.

Moane, G. (1998) 'Violence', in K. Trew and J. Kremer (eds), *Gender & Psychology*, London: Arnold.

Moghaddam, F. M. (1998) 'The self in culture', in F.M. Moghaddam, *Social Psychology: Exploring Universals Across Cultures*, New York: Freeman.

Moscovici, S. (1981) 'On social representation', in J.P. Forgas (ed.), *Social Cognition: Perspectives on Everyday Life*, London: Academic Press.

Moscovici, S. (1984) 'The phenomenon of social representations', in R. Farr and S. Moscovici (eds), *Social Representations*, Cambridge: Cambridge University Press.

Muldoon, O. and Reilly, J. (1998) 'Biology', in K. Trew and J. Kremer (eds), *Gender & Psychology: A European Text*, London: Arnold.

Naus, P. (1987) cited in Daniluk, J. (1991) 'Female sexuality: an enigma', *Canadian Journal of Counselling*, 25(4): 433–46.

Nicolson, P. (1992) 'Feminism and academic psychology: towards a psychology of women', in K. Campbell (ed.), *Critical Feminisms: Argument in the Disciplines*, Buckingham: The Open University Press.

Nicolson, P. (1994) 'Anatomy and destiny: sexuality and the female body', in P. Choi, P. Nicolson, B. Alder, C. Dancey, L. Gannon, E. McNeill and J. Ussher (eds), *Female Sexuality*, New York: Harvester Wheatsheaf.

Nightingale, D. and Neilands, T. (1997) 'Understanding and practising critical psychology', in D. Fox and I. Prilleltensky (eds), *Critical Psychology: An Introduction*, London: Sage.

Oakley, A. (1979) cited in Hudson, F. and Ineichen, B. (1991), *Taking It Lying Down: Sexuality and Teenage Motherhood*, London: Macmillan.

O'Connor, J. (1996) *The Irish Male at Home and Abroad*, Dublin: New Island Books.

Orne, M. (1962) 'On the social psychology of the psychological experiment', *American Psychologist,* 17(11): 776–83.

Oyama, S. (1997) 'Essentialism, women and war: protesting too much, protesting too little', in M. Gergen and S. Davis (eds), *Towards a New Psychology of Gender*, London: Routledge.

Parker, I. (1989) *The Crisis in Social Psychology, and How to End It*, London: Routledge.

Parker, I. (1990) 'Discourse: definitions and contradictions', *Philosophical Psychology*, 3: 189–204.

Parker, I. (1992) *Discourse Dynamics: Critical Analysis for Social and Individual Psychology*, London: Routledge.

Parker, I. (1994) 'Discourse analysis', in P. Banister, E. Burman., I. Parker, M. Taylor and C. Tindall (eds), *Qualitative Methods in Psychology: A Research Guide*, Buckingham: Open University Press.

Parker, I. (1998) *Social Constructionism, Discourse and Realism*, London: Sage

Parker, I. (1999) 'Critical psychology: critical links', *Annual Review of Critical Psychology*, 1: 3–18 (concurrently published in *Radical Psychology*).

Parker, I. and Shotter, J. (1990) *Deconstructing Social Psychology*, London: Routledge.

Parker, I. and Spears, R. (1996) *Psychology & Society: Radical Theory & Practice*, London: Pluto.

Parker, I., Georgaca, E., Harper, D., McLaughlin, T. and Stowell-Smith, I. (1995) *Deconstructing Psychopathology*, London: Sage.

Parlee, M.B. (1975) 'Review essay: psychology', *Signs*, 1: 119–38.

Parsons, T. (1954) *Essays in Sociological Theory*, New York: The Free Press.

Penelope, J. (1992) *Call Me Lesbian: Lesbian Lives, Lesbian Theory*, Freedom, CA: The Crossing Press.

Percy, C. (1998) 'Feminism', in K. Trew and J. Kremer (eds), *Gender & Psychology: A European Text*, London: Arnold.

Perrin, S. and Spencer, C.P. (1981) 'Independence or conformity in the Asch experiment as a reflection of cultural and situational factors', *British Journal of Social Psychology*, 20: 205–9.

Peterson, C., Maier, S. and Seligman, M. (1993) *Learned Helplessness: A Theory for the Age of Personal Control*, New York: Oxford University Press.

Pettigrew, T.F. (1958) 'Personality and socio-cultural factors in intergroup attitudes: a cross-national comparison', *Journal of Conflict Resolution*, 2: 29–42.

Phoenix, A., Woollett, A. and Lloyd, E. (eds) (1991) *Motherhood: Meanings, Practices and Ideologies*, London: Sage.

Pleck, J. (1987) 'American fathering in historical perspective', in M.S. Kimmel (ed.), *New Directions in Research on Men and Masculinities*, Englewood Cliffs, NJ: Prentice Hall.

Plummer, K. (1992) *Modern Homosexuality: Fragments of Lesbian and Gay Experiences*, New York: Routledge.

Potter, J. (1996) *Representing Reality: Discourse, Rhetoric and Social Construction*, London: Sage.

Potter, J. (1997) 'Discourse and critical social psychology', in T. Ibáñez and L. Íñiguez (eds), *Critical Social Psychology*, London: Sage.

Potter, J. and Wetherell, M. (1987) *Discourse and Social Psychology: Beyond Attitudes and Behaviour*, London: Sage.

Potter, J., Wetherell, M., Gill., R. and Edwards, D. (1990) 'Discourse – noun, verb or social practice?', *Philosophical Psychology*, 3: 205–17.

Reavey, P. (1999) 'Child sexual abuse: professional and everyday constructions of female sexuality', unpublished doctoral thesis, Sheffield Hallam University.

Reavey, P. and Gough, B. (2000) 'Dis/locating blame: survivors' constructions of self and sexual abuse', *Sexualities*, 3(3): 325–46.

Renzetti, C. and Curran, D. (1992) 'Sex role socialisation', in J.A. Kournay, J.P. Sterba and R. Tong (eds), *Feminist Philosophies*, Englewood Cliffs, NJ.: Prentice Hall.

Rheinharz, S. (1992) *Feminist Methods in Social Research*, Oxford: Oxford University Press.

Rich, A. (1980) 'Compulsory heterosexuality and lesbian existence', *Signs: Journal of Women in Culture and Society*, 5(4): 631–57.

Rose, N. (1979) 'The psychological complex: mental measurement and social administration', *Ideology & Consciousness*, 5: 5–68.

Rose, N. (1985) *The Psychological Complex: Psychology, Politics and Society in England 1869–1939*, London: Routledge and Kegan Paul.

Rose, N. (1989) *Governing the Soul: The Shaping of the Private Self*, London: Routledge.

Rossi, B. (1977) 'A biosocial perspective on parenting', *Daedalus*, 106: 1–32.

Rothbart, M. (1981) 'Memory processes and social beliefs', in D. Hamilton (ed), *Cognitive Processes in Stereotyping and Intergroup Behaviour*, Hillsdale: Erlbaum.

Sahakian, W.S. (1982) *History and Systems of Social Psychology*, London: McGraw-Hill.

Sampson, E.E. (1977) 'Psychology and the American ideal', *Journal of Personality & Social Psychology*, 35: 767–82.

Sampson, E.E. (1993) *Celebrating The Other: A Dialogic Account of Human Nature*, New York: Harvester Wheatsheaf.

Santa Ana, O.S. (1999) '"Like an animal I was treated": anti-immigrant metaphor in US public discourse', *Discourse & Society*, 10(2): 191–224

Sapsford, R. (1996) *Issues for Social Psychology*, Buckingham: Open University Press.

Sapsford, R. and Dallos, R. (1996) 'Resisting social psychology', in R. Dallos (ed.), *Issues for Social Psychology*, Buckingham: Open University Press.

Sass, L.A. (1992) 'The epic of disbelief: The postmodernist turn in contemporary psychoanalysis', in S. Kvale (ed.), *Psychology & Postmodernism*, London: Sage.

Schegloff, E.A. (1998) 'Whose text? Whose context?', *Discourse & Society*, 8(2): 165–88.

Seale, C. (1999) *The Quality of Qualitative Research*, London: Sage.

Sedgwick, P. (1974) 'Ideology in modern psychology', in N. Armistead (ed.), *Reconstructing Social Psychology*, Harmondsworth: Penguin.

Segal, L. (1987) *Is the Future Female? Troubled Thoughts on Contemporary Feminism*, London: Virgo.

Segal, L. (1990/1994) *Slow Motion: Changing Masculinities, Changing Men*, London: Virago.

Segal, L. (1997) 'Sexualities', in K. Woodward (ed.), *Identity and Difference*, London: Sage.

Semin, G. and Rubini, M. (1990) 'Unfolding the concept of person by verbal abuse', *European Journal of Social Psychology*, 20: 463–74.

Senn, C.Y. (1996) 'Q-methodology as feminist methodology: women's views and experiences of pornography', in S. Wilkinson (ed.), *Feminist Social Psychologies: International Perspectives*, Buckingham: Open University Press.

Sherif, M. (1935) *The Psychology of Social Norms*, New York: Harper & Row.

Sherif, M. and Sherif, C. (1969) *Social Psychology*, New York: Harper & Row.

Shields, S.A. and Crowley, J.J. (1996) 'Appropriating questionnaires and rating scales for a feminist psychology: a multi-method approach to gender and emotion', in S. Wilkinson (ed.), *Feminist Social Psychologies: International Perspectives*, Buckingham: Open University Press.

Shotter, J. (1993a) *Conversational Realities*, London: Sage.

Shotter, J. (1993b) *Cultural Politics of Everyday Life*, Buckingham: Open University Press.

Shotter, J. and Gergen, K.J. (1988) *Texts of Identity*, London: Sage.

Shweder, R. and Bourne, E. (1982) 'Does the concept of the person vary cross-culturally?', in A. Marsella and G. White (eds), *Cultural Conceptions of Mental Health and Therapy*, Boston: Dordrecht.

Siann, G. (1985) *Accounting for Aggression*, London: Allen & Unwin.

Smith, D. (1988) 'Femininity as discourse', in L. Roman and L. Christian (eds), *Becoming Feminine: The Politics of Popular Culture*, London: Falmer.

Smith, P.B. and Bond, M.H. (1993) *Social Psychology Across Cultures: Analysis and Perspectives*, Hemel Hempstead: Harvester Wheatsheaf.

Synder, M. and Uranowitz, S.W. (1978) 'Reconstructing the past: Some cognitive consequences of person perception', *Journal of Personality and Social Psychology*, 33: 941–50.

Spence, J.T. and Helmreich, R.L. (1978) *Masculinity and Femininity: Their Psychological Dimensions, Correlates and Antecedents*, Austin, TX: University of Texas Press.

Spence, J.T., Helmreich, R.L. and Stapp, J. (1974) 'The Personal Attributes Questionnaire: a measure of sex role stereotype and masculinity–femininity', *JSAS: Catalog of Selected Documents in Psychology*, 4(43), (Ms No 617).

Spender, D. (1980) *Man Made Language*, London: Routledge.

Squire, C. (1995) 'Pragmatism, extravagance and feminist discourse analysis', in S. Wilkinson and C. Kitzinger (eds), *Feminism & Discourse: Psychological Perspectives*, London: Sage.

Stainton-Rogers, R., Stenner, P., Gleeson, K. and Stainton-Rogers, W. (1995) *Social Psychology: A Critical Agenda*, Cambridge: Polity Press.

Stanko, E. (1985) *Intimate Intrusions: Women's Experience of Male Violence*, London: Routledge & Kegan Paul.

Stanley, L. (1990) *Feminist Praxis: Research, Theory and Epistemology in Feminist Sociology*, London: Routledge.

Stevens, R. (1996) *Understanding the Self*, Buckingham: Open University Press/Sage.

Still, A. (1996) 'Historical origins of social psychology', in R. Sapsford (ed.), *Issues for Social Psychology*, Buckingham: Open University Press.

Storr, A. (1970) *Human Aggression*, Harmondsworth: Penguin.

Stratton, P. (1997) 'Attributional coding of interview data: meeting the needs of long-haul passengers', in N. Hayes (ed.), *Doing Qualitative Analysis in Psychology*, London: Psychology Press.

Swann, J. (1992) *Girls, Boys and Language*, Oxford: Blackwell.

Szasz, T. (1961) *The Myth of Mental Illness*, New York: Harper & Row.

Tajfel, H. (1978) *Differentiation between Social Groups: Studies in Intergroup Behaviour*, London: Academic Press.

Tajfel, H. (1981) *Human Groups and Social Categories*, Cambridge: Cambridge University Press.

Tajfel, H. and Billig, M. (1973) 'Social categorization and intergroup behaviour', *European Journal of Social Psychology*, 1: 149–78.

Tajfel, H. and Turner, J.C. (1979) 'An integrative theory of intergroup conflict', in W. Austin and S. Worchel (eds), *The Social Psychology of Intergroup Relations*, California: Brooks-Cole.

Tajfel, H. and Turner, J.C. (1985) 'The social identity theory of intergroup behaviour', in S. Worchel and W. Austin (eds), *Psychology of Intergroup Relations*, Chicago: Nelson-hall.

Tavris, C. and Wade, C. (1984) *The Longest War: Sex Differences In Perspective*, New York: Harcourt Brace Jovanovich.

Terman, L. and Miles, C. (1936) *Sex and Personality*, New York: McGraw-Hill.

Thompson, J. (1984) *Studies in the Theory of Ideology*, Cambridge: Polity.

Thomson, R. and Scott, S. (1991) *Learning About Sex: Young Women and the Social Construction of Sexual Identity*, London: The Tufnell Press.

Tiffin, J., Knight, F.B. and Josey, C.C. (1940) *The Psychology of Normal People*, Boston, Mass.: Heath.

Toffler, A. (1981) *The Third Wave*, London: Pan Books.

Trew, K. and Kremer, J. (1998) *Gender & Psychology: A European Text*, London: Arnold.

Triplett, N. (1898) 'The dynamogenic factor in pace-making and competition', *American Journal of Psychology*, 9: 507–33.

Trivers, R. (1985) *Social Evolution*, Menlo Park, CA: Benjamin/Cummings Publishers.

Turner, B. (1984) *The Body and Society*, Oxford: Blackwell.

Turner, C.W. and Goldsmith, D. (1976) 'Effects of toy guns on children's anti-social free play behaviour', *Journal of Experimental Child Psychology*, 21: 303–15.

Turner, J.C. (1982) 'Towards a cognitive re-definition of the social group', in H. Tajfel (ed.) *Social Identity and Intergroup Relations*, Cambridge University Press.

Turner, J.C., Hogg, M.A., Oakes, P.J., Reicher, S.D. and Wetherell, M. (1987) *Rediscovering the Social Group: A Self-Categorization Theory*, Oxford: Blackwell.

Unger, R. K. (1996) 'Using the master's tools: epistemology and empiricism', in S. Wilkinson (ed.), *Feminist Social Psychologies: International Perspectives*, Buckingham: Open University Press.

Ussher, J. (1991) *Women's Madness: Misogyny or Mental Illness*, London: Harvester Wheatsheaf.

Vance, C. (1984) *Pleasure and Danger: Exploring Female Sexuality*, London: Routledge.

van Dijk, T. (1984) *Prejudice in Discourse: An Analysis of Ethnic Prejudices in Cognition and Conversation*, Amsterdam: John Benjamins.

Waddell, N. and Cairns, E. (1986) 'Situational perspectives on social identity in Northern Ireland', *British Journal of Social Psychology*, 25: 25–31.

Walby, S. (1990) *Theorising Patriarchy*, Oxford: Blackwell.

Walkerdine, V. (1981) 'Sex, power and pedagogy', *Screen Education*, 38: 14–23. Reprinted in M. Arnot and G. Weiner (eds) (1987) *Gender and The Politics of Schooling*, London: Hutchinson.

Walkerdine, V. (1987) 'No laughing matter: girls' comics and the preparation for adolescent sexuality', in J.M. Broughton (ed.), *Critical Theories of Psychological Development*, New York: Plenum Press.

Walkerdine, V. (1991) *Schoolgirl Fictions*, London: Verso.

Walkerdine, V. (1996) Special Issue on social class, *Feminism & Psychology*, 6(3).

Weedon, C. (1987) *Feminist Practice and Post-Structuralist Theory*, London: Blackwell.

Weeks, J. (1977) *Coming Out: Homosexual Politics in Britain from the Nineteenth Century to the Present Day*, London: Quartet Books.

Weeks, J. (1981) *Sex, Politics and Society: The Regulation of Sexuality since 1800*, London: Longmans.

Weeks, J. (1985) *Sexuality and its Discontents*, London: Tavistock Publications.

Weeks, J. (1991) *Against Nature: Essays on History, Sexuality and Identity*, London: Rivers Oram.

Weisstein, N. (1993) 'Psychology constructs the female; or the fantasy life of the male psychologist (with some attention to the fantasies of his friends, the male biologist and the male anthropologist)', *Feminism & Psychology*, 3(2): 195–210. (First published 1968).

West, D., Roy, C. and Florence Nichols (1978) *Understanding Sexual Attacks*, London: Heinemann.

Wetherell, M. (1982) 'Cross-cultural studies of minimal groups: Implications for the social identity theory of intergroup relations', in H. Tajfel (ed.), *Social Identity and Intergroup Relations*, Cambridge University Press.

Wetherell, M. (1995) 'Romantic discourse and feminist analysis: interrogating investment, power and desire', in S. Wilkinson and C. Kitzinger (eds), *Feminism & Discourse: Psychological Perspectives*, London: Sage.

Wetherell, M. (1996) *Identities, Groups and Social Issues*, London: Sage/Open University Press.

Wetherell, M. (1997) 'Linguistic repertoires and literary criticism: new directions for a social psychology of gender', in M. Gergen and S. Davis (eds), *Towards a New Psychology of Gender: A Reader*, London: Routledge.

Wetherell, M. (1998) 'Positioning and interpretative repertoires: conversation analysis and post-structuralism in dialogue', *Discourse & Society*, 9(3): 387–416.

Wetherell, M. and Edley, N. (1999) 'Negotiating hegemonic masculinity: imaginary positions and psycho-discursive practices', *Feminism & Psychology*, 9(3): 335–57.

Wetherell, M. and Griffin, C. (1991) 'Feminist psychology and the study of men and masculinity: Part one: Assumptions and perspectives', *Feminism and Psychology*, 1: 361–93.

Wetherell, M. and Maybin, J. (1996) 'The distributed self: a social constructionist perspective', in R. Stevens (ed.), *Understanding the Self*, London: Sage/Open University Press.

Wetherell, M. and Potter, J. (1992) *Mapping the Language of Racism: Discourse and the Legitimation of Exploitation*, Hemel Hempstead: Harvester Wheatsheaf.

Wetherell, M., Stiven, H. and Potter, J. (1987) ' "Unequal egalitarianism": a preliminary study of discourses concerning gender and employment opportunities', *British Journal of Social Psychology*, 26: 59–71.

Wilkinson, S. (ed.) (1986) *Feminist Social Psychology: Developing Theory & Practice*, Milton Keynes: Open University Press.

Wilkinson, S. (1988). 'The role of reflexivity in feminist psychology', *Women's Studies International Forum*, 11.

Wilkinson, S. (1991) 'Feminism and psychology: from critique to reconstruction', *Feminism & Psychology*, 1(1): 5–18.

Wilkinson, S. (ed.) (1996) *Feminist Social Psychologies: International Perspectives*, Buckingham: Open University Press.

Wilkinson, S. (1997) 'Prioritising the political: feminist psychology', in T. Ibáñez and L. Íñiguez (eds), *Critical Social Psychology*, London: Sage.

Wilkinson, S. and Kitzinger, C. (1993) *Heterosexuality: A Feminism & Psychology Reader*, London: Sage.

Wilkinson, S. and Kitzinger, C. (1994) 'The social construction of heterosexuality', *Journal of Gender Studies*, 3(30): 307–16.

Wilkinson, S. and Kitzinger, C. (1995) *Feminism and Discourse*, London: Sage.

Williams, J. (1984) 'Gender and intergroup behaviour: towards an integration', *British Journal of Psychology*, 23: 311–16.

Williams, T.P. and Sogon, S. (1984) 'Group composition and conforming behaviour in Japanese students', *Japanese Psychological Research*, 26: 231–4.

Willig, C. (1998) 'Social constructionism and revolutionary socialism: a contradiction in terms?', in I. Parker (ed.), *Social Constructionism, Discourse and Realism*, London: Sage.

Willig, C. (1999) *Applied Discourse Analysis: Social and Psychological Interventions*, Buckingham: Open University Press.

Willis, P. (1977) *Learning to Labour: How Working-Class Kids Get Working-Class Jobs*, Farnborough, Hants: Saxon House.

Willott, S. and Griffin, C. (1997) ' "Wham, Bam, Am I a Man"?', Unemployed men talk about masculinities', *Feminism & Psychology*, 7(1): 107–28.

Wilson, E. O. (1975) 'Human decency is animal', *New York Times Magazine*, October 12: 38–50.

Wilson, E. O. (1978) *On Human Nature*, Cambridge, Mass.: Harvard University Press.

Wilson, G. (1994) 'Biology, sex roles and work', in C. Quest (ed.), *Liberating Women ... From Modern Feminism,* London: Institute of Economic Affairs, Health & Welfare Unit.

Winterson, J. (1985) *Oranges Are Not the Only Fruit*, London: Vintage.

Zajonc, R.B. (1965) 'Social facilitation', *Science*, 149: 269–74.

Zillman, D. (1979) *Hostility and Aggression*, Hillsdale NJ: Lawrence Erlbaum Associates.

Index